DAMS, PARKS & POLITICS

Elmo Richardson

DAMS, PARKS & POLITICS

Resource Development & Preservation in the Truman- Eisenhower Era

The University Press of Kentucky

ISBN: 0-8131-1284-2

Library of Congress Catalog Card Number: 72-91670

Copyright © 1973 by The University Press of Kentucky

A statewide cooperative scholarly publishing agency
serving Berea College, Centre College of Kentucky,
Eastern Kentucky University, Georgetown College,
Kentucky Historical Society, Kentucky State University,
Morehead State University, Murray State University,
Northern Kentucky State College, University of Kentucky,
University of Louisville, and Western Kentucky University.

Editorial and Sales Offices: Lexington, Kentucky 40506

To Rod & Sharon,
Kiendra & Koy

*Love was the greatest
of all the things
we shared.*

Contents

[ILLUSTRATIONS FOLLOW PAGE 96]

Prologue

THE
NEW DEAL
LEGACY

The United States inherited a seemingly inexhaustible fortune in natural resources, yet it has responded to its environment with a dismaying mixture of materialism and inertia. The nation was virtually founded upon a ubiquitous desire for access to the land and its contents. Its amazing growth during the nineteenth century was based directly upon exploitation—immediate, unplanned, full use of soils, minerals, forests, and rivers. Equitable access to these natural bounties rather than constitutional guarantees would be the practical basis for democracy. Subsequently, political institutions were shaped in such a way that they could facilitate the disposition of the public domain. But that expectation, as later generations ruefully observed, did not materialize. The combination of economics and government had instead produced a handful of owners and policy makers who were beyond the control of the ballot box.

As the twentieth century began, it was not the people who took up the task of reasserting the public interest but a few perceptive technicians and their political disciples. The managers and engineers who served Theodore Roosevelt and his successors were determined to make federal resource policies more equitable and at the same time more efficient. Initially, they encountered the opposition of local economic and political interests who feared that the new regulations would short-circuit traditions of patronage and pork barrel. By pointing out the material advantages of planned, diverse use of resources, the federal administrators soon won the support of influential elements of the population. Although monopolies continued to grow, now there were much greater opportunities for many more enterprisers

in federally financed multiple-use projects for land and water development. There were some small operators who predicted accurately that federal forest reservations and dam projects would
strengthen the control of already powerful capitalists in and beyond
the area involved. Nevertheless, every man believed in the paramountcy of material progress whether he was at the top or the
bottom rung of the economic ladder.

That consensus was not altered by the inauguration of a system of
national parks—seemingly the antithesis of multiple use—as a result
of the publicity and pressure of a few aesthetes and sportsmen who
hardly represented the pragmatic public. But the officers of the
National Park Service, created in 1916, fully recognized the need
for arousing and cultivating popular understanding of the parks and
pride in them. They deftly used a chamber-of-commerce rationale:
the preserves would serve as a permanent magnet to attract an endless
stream of visitors who would spend or invest in adjacent communities.
At the same time, however, they were obligated by law to protect
these units from commercialization and overuse. Therefore, they
relied upon increasingly influential nature and outdoor sports groups
and scientific organizations—not multiple-use conservationists but
preservationists—to help uphold the principle of park inviolability.
Because that crusade was a matter of eternal vigilance and because
the enemy had to win only once to mar the ecology permanently,
the preservationists employed the style and techniques of the old
muckrakers. Yet all their rhetoric about "selfish interests" obscured
the truth that the greatest obstacle to preservation of the natural
environment was the American tradition of progress. That faith
held that uncontrolled nature was a danger; wilderness meant barren
and malevolent waste. It was almost a godly necessity for men to
carve farms, towns, and fortunes out of these so-called unused natural
resources. The public interest was unquestionably served by their
development.

For the subsequent generation that experienced the depression
and war of the 1930s and 1940s, renewed development of resources
was elevated into one of the primary tasks of the federal government.
Short- and long-term plans for such a policy were proposed by
Franklin Roosevelt's New Dealers. One of these was the work done
by the popular Civilian Conservation Corps (CCC) in protecting
forests, soil, and water supply, and in constructing roads and other
facilities near thousands of communities. Only a few purists objected

to the way in which these projects altered the ecology of the areas involved. Most Americans—whether Democrats or Republicans—were pleased that the work enhanced property values and aided local businesses. The far larger portion of federal largesse was the long list of reclamation and power projects constructed in the river basins of the nation. Segments of every state vied with each other to secure more of these constructions without delay. Even when the vast Tennessee Valley Authority was established, the theoretical doubts of a few Republicans and states'-rights Democrats gave way to general enthusiasm. Indeed, they contended thereafter that government-built projects should ultimately become part of privately owned water and power distribution companies. Although they insisted that they were defending private enterprise and democracy, such a policy in fact would mean that a few local monopolists would reap the benefits of highly profitable projects financed by the taxes of the entire population.

These problems of development and preservation were the concern of the Department of the Interior. Because it administered regulations which greatly affected the economy of the resource-rich western states, that region had always considered its directors as important as any of the members of a presidential staff. Leaders and enterprisers of the West often recommended the men chosen for the secretaryship of the Interior, but the patronage advisers to the presidents actually selected the nominees on the bases of availability, party service, and balance among political factions in the region. Moreover, the Interior secretary was obliged to share the concerns uppermost in the plans of the White House and the Congress, whether that was to dispense jobs, distribute lands, or encourage extractive industries. After the beginning of the twentieth century, the West was no longer a frontier land with a simple pattern of economic and political loyalties. New immigration, new technology, and new leadership destroyed its isolation and its uniqueness. Moreover, a westerner in the secretaryship would be committed to specific enterprises and party factions not necessarily representative of those interests in other parts of the region or even his own state. As a result, whether these policy makers were sympathetic toward development, preservation, or budgets, they were criticized by westerners as well as easterners. Often branded as inept, unfair, or corrupt, the men in that department rode a fitful tiger. Their tenures usually began in obscurity or high hopes and often ended in notoriety and vilification. Not coincidently, their alleged villainy served the purposes of the political party not then in power.

Roosevelt appointed Harold Ickes as secretary of the Interior in order to demonstrate the continuation of the old Bull Moose Progressive reform in his administration. The Chicagoan had sought a lesser post in the department, but when he took over as secretary his modest ambitions gave way to one overriding personal goal. Recalling the earlier scandals of the Ballinger-Pinchot affair, which had contributed to the formation of the Progressive party in 1912, and the Teapot Dome scandals of the 1920s, he was determined to remove the stigma of corruption and restore public confidence in the department. By the time he left office nearly thirteen years later, Ickes's power had reached an extent unmatched by any of his predecessors. His substantial accomplishments were made possible because the American people were receptive both economically and politically to any resource policy insuring expenditures and jobs. During the continuing national economic emergency, the decisions of the department were as important to the nation as any made by the Roosevelt administration. Millions of westerners were affected by them— from oil and mining men to stockraisers and farmers dependent upon range and watershed protection and renewal. Only the system of national forests, under the jurisdiction of the Department of Agriculture, was beyond Ickes's control; he spent several years in a frustrated attempt to bring its Forest Service over to Interior.[1]

Above all, the secretary's personality shaped the emphases and procedures involved in his distinctly imperial policies. Zealous and self-righteous, Ickes was an uncomfortable combination of paranoia and megalomania and a man convinced that the public interest could not be compromised. Although an adept politician himself, he expressed undisguised disdain for what he felt was the inveterate myopia of politicians. In radio addresses that became something of a public entertainment during those years, he took swipes at plutocrats and pork barrelers. Those who differed with him in and beyond the department he suspected not only were detrimental to the New Deal's crusade but were enemies of the American people. Such opinions quickly earned for him such epithets from the press as "Donald Duck," "Honest Harold," and "Old Curmudgeon." Yet passions did not displace subtle tact when he had to work with congressional committees acting on departmental proposals and budgets. There, conflicting demands by local western interests produced ill feelings on the part of many members. Ickes's first critics were those who wanted the government to build waterways in their states before any others and those seeking the appointment of favorite sons to preside over reclamation policy. The secretary was confident that he could overcome these pressures because he had the full support of the president even in politically sensitive matters. Indeed, the two men shared a detailed knowledge and personal concern for resource programs. Both were determined to make them into the basis for a restored national prosperity and a more responsible political foundation for the American economy.[2]

Secretary Ickes's unconcealed doubt about the enlightenment of business interests undercut the general popularity of the New Deal's land and resource programs among westerners. His feelings were a heritage of his early association with the reform movement. During the late 1920s, he had been critical of the Herbert Hoover administration's excessive scruples on behalf of private enterprises whose profits were made possible by federally financed hydroelectric projects. He was also angered by Interior Secretary Ray Wilbur's promotion of state control of the public lands. When Ickes became secretary of the Interior, he invariably suspected that the appeal to public opinion was a mask to conceal the machinations of selfish private operators. He was able to make up his own mind about the inclinations of alleged public opinion. His subordinates assured him that the West was hopelessly divided on questions of regulation and construction. They seemed unable to agree on legislation. Their suggestions for alternatives, usually economically naive, required the action of the states that were already financially strapped. Ickes was willing to promote interstate compacts rather than federal regulation for such matters as water pollution. On most problems, however, he placed national control before state or local initiative.[3]

Having made up his mind on what was the public's best interest, he then defined public opinion to mean anything that confirmed that analysis. As he assured a congressman from the Pacific Northwest in 1941: "Since my arrival in the State of Washington . . . I have concluded as a result of many conferences with the people of this area, that the policies of the Department of the Interior meet with the approval of a far greater majority than even I had expected. Especially do they favor the orderly development of the natural resources of this State. Monopolistic critics of those policies are, undoubtedly, but a small although vociferous minority."[4]

Ickes's impatience with parochial pressures was at the heart of his many quarrels within and beyond the department. Whenever he found members of his own staff overly sympathetic to the demands of local land and resource users, he felt an overwhelming urge to purge them. For example, he never really trusted his first assistant secretary, Theodore Walters of Idaho, a political appointee who, he felt, had been foisted on him by western congressmen seeking reclamation projects and grazing privileges. Similarly, he grew highly suspicious of Walter's subordinate, Farrington Carpenter, a cattleman from Colorado who was in charge of the Grazing Service.

Carpenter had seemed to be an ideal choice to preside over the administration of the new Taylor Grazing Act, a 1934 measure hailed throughout the West as a happy combination of federal supervision and local participation in rangeland use. Not long after his appointment, however, even the Coloradan who had sponsored him, Assistant Secretary Oscar Chapman, admitted to his chief that he was "becoming a little concerned about Mr. Carpenter's indiscretions." After two more years, Carpenter seemed set on undermining Ickes's centralization of grazing policy. He refused to consult the heads of other agencies within the department, especially the Park Service, whose preserves adjoined national grazing areas. He was particularly opposed to one of the secretary's pet projects, a proposed Escalante National Monument in the midst of the stockraising area of Utah. Carpenter urged Ickes to adopt a new policy that would bring about "a large degree of home rule in the handling of western matters." In the meantime, he pleased audiences of stockmen by promising to give them long-term leases to the public lands they wanted to use. In 1938, acting on his own initiative, he asked congressmen to reduce federal grazing fees. After the elections that November Ickes unleashed his famous temper. He summoned the Grazing Service director to his office and asked him to resign. Carpenter replied that he would think it over, whereupon the secretary jumped out of his chair and shouted: "You're out of a job! You're out of a job!"[5]

Ickes's tight supervision of his bureau chiefs also expressed personal interest as well as distrust. This was clearly the case in his relations with the men of the National Park Service. Although most of the department's work was oriented toward the utilitarian emphasis of conservation for development and employment, the preservationist concept of the national parks was close to his heart. The striking enlargement of that system accomplished during his administration was a personal victory made possible by his great knowledge of local geographical and economic conditions and by his accurate assessment of the political vulnerability of state officials. Usually, he would respond to a local petition which coincided with the Park Service's own plans, present the idea to state officials in an attractive package, and then rely on commercial and preservation organizations to mold a base of public approval. He could also drop his anti-big-business bias when it served his larger purpose.

In every case, the secretary relied upon the shrewd lobbyists of preservationist organizations. These men worked beyond the limits of government discretion and drew upon scientific and political information that was beyond the grasp of their opponents. In the process of overwhelming their foes, however, Ickes and his advisers alienated many westerners. By 1938 his heavy-handed procedures prompted some critics to compare him with Adolph Hitler and refer to his creation of large preserves as an "Anschluss." It was "dictator Ickes" and his Park Service that a Wyoming editor, angry over the proposed enlargement of Grand Teton National Park, had in mind when he wrote that the New Deal had "long since shown its disrespect for the wishes of the people who have builded the West."[6]

The political consequences of the inevitable clashes between the public's attitudes and the requirements for resource development were less important to Ickes than their effect on the reputation for integrity which he was trying to restore to the Interior Department. He knew well how even the finest intentions could produce irrevocable mistakes. In the years of the reform movement, he had been a devoted adherent of Theodore Roosevelt and his conservation lieutenants, Interior Secretary James Garfield and Chief Forester Gifford Pinchot. But when they approved of San Francisco's use of the Hetch Hetchy Valley as a reservoir within Yosemite National Park, he never forgave them. When he became secretary, the same vexatious problem of determining priorities in resource access dominated every program. In the case of national park policy, he profited from the advice of the outgoing Republican Park Service director, Horace Albright. The latter pointed out that there were advantages in having some parks that would serve large numbers of visitors while other units in the system could be preserved intact as wildernesses.[7] Ickes was eager to promote the concept of wilderness parks even though he realized that the public had a minimal understanding of it.[8] Over the objections of real estate investors, lumber and mining companies, dam promoters and their legislators, he added three major wilderness parks to the system by the end of the peacetime period of his tenure:

Kings Canyon in California, Olympic in Washington State, and Everglades in Florida.[9]

Ickes's obsession with principle determined his selection of men to
direct the Park Service. In 1939 he sought "new blood and a strong
man" for that post to continue the tradition of Albright and Stephen
Mather, "Father of the National Parks." When he had taken over the
department in 1933, he had offered the position to Newton Drury
of California. The former associate of Albright, however, preferred
to remain as adviser to the state park commission and executive
secretary of the Save the Redwoods League. The job was then twice
offered to Robert Moses of New York City. He declined it—fortunately
perhaps, because he firmly believed that man could and should improve on nature. Finally, on the advice of Albright and others, Ickes
appointed Arno Cammerer. The new man proved to be thoroughly
dependable, but he was not much of an innovator. When he resigned
for reasons of health in 1939, Ickes considered appointing Michael
Straus, a fellow Illinoian who had served him as director of public
relations for the department's Public Works Administration. In retrospect, that may have proved to be a mistake too. Ickes once again
turned to Drury who, in the intervening years, had become even more
of a preservationist. He now thoroughly opposed commercial concessions in the parks, except in units that were isolated, and considered any improvement of visitor access roads as undesirable if it
meant marring the natural terrain. "I am against roads," he once
told wilderness advocate Robert Marshall, "I am death on roads."
Drury was also critical of the sometimes careless damage done by
CCC projects in parks and of the local politics said to be involved in
that program. When his sponsors admitted to Ickes that Drury was
a Republican, the secretary reportedly barked: "I don't give a damn."
Though a Republican, Drury was perceptive enough to see that the
Democrats were willing to spend more money than the Republicans
for the national park system. Concluding that the department needed
a purist, he finally agreed to accept the appointment.[10]

If the Park Service was Harold Ickes's favorite child, it was hardly
favored by the westerners in Congress. They preferred to give the
Bureau of Reclamation the larger appropriations, especially after 1936.
Development-minded legislators, businessmen, and farmers welcomed
the bureau's surveys as harbingers of more votes, more jobs, more
contracts, and community growth. Whether they advocated private
control of water and power transmission or the organization of public

utility cooperatives, all of them considered federal dam construction an essential program. Because the Army Corps of Engineers shared jurisdiction over river control with Interior's Reclamation Bureau, however, many westerners favored the Corps's emphasis upon the participation of local private enterprise. As a result, a certain rivalry developed between the two. The bureau had more money to spend and therefore built many more dams and reservoirs than the Corps, but it also carried the stigma of government interference by bureaucrats who were not always professional engineers. Indeed, the absence of engineers at the head of the bureau was a persistent criticism heard in the West.

Ickes was naturally suspicious of the Corps's infringements on Reclamation's territory, but at first he was only slightly interested in the bureau's programs. As he became increasingly determined to enlarge the jurisdictions of his department, however, he realized that the popularity of dams and reservoirs in the West could boost support and increase budgets. By 1940 he was eagerly endorsing his department's surveys for large river basin development. When Michael Straus was appointed assistant secretary of the Interior in 1943, Reclamation's influence in the department was substantially increased. Ickes admired the man's skill in public relations, but he also questioned some of the bureau's activities. Preservationist friends warned him that Reclamation was extending its investigations for potential dam sites to the units of the national park system.

Conflicting priorities were dramatically involved in the Big Thompson aqueduct proposal of 1936. Coloradans, seeking a conduit from the western slope of the Rocky Mountains to the cities and farms concentrated on the eastern side of the state, obtained congressional approval of the project. Although a small number of preservationists were convinced that this violation of Rocky Mountain National Park would be a foothold for developers elsewhere in the system, Ickes reluctantly gave it his endorsement. Alternative routes would be too costly, he explained, and the water tunnel would burrow beneath the parkland without damaging its surface features. Yet the whole episode must have reminded him of the Hetch Hetchy affair and sharpened his already keen sense of what constituted sin in resource policy.[11]

Some of the crises which seemed to beset Ickes's defense of the national parks arose naturally from the workings of the democratic process. One of these loomed in 1940 when Wendell Willkie campaigned as Republican nominee for the presidency. Leading preservationists wondered at first who would be available to advise him on resource issues. They racked their memories but could think of only one member of their persuasion who was a Republican: Franklin Roosevelt's cousin Nicholas Roosevelt. These same observers bought newspaper space to broadcast a warning against the candidate after Willkie referred to the Democrats' national park "grabs" and told western audiences that he would appoint a man of their region to the Interior Department if elected. They finally concluded that he was depending upon Congressman Frank Horton of Wyoming for his statements on resource policies. Horton had recently been elected by a protest vote against Ickes's efforts to add the large Jackson Hole countryside to Grand Teton National Park. He spoke for many citizens who still clung to the tradition of progress through use. "It was never indicated," he said during that campaign, "that the federal government should be an arbitrary landlord, but merely a trustee of these lands until they could be put to use by the people." This was the man, preservationists assumed, whom Willkie would put in charge of the Interior Department. They did not rest easy until both men were defeated in November.[12]

Roosevelt's margin of victory in Wyoming was small and he lost Colorado, but the other western states gave him substantial victories. Afterwards, there was a flurry of demands from westerners that he replace Ickes with a man from their region. Preservationists were quick to object. Any such appointment would be "just another Ballinger." Distinctions between supporters and critics of federal resource policy in the West were blurred by partisanship, however. The Democratic senator from Wyoming, Joseph O'Mahoney, had opposed the enlargement of Teton Park, yet the Democratic governor, Leslie Miller, had supported it. The latter had not stood for reelection and was now mentioned as a possible assistant Interior secretary or even as Ickes's replacement. The second idea did not appeal to the nominee, however. Miller advised Roosevelt to retain Ickes, maintaining that no stouter champion of the New Deal's policies could be found. Ickes was "the right man in the right place. Keep him."[13]

The greatest challenge to the continuation of Ickes's policies came as the nation mobilized for war in 1940. The defense program and subsequent total mobilization greatly intensified the demands for access to resources. Anything could be done under conditions of war hysteria, preservationists believed. Members of the Emergency Conservation Committee of New York City who had helped fight the battles for the wilderness parks decided to remain watchful. Their caution was wise. After Pearl Harbor, some developers actually exulted. "Now that we are at *War*," wrote a Wyomingite who had felt the weight of the crusaders' swords, "the conservation extremist bureaucrats in the Interior Department must of necessity be at an end." Several bills were introduced in Congress to permit mining exploration, lumbering, and grazing inside the boundaries of the national parks, but none passed. The War Department threatened wildlife refuges with its mushrooming facilities and refused to consult the Interior Department on the matter. Another potential danger was foreseen by very few. Wartime conditions in Washington caused Interior to relocate nonessential bureaus such as the Park Service, which was moved to Chicago. At that distance, Ickes retained less personal touch with his favorite program, and dislocation weakened normal communication and mutual understanding. As director Drury would ruefully recall, these conditions created administrative confusion whose consequences would rebound for years afterward.[14]

The watchdogs produced their loudest barks of protest in 1941 when they foresaw trouble in Olympic National Park. Irving Clark of Seattle informed journalist-historian Irving Brant of the Emergency Conservation Committee that Forest Service officials were casting covetous eyes on timber stands in the preserves. The following year fears were confirmed when local lumber companies asked their congressmen to obtain access to these forests so that they could meet the need for wartime housing material and aircraft production. During peacetime, the department had been able to restrain their appeals about profits and payrolls, but Ickes wondered if he could resist those arguments in the war emergency. Ominously, the War Production Board's Division of Lumber promptly supported their demand. As Brant wrote privately, it was unfortunate that the recently announced war aim of unconditional surrender could not be used against the "timber hogs." In December Ickes admitted that the two newest additions to the national park contained Sitka spruce used for airplane production. He explained that timber could be sold legally from them because they had not yet been given full park status; indeed he calculated that "a substantial amount of Sitka spruce . . . could be removed without serious impairment of scenic and recreational values." His letter to the president concluded that wartime needs could compel a "temporary deviation" from the department's adherence to the principle of park inviolability.[15]

Roosevelt also learned from Brant that local lumber interests on the Olympic Peninsula had spurned spruce stands in adjacent state-owned areas. Brant and Ickes agreed that there were actually several alternatives to harvesting parkland timber. If funds and manpower were made available, if the embargo on lumber imports from nearby British Columbia were lifted, or if Alaskan timber as a substitute for spruce were used, then no invasion of the park would be necessary. Drury was dispatched to the area in June 1943. When he returned to Chicago, he wrote to his chief. If any cutting were to be done, he stated, it would have to be done before the onset of winter, and such cutting should be confined to well-designated areas. Moreover, both lumber and preservationists organizations should be advised that no further cuttings would be permitted. If any section of the park were thus despoiled, it should be eliminated from the preserve by presidential action in order to maintain the park principle. Then he repeated the alternatives proposed by Brant and concluded: "It may therefore be fairly asked whether in view of the national acceptance of these last remnants of the once vast virgin forests of the Peninsula, the alternatives should not be exhausted *before* rather than after" the preserve was nibbled on.

Drury's letter was a conscientious effort to outline a solution to the problem, but the sequence of his statements seemed to Brant to chart a line of retreat just when it was time for an "offensive defensive." The preservationist thought that the matter could be solved with one action. The forests in the park were desired by lumbering companies mainly because they were easily accessible; the shortage of workers made it difficult to get to isolated stands of timber. Therefore, Drury felt that the president could merely issue an order that would shift lumber workers from their wartime jobs in the cities on the Puget Sound back to the peninsula. Ickes did not comment on that suggestion, but did agree with Brant that Drury was simply "not a fighter." When he first heard the director's recommendations, he reportedly snapped: "I am not interested in logging in the park." Moreover, the department solicitor advised him that even the president could not authorize such a violation of the statutory definition of the national parks. The only way he could make the tracts available for lumbering would be to transfer them to the adjoining Olympic National Forest by executive order. Ickes rejected Drury's further suggestion that the crisis called for widespread publicity.

Democratic Congressman Henry Jackson conducted hearings in

his home constituency of western Washington, although he did not commit himself to sponsoring legislation to open the Sitka spruce tracts to lumbering. Meanwhile, Drury and Chapman reluctantly prepared an order that would authorize a limited lumbering operation in the park. They inserted Brant's alternatives in the draft, but used phrases that Ickes thought were "weak and yielding." He decided not to sign the document, therefore, and instead sent his own stronger version to the War Production Board's Lumber Division. This insisted that all alternatives be exhausted before any violation of the park was approved. The federal agencies, he added, owed that much to the groups who had helped to create Olympic. The head of the War Production Board (WPB), Donald Nelson, evidently knew no more about the matter than what his subordinates told him. He did not even know that the president was personally concerned about the problem. Brant therefore urged Ickes to ask the White House to tell Nelson about Roosevelt's concern. This information was evidently dispatched because the WPB soon announced that spruce production did not depend on the availability of stands in the national parks; a substantial amount of the wood was already on hand.

The Interior Department subsequently directed lumbering companies to timber on nearby tracts owned by the University of Washington and to stands of spruce in Alaska. The operators quickly complained that the former was not of good quality and the latter was delivered too slowly. "This is certainly an example of governmental inefficiency and ineptitude," one of them complained to Drury, "to go 1000 miles away and be a year late when there is a fine supply of suitable timber controlled by you right in the backyard of mills available for use during this war when, if ever, the need is most urgent." In an expression of the American belief in practicality first he added: "The claim that the park timber is sacred and should be saved for posterity is poorly taken, especially as against the demand of this world-struggle . . . do you mean to take the stand that scenery and logs are more important than winning the war and [saving] human lives?" Drury adhered to his convictions. He also remembered how sheep and cattle had been permitted to graze in federal preserves in California during World War I. They had destroyed both natural and archaeological values for years to come. Although applications for grazing privileges continued to come in from western stockmen, Drury rejected all of them. No legislation granting access to the parks by grazers was approved by Congress.

Other challenges to the principle of park inviolability came from within the Interior Department itself. Just as the war was coming to an end, Assistant Secretary Michael Straus asked Drury to consider the consequences of an anticipated postwar increase in the number of dams built by the Bureau of Reclamation. Responsibility for the recreational use of the man-made lakes behind many of these structures, he believed, could properly be assumed by the Park Service. Drury objected. He had spent part of his Chicago "exile" drawing up plans for the postwar improvement of the park system, apparently at Roosevelt's own request. The idea of adding lesser recreational sites to the park system seemed ill suited to those plans. Besides, he resented Straus's interference in the service's programs. The National Park Advisory Board, a quasi-official group serving the department and including such prominent preservationists as journalist-historian Bernard De Voto agreed that the Park Service should not waste its efforts on such an inferior and extensive responsibility. Such recreational areas might produce an undesirable modification of the preservationist emphasis that was central to the national park system.[16]

Straus chided his colleague for taking an ivory-tower attitude, and both men appealed to their chief for a decision. Once again, Ickes's interests clashed with his responsibilities. Although he shared Drury's belief in the highest purpose of the Park Service, he also thought about the increase in the department's appropriations if the additional responsibility were assumed. He had been willing, moreover, to use potential recreation areas in order to outflank his opponents in the attempt to create Escalante Monument in Utah a few years earlier. Finally, the change could ease increasing pressures from visitors using the system's units in the near future. Perhaps for these reasons he felt compelled to reject Drury's argument. At the time, the issue seemed a minor administrative matter, but it would shortly contribute to a major policy controversy.[17]

Harold Ickes was preoccupied at this time with the subject that would become his department's principal concern in the postwar years: the development of river basin systems for reclamation and hydroelectric power production. During the war years, the Bureau of Reclamation had compiled numerous surveys for large-scale projects similar to the Tennessee Valley Authority (TVA), the showpiece of the New Deal's resource program. In October 1944, when the course of the war seemed to forecast early victory, the president asked Congress to approve "regional conservation authorities" for several

other rivers, including the Missouri and the Columbia. Senator George
Norris of Nebraska, the "father" of TVA, had introduced such a bill
in 1937 but subsequent congressional disenchantment with Roosevelt's proposals prevented any further action on it. The same mood
had returned during the campaign of 1944, but the president preferred
to set the nation's sights high by outlining a program for postwar
progress. Characteristically, he also started a rumor that he was
thinking of putting TVA's able but controversial administrator, David
Lilienthal, in charge of the new valley authorities. The news pleased
neither opponents of the New Deal nor Ickes, who was jealous of
Lilienthal's jurisdiction.[18]

Several western Democrats eagerly responded to the president's
proposal with plans of their own. Senator James Murray of Montana
tried to attach a rider to a flood control measure which would authorize
a Missouri Valley Authority (MVA). He was dismayed to learn that
opposition to it came not only from his colleagues but from his own
region. The reaction was evidence that the Northwest's political and
economic patterns had changed since the depression years. Many
residents wanted more federal dam construction on the upper Missouri
River, but they were increasingly opposed to further centralization
of federal control over water and power distribution. All that was
needed, some believed, was for the conflicting jurisdictions of the
Bureau of Reclamation, the Corps of Engineers, and the state agencies
to be properly coordinated.

When Murray held hearings on his bill late in 1944, he was angered
at the appearance of a veritable anti-MVA lobby in his own state. At
its head were two prominent Republicans: Wesley D'Ewart, secretary
of the Montana Reclamation Association, and the governor, Sam Ford.
These men maintained that the reclamation needs of the basin could
be met by private enterprise, while flood control on the lower course
of the river could be more wisely handled by the army engineers' so-
called Pick-Sloan plan for interagency, interstate compacts. Local
support for their argument was strong enough to put D'Ewart into
Congress in a special election that year. Murray and his lieutenants
charged that the Republicans were frontmen for the Montana Power
Company and other power monopolies in the region. Their opponents
in turn employed another bugaboo from the political rhetoric of the
previous decade. As Governor Ford said: "We are facing a pretty
cunning bunch of socialists and communists who seem to have un-
limited funds in their campaign to sell river authorities to the people

of the country." By April 1945 even the Interior Department concluded that Murray's proposal had no chance of adoption.[19]

During the same period, adherents of the Democratic administration
in the Pacific Northwest sought implementation of Reclamation's surveys on the Columbia River, already the site of large federal dams
at Grand Coulee and Bonneville. Roosevelt had learned of the potential of that basin from former Democratic Senator Clarence Dill of
Washington and from Charles McNary, Republican senator from
Oregon. Together, these men intended to apply the lessons of TVA
to a super power system involving the large river valleys of the nation.
Like TVA and the proposed MVA, a Columbia Valley Authority (CVA)
would epitomize the faith and promise of federal responsibility for
progress through development. They recognized the political appeal
of these projects, of course. But Roosevelt's concern may also be
interpreted as a latter-day populist-progressive doubt about the sensitivity of business to the public's best interests. He was interested
incidently in bringing about a redistribution of concentrated urban
population into agrarian areas. Still other supporters of the regional
authority idea observed that it would act as a countervailing force
to the increasing consolidation of private corporations in the nation's
economy.[20]

When McNary died in 1944, Republican Congressman Walt Horan
of eastern Washington decided to "carry the ball" for the Columbia
River development. He was determined, he told his constituents, to
fulfill the dreams of the people "who have made capital out of sweat
and sand." When he and his aides approached the Interior Department, they were heartened to learn that Under Secretary Abe Fortas
would agree to their version of a CVA if it emphasized a plan to
provide work and housing for ex-servicemen. Horan was willing to
support the administration's idea because he was convinced that only
federal action could develop the full potential of the Columbia. But
he insisted that bureaucratic control be decentralized and that participation of local private enterprise be fully recognized in the legislation creating the authority.[21]

With the war's end and the death of Roosevelt, bipartisan interest
in the idea of CVA declined among westerners. When Democratic
Congressman Hugh Mitchell of Washington introduced a bill to
authorize a Columbia Valley Authority in 1945, Republicans began
organizing opposition to it. Led by Wesley D'Ewart of Montana and
Robert Sawyer, Oregon newspaper publisher and executive secretary

of the National Reclamation Association, they formulated a strategy to delay the bill indefinitely. When the reclamation associations of the Pacific Northwest states met, discussion of the subject was so heated that the representative of the Bureau of Reclamation thought it wiser to withdraw from the session. Subsequent reference to the bill was equally divided between assertions that it was a triumph of federal planning and those predicting that it would be a victory for communism. Some opponents warned Horan that even if the word authority were deleted from the title, the program would still be "plain Revolution with a big 'R.'" The congressman did not agree. He did not think it was sufficient merely to block his colleague's measure, however, but proposed amendments that would transform it along the lines of his own plan. Federal administration, he argued, should be based on an interstate compact that would organize inter-agency regulation of dams and distribution systems. He took no satisfaction in seeing Mitchell's bill ignored at the end of the session because he noticed an ominous lack of interest on the part of legislators from the Midwest and East in any plan for more federal expenditures for western resource development.[22]

The advocates of CVA also encountered the phenomenon that Ickes knew so well: intraregional arguments over the location and extent of the projects. Lilienthal had urged Roosevelt to avoid a piecemeal approach to river basin development, but he did not endorse Ickes's alternative program to be unified under Interior's jurisdiction. The secretary had appointed Paul Raver, a friend who had served with the Illinois Commerce Commission, to head the Bonneville Power Administration in 1938. Since that agency would be the cornerstone of the CVA, supporters of federal power development in the West feared that Ickes would have considerable influence in the proposed basin authority. If his department gained control, they felt, the whole program would "degenerate into a political machine and . . . ultimately prove to be a stupendous failure." It was too big a plan to become the personal tool of any secretary or single administrator.[23]

Secretary Ickes already had substantial influence on Roosevelt's thinking about the subject. It was he who drafted the president's statement of intention for a marriage of federal supervision and local participation. Writing to Senator George Norris in 1941, he said that he wanted to "set up a strong public power area in the Northwest so that local people will be distributing the power that is sold to them by the Federal authority. When this partnership has been firmly established it will be impossible for any less progressive administration to seriously impair the work we have done."[24] Indeed, in subsequent administrations that were both more and less progressive, the definition of desirable "partnership" and the proper relationship of the Interior Department to river development would become contentious issues. By the time Roosevelt's presidency came to an end, Americans were committed to resource development, but still divided on the means to achieve it.

The New Deal's legacy in the area of natural resource policy was, to a great extent, the record of the old warhorse, Harold Ickes. No other official could match his mastery of the problems that faced the government or the means that might be used in postwar programs. Yet that same legacy contained two weaknesses. First, however efficient the "doctor" was in administering medicine that was good for the public interest, his methods left a bad taste in the mouth of many of his "patients" in the West and his competitors in the bureaucracy. A second weakness lay in his relationship to the president. No successor could possibly accomplish as much as he did unless that person served a president who was either greatly informed about resource problems or one who was willing to endorse all his secretary's proposals. By April 1945 a new president was in the White House with his own problems, programs, and advisers. Ickes, the old Progressive, must have remembered how Theodore Roosevelt's policies had seemed endangered by his successor of the same political party, William Howard Taft. So the "Old Curmudgeon," a veteran lieutenant of the New Deal, decided that it was clearly his responsibility to transmit its legacy in resource policies to the administration of Harry S. Truman.

Chapter One

CVA:
THE ROAD
NOT TAKEN

Before the end of Harry Truman's first month in the White House, he made the expansion of regional water power projects a primary domestic goal of his administration. It was, he told a meeting of advisers and legislators, "a subject close to my heart and vital to the future of the nation." He intended to resume the course set by Roosevelt by seeking congressional authorization of the programs outlined in the Bureau of Reclamation's wartime surveys. In September 1945 he presented a twenty-one point agenda to Congress, including an appeal to apply the lessons learned at TVA to other river basins, especially those of the Missouri and the Columbia. Naturally he took a personal interest in bringing federal development to the water course that traversed his native state, Missouri, but he felt that a Columbia Valley Authority stood a better chance of being accepted. The upper and lower stretches of the mighty Missouri involved distinctly different problems of silting, flooding, irrigation and power needs so that it was less likely that the senators and representatives of the nine affected states could readily agree on a Missouri Valley Authority. The Columbia was shorter and more homogeneous, and a majority of Democrats from the three states watered by it and its tributary, the Snake River, already favored a CVA. If that plan was authorized, moreover, it might break trail for acceptance of MVA.[1]

The president's request caused the debate over regional valley authorities to explode from the Pacific Northwest to the national political scene. Spokesmen from the region stated that a variety of water and power administrative arrangements already existed in their area. These included private monopolies, municipally owned utilities, and public utility districts. Yet these residents readily adopted the irrelevant stereotypes used by commentators elsewhere in the nation, men who did not know that both private and public enterprise were already accepted by the people of the region in these varying combinations. The publicity and oratory poured out on the subject of CVA nevertheless insisted on the false dichotomy: public versus private power. The supporters of CVA claimed that it would be more efficient than any private combination and more democratic because it would act in the people's interest rather than for the profits of a monopoly. Its critics predicted that it would be a victory for the forces of socialism and communism already threatening to subvert democratic governments throughout the world. But the most disturbing part of their charges was that CVA would not be controlled locally.[2]

Just as the debate began, the advocates lost one of their best spokesmen: Secretary Ickes. Having convinced Roosevelt that his department should have extensive jurisdiction over the program, he had quickly presented his arguments to Truman. MVA, he claimed, had been stymied the year before because "existing agencies of the Government which have proved their worth in the construction and operation of multiple-purpose projects [he meant his Bureau of Reclamation] should not be superseded by new instrumentalities." Interior's administration would set a "middle course," retaining the advantages of an independent authority like TVA, yet preserving the necessary measure of central control over all federal bureaus involved. Some highly placed officials supported the secretary in his idea, but others thought that his scheme would undermine existing programs as well as future ones.[3]

TVA's David Lilienthal also hastened to present his views to Truman on several occasions during that hectic first year of his presidency. Together with Samuel Rosenman, former adviser and speech writer to Roosevelt, he urged Truman not to approve the Ickes plan. The president was already aware that bureaucratic jealousies had contributed to the rejection in 1937 of Roosevelt's proposal for river valley authorities. It was not just a matter of building dams, he told Lilienthal. He wanted CVA to be "essentially a local affair." The public interest would be served when Congress passed the legislation and when he appointed the governing board of three men, but he emphasized that the states and communities must "do their job" too.[4]

Ickes got "too big for his breeches," as Truman saw it, in another controversy during the same spring months of 1946. Without warning his new chief, Ickes publicly criticized confirmation of the president's nomination of California oil magnate Edwin Pauley to be under-secretary of the navy. Just as Ickes had guarded the national parks, he had also served as watchdog over the oil industry and, remember-ing the Teapot Dome scandals, was particularly mindful of the oil reserves on the public domain under the Navy Department's jurisdic-tion. That stance now seemed to cast doubts upon the motives of his own chief. Truman respected Ickes, especially because "he was not a special interests man." He took "a lot" from his volatile lieutenant, as Irving Brant observed, "even if he does make him mad, because he knows his value." The two men did not clash personally, but the president could not permit this embarrassing insubordination to stand. On Ickes part, he was already looking for a suitable successor and may have used this affair as a good opportunity to resign in righteous protest. He had employed that gesture several times in the past, but unlike Roosevelt, Truman refused to pamper him. After reading Ickes's "not very courteous letter," he accepted the resignation.[5]

The White House was deluged with letters of congratulations from some Democrats who had long considered Ickes a disturber of the party's peace and some westerners who felt that they had "groaned under his dictatorship" long enough. But three times as many com-plaints arrived in the mail. These reiterated that the secretary had been fired for exercising the same honesty and defense of the public interest that had made him such a valuable administrator. For many, the loss of the old warrior seemed to sever an element of continuity between the New Deal and its heir. In retrospect, the affair was part of a larger cabinet crisis that marked the opening of a Pandora's box of troubles for Truman.[6]

During the ensuing weeks, the president toyed with the press's curiosity on the subject of the Interior secretaryship. He told them that he had considered several men. One, Joseph O'Mahoney of Wyoming, he felt, would be more valuable in the Senate where he could draw upon his great understanding of water problems. An-other, Governor Monrad Wallgren of Washington, had been Truman's colleague during the war years and was a very close friend. From the same state, Supreme Court Justice William O. Douglas was a leading publicist for wilderness preservation. Douglas indicated, how-ever, that he would take the post only if ordered to do so. Justice Harlan Stone soon afterwards easily talked him into remaining on the Court, his first love. It seemed most likely, Brant decided, that Wallgren would be named. In view of the man's record in support of the creation and protection of Olympic National Park, it would be a most desirable selection. Then Truman announced that the new secretary of the Interior would be Julius Krug of Wisconsin. Ickes, who always believed that an easterner was far more trustworthy than any westerner, must have been pleased. But the White House newsmen, remembering the West's claim to the office, greeted the announcement with laughter.[7]

"Cap" Krug, handsome, genial, monolithic in size, had been chosen to preside over the establishment of the administration's river valley authorities. Few men were better qualified for that task. He had served a well-publicized term as chief of his state's public utilities commission, a veritable model of public power administration. He then entered the federal service as a staff member of TVA and later became chairman of the War Production Board. In that post, his abilities first came to the attention of Senator Truman whose committee was investigating war contracts. The offer of the secretaryship came to him just as he was receiving attractive invitations to join private corporations. As a result, he did not intend to remain in that post for very long. Lilienthal thought it would be well enough if he could do no more there than reverse the "40 year decline of western development" by securing adoption of the president's water power program. Yet it was said that liberals "from Cheyenne to Seattle" were disappointed by the choice precisely because Krug was no politician and because he shunned controversy. Preservationists like Horace Albright were also disappointed that Assistant Secretary Oscar Chapman had not been appointed. Truman had considered him, but Chapman seemed reluctant to appear to profit from the demise of his old chief. At least Krug would not be one of the usual faceless westerners who ran the department with a marked solicitude for local economic interests, Albright observed. Still, Lilienthal shook his head in wonder at the "curious turn" in his own long feud with Ickes: "one of our boys, as close to me as 'Cap,'" he wrote, was now sitting where "the old devil" had sat.[8]

Secretary Krug did not assume the mantle of Ickesian omnipotence even though he retained all his predecessor's jurisdictions. He immediately set about to alter the chain of command in the department, relying upon the advice of O'Mahoney and Chapman, now under secretary, and upon Michael Straus. The former assistant secretary had just taken over the commissionership of the Bureau of Reclamation, a place secured for him by Ickes who had recommended him to Truman as a man with "vision, enthusiasms, and a full appreciation of the necessity for sound planning." Straus was especially adept at working with representatives of western states and western organizations. Some indication of his high level of influence was the fact that Assistant Secretary Warner Gardner often approved Reclamation's budget requests even when they were not presented in customary detail.[9]

Since water and power had priority in the Krug administration, his principal lieutenant was Assistant Secretary C. Girard "Jebby" Davidson. A native of Louisiana, as brash and zealous as Straus, he had moved to Oregon to serve under Paul Raver at Bonneville. When he came to Interior, he "practically took charge" of the department's budget. His preoccupation with resource development particularly disturbed Newton Drury of the Park Service. It looked as if everything now had to be processed through a series of new personnel, "bright young men and good looking young women" just out of college, holding "lots of ideas . . . out to remake the world" without practical touch with reality. None of them were aware that the department had obligations to preserve as well as to develop, Drury felt. Privately he wondered whether his cause would be quickly forgotten.[10]

Secretary Krug adhered to the principles of public power policy that had been outlined by his predecessor in January 1946. Because the federal dams were built with public taxes, the public's interest would be paramount in every consideration of water and power distribution from those dams. This had been the sense of the acts of Congress on the subject in 1937, 1938, and 1939. Public preference would be specifically designated in every contract negotiated between federal agencies and any consumer. As a result, the needs of local cooperatives would be favored over those of private companies that intended to profit from the public facilities. No contracts would be made which would limit sales to specific areas or favor specific users.

President Truman emphasized these same guidelines in his messages to Congress and his communications with water development organizations in the West. He told the National Reclamation Association, for example, that he deeply shared the region's desire for growth and prosperity through development of water resources. The public preference clause and the 160-acre user limitation on land held by every consumer were proper safeguards for the requirements of an expanding population, for the opportunity of the ordinary citizen, and for the benefit of the returning veteran. Interior's Bureau of Reclamation, he reminded them, was "a mighty force" working toward those aims. He urged the members of every such organization to use their influence to secure public support and congressional appropriations for the proposals of his administration. That same month, January 1946, Democratic Senator Hugh Mitchell of Washington introduced a bill to authorize a Columbia Valley Authority embodying these principles.[11]

Later that year, Krug went out to the Pacific Northwest "to listen and learn what's going on." In Mitchell's home state, he found what he believed was substantial support for the CVA proposal and sentiment favoring regional authorities elsewhere in the nation. His lieutenants shared in the fieldwork. Warner Gardner addressed the National Reclamation Association meeting in Nebraska. He apologized for not being a westerner himself, but assured them that he nevertheless knew enough about western economics to believe that the public preference clause was wise. "None of you would consider it good business to sell your crops to none other than one person," he explained. "No more should the United States be forced to sell at the dam to only one private power company." Almost all the single-purpose reclamation dams planned by the New Deal were already functioning. Now the emphasis would be on multiple-purpose structures, he announced, and upon the widest distribution of water and power. Such programs could be administered only by regional valley authorities. "Jebby" Davidson returned to Oregon at this same time and talked to many former associates among utility and farm organizations. To help allay their doubts about the status of local interests in the CVA proposal, he promised that the Interior Department's policies would reflect the needs and wishes of the people of the West.[12]

The voices of the administration's spokesmen were nearly drowned out by the uproar over the CVA issue. The Republican governors of the three basin states joined forces to state that the proposal was not wanted or needed in their region. While Congress held hearings on the Mitchell bill, western meeting halls and newspapers were filled with the arguments and warnings of each point of view. Farm and labor organizations, engineers and businessmen eagerly extended invitations to speakers from such authority proponents as the Northwest Public Power Development Association and from such critics as the Pacific Northwest Development Association. Underneath the usual clichés about "socialism" and "free enterprise," these comments focused on the question of centralism over localism. Federal dams were unquestionably desired. Federal administration by a handful of appointed officials thousands of miles from the region was widely questioned. Moreover, some asked why the "accumulated wisdom" of the working agreement between the Corps of Engineers and the Bureau of Reclamation on the Missouri should be rejected in order to bring in a new "conflicting layer of authority." Why place Columbia River development into the hands of "a few politicians whose power would supercede that of the state"? Others regarded these challenges as mere scare tactics. The region needed any and all arrangements that could substantially stimulate economic growth. As one Portland banker concluded: "I believe the regional authority idea is coming, and when it comes I do not believe that the country will fall into Communism."[13]

It was not possible accurately to assess public opinion on the CVA issue, although both sides insisted that they knew what it was. There was some talk of holding a regionwide referendum on the subject, but the proposal's critics feared that the administration would make political capital out of any sized margin of support. When the press corps asked President Truman whether he would call for such a vote, he replied that action by the Congress, as the elected representatives of the people, would in fact be a referendum. That remark seemed a bit embarrassing when the results of the general election were known that November. The Republicans won the strongest majority control of Congress since the 1920s, and one of the Democrats who lost his seat was Senator Hugh Mitchell, author of the CVA bill. Senator Henry Dworshak of Idaho and Congressman Walt Horan of Washington immediately sent out a call to all Republican members from the Northwest for a discussion of common strategy and committee assignments. But Horan at least knew that parliamentary tactics would not necessarily express the region's interests. If his colleagues were able to destroy the water proposals of the Truman administration, they would thereby jeopardize federal activities essential to the West's economy. One of his constituents, a staunchly Republican member of the Spokane, Washington, Chamber of Commerce, foresaw the horrible result: "if the Republican organization in Congress attempts to throttle our western irrigation program," whether for reasons of cutting federal spending or for political purposes, "it will simply drive the West back into the lap of a second New Deal."[14]

Few westerners had as knowledgeable and realistic a grasp of the political implications of the CVA controversy as Walt Horan had. Ever since he had been a candidate for Congress in 1944, his interest in federal power programs had earned him the continuing condemnation of Spokane's Washington Water Power Company, one of the few large private utilities in the state. He insisted that he was not an enemy of free enterprise, however, but an advocate of comprehensive development of the Columbia basin. The political climate of guilt by association prevailing in that period tended to cloud all distinctions. As a result, Republicans set a man who favored federal development against Horan in the primary campaign of 1946, and the Democrats chose a supporter of the Mitchell bill to face him in the general election. He beat both of them and returned to the House to submit a plan of his own to turn the federal proposal toward more local control.[15]

After the establishment of a Columbia Basin Interagency Commission that same year, Horan decided that it could be the basis for an acceptable alternative to CVA. He sponsored a bill calling for federal authorization of a Columbia Interstate Compact (CIC) which would draw upon the ideas of TVA yet protect state power from federal dominance. "I certainly have no brief *against any* agency," he told water engineer James O'Sullivan, "It is merely that the eventual prerogatives should come from this area and not from Washington, D.C. My bill is an attempt to effect a workable interstate compact with all of the court tested powers of TVA. I have tried, however, to eliminate the dangers of administrative power inherent in the TVA act." Politically, the bill would have the effect of transforming the negative attitude of the Republican majority into a positive program as the best offense against the CVA. He felt that if they did not adopt that alternative the party would be "missing a glorious opportunity to take the lead in this matter."[16]

Observing that a Californian headed the Public Lands Committee in the House and a Nebraskan was chairman of the Senate Interior Committee, Horan was confident that the Republican Congress "did not intend to short-change the West." But the new leadership immediately laid plans to cut every aspect of the Truman water development program. They appealed to southern conservative Democrats on the grounds of states' rights and to eastern representatives of both parties who resented spending money on western projects. Horan reintroduced his CIC bill, but watched helplessly as his own Interior appropriation subcommittee slashed away at the department's budget requests for reclamation projects and transmission lines. Funds sought by the Bureau of Reclamation and by the Bonneville Power Administration were trimmed because western Republicans felt that they would be used to spread CVA propaganda.[17]

In several instances, the lead for this surgery was taken by another subcommittee member, Wesley D'Ewart, the old foe of James Murray's aborted MVA. Other reclamationists joined him in permitting partisan vengeance to override the economic interests of their region. The Republicans also proposed alterations in the Reclamation Act of 1939 which would give Congress the right to initiate new projects and to prohibit the use of any appropriations for public power publicity. This move was echoed when the Washington state legislature resolved that funds designated for Grand Coulee Dam should not be spent on publicity to support CVA. Democratic Congressman Henry Jackson decried these attempts to "strangle the West," and Governor Monrad Wallgren asked his fellow state chief executives of both parties to unite in a demand that the reclamation appropriations at least be restored. The Republican governors refused to join his appeal, however. Wallgren was obviously embarrassed when the state engineers of the West met in his own state and publicly criticized the Bureau of Reclamation's policies. Moreover, private power men spread the rumor that the Democrats were planning to divert the region's water supply to California by means of an intertie pipeline. Advocates of public power in the Pacific Northwest feared that the Republicans were willing to do anything to thwart the "bastards" in the Truman administration. Western Republicans hastened to assure their constituents that these were merely temporary tactics, no more damaging than other expressions of disgust with the Interior Department's "continued arrogance."[18]

The Democrats were angry, but they saw in the blatant actions of the Republicans in the Eightieth Congress a great opportunity for themselves. In the spring of 1948, presidential adviser Clark Clifford submitted a memorandum to Truman for planning the coming election campaign. Arguing that the traditional Democratic alliance of the West and the South was the cornerstone of victory, he wrote: "therefore, political and program planning demands concentration upon the West and its problems, including reclamation, floods, and agriculture. It is the Number One priority for the 1948 campaign." The Republicans, he dryly observed, had already done their part "to give the

West to the Administration." Resource policy was to be one of six major issues stressed in the contest, with specific emphasis upon the need for reclamation projects, "and lots of them," public power, and "help in the development and protection of their resources." The Democratic National Committee opened that strategy by lamenting that the western states had been "especially badly treated" by the Republican Congress. Commissioner Michael Straus toured the six states of the Northwest early that summer. When he returned he told the president that the administration's policies were supported by a majority who wanted and needed federal water and power development. Truman commented: "I think this last Congress amply demonstrated what the attitude of the Republicans would be toward Reclamation if they had complete control of the Government."[19]

The president made a dramatic swing through the West during the the summer and fall months. He enlarged upon the Clifford strategy by employing the current rhetoric of conspiracy and the time-honored Democratic devil theories. At Seattle, with Julius Krug at his side, Truman said he did not believe that westerners would exchange public interests for the "selfish interests" of "private power lobbyists." Speaking against the impressive backdrop of devastating floods along the Columbia River, he reminded his audiences that the forces of evil were cunning. "You know what they are doing with those appropriations now? They are tieing them up in such a way that even if we get them, we can't use them to the best advantage and the best interests of the public."

Truman addressed other gatherings in Colorado and predicted that a Republican administration would be interested only in the demands of "the real estate lobby . . . the power lobby." Every appropriation that affected the West, he pointed out, had been "slashed with malice aforethought." It was easily explained: easterners were in charge of the appropriations committees. Using his famous humor, he admitted that one of them had perhaps come into the region "at some time or other on some Senate jaunt . . . but he didn't know what he was looking at when he saw it." In the Mormon tabernacle at Salt Lake City, the jaunty campaigner told another crowd that the West's real friends were those who had helped it obtain needed water and power. By the same token, those who had hampered that assistance "are not your friends." It was an old story, he pointed out: selfish men had always controlled the Republican party over the years and they had "done their best to make the West an economic colony." Their record on resource policy was easily summed up: "Never before in history had so much been wasted by so few."[20]

The Republicans in Congress belatedly realized that their defiant gestures were harming the party's image in the West. Just before the session ended in late summer, they restored some of the cuts in the Interior budget. Yet that action was obviously politically motivated and merely served to underscore Truman's charges. Horan protested that there was no truth in the equation of party allegiance and attitude toward appropriations. Democrats in the House had purposely refused to cooperate, he claimed, in order to make political capital out of the Republicans' actions and had even criticized their opponents for spending too much on reclamation projects. Other Republicans pointed out, moreover, that their nominee for the vice presidency, Governor Earl Warren of California, was a long-time supporter of federal water and power development.[21]

The same could not be said of the Republican nominee for the presidency. Governor Thomas E. Dewey of New York made few extended references to the issues of resource policy during his campaign, and these were dismayingly ambiguous. Goaded by Truman's jabs about easterners, he branded Krug and Davidson as "carpetbaggers" themselves. He condemned "socialized power" but confused many voters by defending federal control of "main line" power transmission. Although he said he favored federal hydroelectric programs, he insisted that he would assert his state's control of the administration of the proposed St. Lawrence-Niagara navigation and power project. Westerners must have wondered about his personal interest when he referred to power development as "a dreary but vital subject." In that context, his promise to appoint a westerner as secretary of the Interior looked somewhat like a proferred carrot. When Republican candidates in the West talked about resource issues, they could say little more about Dewey than to assert that he would bring a change. Generally, they preferred to raise the effigies of federal bureaucrats and hope that western irritation would be stronger than the desire for the largesse dispensed by those bureaucrats.[22]

Clark Clifford's strategy concerning use of the issue of resource development proved to be accurate and effective. Every voter in the western states could read clearly the simple dichotomy presented by the Democrats: their concern for the needs of the region during the preceding fifteen years and the contrasting, devious record of the Republicans during their two-year control of Congress. To point up that comparison, several veterans of the Interior Department traveled throughout the West to address resource-minded organizations. Under Secretary Oscar Chapman did yeoman service in that task and confirmed his image as a bureaucrat-westerner worthy of western trust. New Dealers also cheered Ickes, who issued a strong endorsement of Truman after Chapman and Straus convinced him that the president's stand on resource development and preservation was exactly like his own.[23] All these factors contributed to the impressive total: Truman won ten of eleven western states. Washington gave the Democrats a margin of four to three and sent former Senator Hugh Mitchell back to Congress as a representative. Oregon remained Republican only by a slim margin. Senator Guy Cordon retained his seat by 60 percent of the votes cast, but Democrats noticed a substantial increase in their party's registration in Oregon as well as in several other strongly Republican states of the region. A Utah reclamationist offered one explanation of the outcome: the West had resented Republican attacks on Krug, Straus, and Lilienthal. Generally speaking, however, it was a case of economics outweighing political interests. Westerners might well have preferred to halt Democratic spending and throw out "arrogant" bureaucrats, but not halt the spending for dams and not throw out bureaucrats who were eager to build more of them. The few irreconcilable critics of federal water policies sighed with resignation and prepared themselves for the "rough time" that would "undoubtedly" be their lot for the next two and possibly four years.[24]

The men of the Truman administration were exultant and confident after their surprise victory. Davidson shrugged when he heard that CVA's opponents were still planning to fight it: "So far the Republicans and power companies are against it, and the Democrats, labor and farmers are for it. What more could we ask?" The president was certain that the West had given him a mandate. The people of that region, he informed the National Reclamation Association, had "reaffirmed their adherence" to the emphases and programs of Democratic administrations. His White House advisers and officials at the Interior Department at once began drawing up plans for the reintroduction of regional valley authority legislation. David Bell, an expert on reclamation matters, and Charles Murphy, special assistant to the president, decided to unfold the CVA proposal gradually this time, in order to forestall its critics. They saw two major problems involved in drafting a new measure. The first problem was the extent to which the authority would conduct operations as well as control planning for water and power projects. Second, they would have to decide the precise extent to which states and localities should participate in both plans and operations. River valley development already underway in California and Arizona, for example, could be handled by a limited coordinating body, the Southwest Power Administration. The Pick-Sloan arrangement seemed to be adequate for the conditions in the Missouri Valley, but neither variation was desirable for the Columbia. Objections to a "superbureaucracy," Bell thought, might be met by emphasizing that CVA would simply be a more efficient, more far-sighted replacement for the machinery already working at Bonneville.[25]

Chapman reported the sense of the White House plan to Krug, and the latter issued a special report on regional resources development which reiterated the emphases of the president's advisers. CVA would not create a "super Federal Government," he said. It would merely relocate the focal point of certain federal powers and functions already in existence—but instead of being performed in Washington, D.C., they would be carried out on home grounds. The proposal did not give the government authority which it did not already have and exercised by remote control. In effect, federal control was thus to be transferred to the grass roots. Evidently Chapman, Davidson, and Assistant Secretary William Warne concluded that it was unrealistic to expect major support among the people of any other river valley except the Tennessee and perhaps the Columbia. They therefore recommended that the Bureau of Reclamation construct the dams in the Columbia Valley and the Upper Colorado River basin. Truman agreed.[26]

In April 1949 the president sent a special message to Congress asking for the establishment of a Columbia Valley Administration. The alteration in the title undoubtedly reflected his advisers' hope of overcoming the implication of supergovernment. Truman pointed out that the interstate compact idea had obvious limitations which rendered it incapable of meeting the larger agricultural and industrial needs of the region. The basic planning for a CVA was already completed and would involve no expansion of federal power, no encroachment on the rights of states, counties, or individuals. It would bring government closer to the grass roots and would therefore be more responsive to the people's needs. Legislation was thereafter introduced by Senator Warren Magnuson and Congressmen Mitchell and Jackson of Washington State. Senator Glen Taylor of Idaho also championed the measure. Although Taylor's support may have seemed surprising in view of his recent criticism of Truman while vice presidential nominee of the Progressive party, he had in fact long been a strong advocate of CVA. The measure's adherents claimed that their bill was very different from the original Mitchell bill of 1946. Bell was pleased to see that it was already helping to bring about a "shotgun" agreement between Reclamation and the Corps of Engineers on future planning in the West. He felt that it could be the basis for converting critics in the region. Those in eastern Washington perhaps could be pacified by designating Spokane as CVA's headquarters.[27]

The first response to the president's request was heartening. The White House was flooded with endorsements of CVA, and the Washington state legislature passed a resolution in its favor by a vote of 71 to 26. But Truman also received telegrams from the Republican governors of the region: Arthur Langlie of Washington, Douglas McKay of Oregon, and C. A. Robins of Idaho. These executives insisted that the people of their states did not want a CVA; water and power development could be accomplished more properly by existing interagency commissions. Truman was unmoved. "I think the people of those . . . States are entitled to the development of this Great River Valley," he replied, "and I am going to try to get it done."[28]

The president and his supporters were assuming that only Republicans found the CVA proposal unacceptable. But such a veteran Democrat from the Pacific Northwest as Clarence Dill feared that the bill could not garner local support until it included a guarantee that state water laws would be protected and that residents of the region were named as its administrators. Another Democrat urged Mitchell to redesign the measure "to fit the political pattern of the Northwest." The existing public utility districts, municipal power plants, and rural electrification units were quite able to assume their full degree of responsibility in policy making. Their advice on the governing board would prevent federal bureaucrats from "getting too uppity and making mistakes." Those officials *"must be instructed"* to act in substantial agreement with the public agencies owned and controlled in the region. Even though Republicans also advocated the localist approach, it had the advantage of being slow but safe.[29]

Among Republicans from the Pacific Northwest there were similar voices urging reasonableness. Congressman Walt Horan wrote with apprehension to Governor Langlie: "we cannot simply oppose a program which may be distasteful to us. We must take the lead in evolving a solution to a real problem and offer it constructively and forcefully. If we fail to do so, we may get a program shoved down our throats, like it or not." Believing that he could satisfy the needs and prejudices of all factions and aware that even members of the Democratic majority had private misgivings, Horan tried to establish communication on the matter with the opposition. The new CVA bill, he privately believed, was no different from the old; Mitchell, Jackson, and Taylor had not "changed a semicolon." Yet the president said that the lessons learned at TVA should be applied to the administration of the Columbia. Consequently, he sent a draft of an alternate plan to the Interior Department. It proposed a four-member governing council with basic control over policy making but one that would rely on local agencies whenever practical. The council members would be appointed by the president from names recommended by the state governors, and they would serve for seven years. Their projects would be self-supporting and self-liquidating, an arrangement often demanded by critics of federal power production.[30]

The department passed Horan's letter on to Mitchell for "a friendly analysis." The Democrat found it wholly unsatisfactory. It would limit the president's appointive power, he replied, and it was a fallacy to assume that just because governors recommended the councilmen they would in turn represent popular, local will. There was no provision to prevent men with financial ties to private utilities from gaining those places. On the other hand, there was no provision for the representation of other public economic interests or other federal agencies. Horan's plan contained no set of priorities to meet the needs of cooperatives and no recognition of such related activities as research and flood control. Most objectionable, the council would be making policy without direct congressional mandate and would have an independent veto over the plans of other federal and state legislative bodies. It would be, Mitchell implied, as unresponsive to the public interest as the critics claimed CVA would be.[31]

When Arthur Langlie read Mitchell's assessment he was indignant. "We hold no brief for private power interests," he replied hotly, "and take issue with your comparison." The opponents of CVA were only seeking a better method of bringing about federal development, not trying to replace it. But the behavior of the Republican opposition belied protestations of good intention. Horan's own colleagues were not interested in his suggestions. One constituent described his plan as "just another shingle on the political roof." Senator Harry Cain of Washington declined to help sponsor the bill, although he later introduced his own pale facsimile of it. By the end of 1949, the congressman realized that his proposal was "too conservative to satisfy the radicals, too liberal to satisfy the reactionaries, and doesn't promise enough special privilege to anyone." When the session ended, neither party had given an inch on CVA or any alternative. In 1950 both sides took up the issue again but this time with markedly less enthusiasm.[32]

President Truman praised the Democratic Congress for adopting the most far-reaching reclamation program ever, one that maintained public preference in the transmission and marketing of water and power. But neither his friends nor his enemies overlooked the fact that his greatest desire, CVA, had again been thwarted. Perhaps to substantiate his proposals on the subject of water resource development, he appointed a Water Resources Policy Commission under the chairmanship of Morris Cooke, onetime director of Roosevelt's Rural Electrification Administration. For most of 1950, the commissioners traveled throughout the West, taking testimony from state officials and from spokesmen for public and private utilities, professional and farm organizations. Inadvertently, the hearings provided a forum for the critics of the administration's proposals. Governor Douglas McKay of Oregon submitted a defense of state control to them. Federal water development, he maintained, should correspond to the requirements and policy of each state and all projects should be determined by the extent to which they satisfied local requirements. Not one who believed that federal policy should be determined by political philosophy, he did not think that mere engineering efficiency should be the major consideration either. He was positive about one thing, however: no additional federal legislation was necessary or desirable so far as Oregon was concerned. A spokesman for the Montana Chamber of Commerce repeated that assertion. Localism was a way of life in the West; the region's people were the proper judges of the many conflicting aspects involved in water resource development— not "alien" federal agencies. Other testimony revealed intraregional jealousy, however. One witness asserted that the debate over CVA had obscured the need for development in other river valleys. Moreover, a federal super grid system would favor areas with concentrated population rather than encourage growth elsewhere. As a result, the allegedly insatiable dominance of California would be perpetuated by diversion of Pacific Northwest and Upper Colorado basin waters southwestward. Finally, a few lone voices registered objection to any federal water programs. A member of the preservationist Izaak Walton League in Denver described dams as "a popular fad" used by developers to hypnotize the West. Other human needs besides finance and engineering warranted consideration by the planners at all levels of government. Even such a prominent advocate of reclamation projects as Robert Sawyer of Oregon privately wondered whether the programs had gone too far already in view of the mounting agricultural surpluses. Former governor Leslie Miller of Wyoming urged the commissioners to recommend a slowing up of river basin development in order to preserve water for probable future demands.[33]

Throughout 1949 and 1950, criticism of CVA from every point of view worked to the advantage of the Republicans as they stepped up their attacks on the Truman administration. Many of the newspapers of the Pacific Northwest printed editorials that equated CVA with internal subversion.[34] The president's nomination of Monrad Wallgren as chairman of the Federal Power Commission was blocked by a group led by Senator Cain. Rumors were spread alleging that the administration was planning to divert Columbia River water to California. Idahoans learned that the Democrats wanted to build a high, multiple-purpose dam at Hells Canyon on the Snake River. Many economic organizations in that state preferred authorization of the Idaho Power Company's application to the Federal Power Commission (FPC) for the construction of three low single-purpose dams. These units were needed for irrigation storage in the agricultural part of Idaho. Because they found the service of a single private utility company to be satisfactory, Idaho people appeared to federal planners as the most hostile critics of federal projects in the region. When the Interior Department applied to the FPC to withhold approval of the Idaho Power Company contract, the issue of Hells Canyon elicited as much debate as CVA. Republicans everywhere pointed to it as evidence of the way that the federal leviathan threatened the small farmer and as proof that the people had to be rescued by the intercession of those who believed in private enterprise.[35]

As the elections of November 1950 approached, there was a distinct feeling that political change would determine resource policy. When Senator Warren Magnuson reintroduced the CVA bill in a form that contained some modifications of the earlier versions, Republicans read it as a sign that the administration was weakening and that prominent

Democrats opposed the plan. Even Oscar Chapman at Interior admitted that interest in it was declining. Seeing their adversaries weakening, the Republicans took the offensive. Senator Sheridan Downey of California selected Commissioner Straus as a personal target, threatened to investigate his handling of the Bureau of Reclamation, and called for suspension of his salary until the investigation was concluded. Senator Andrew Schoeppel, called the "Kansas McCarthy," announced that Chapman had been a member of several Communist-front organizations and along with Straus had crossed out the loyalty portion of his oath of office. Their colleague "Jebby" Davidson had had the temerity to criticize the House Un-American Activities Committee. The charges continued, claiming that Straus was "known and understood to be an ardent follower of the concept of nationalization of land, water, and power." According to the senator, the "scarlet 'left of left' record" of all these men extended back many years, "even to the early days of the New Deal." Perhaps Straus had made too many enemies in his zeal for federal reclamation, but the senator could not have picked on a man with more friends and admirers than Chapman. The under secretary deftly answered the charges; the president was obviously pleased with his defense. When Schoeppel threatened further investigation, Joseph O'Mahoney of Wyoming, chairman of the Senate Interior Committee, bluntly replied that there would be none.[36]

The three "subversives" of the Interior Department, Chapman, Straus, and Davidson, once again took to the hustings during the campaign that summer. There they encountered the same acidic fog of innuendo and non sequitur. In California, Congresswoman Helen Gahagan Douglas's support of Reclamation's 160-acre limit on Central Valley projects was cited as evidence of her adherence to communistic ideas. In Idaho, the CVA issue lent ammunition to the opponents of Glen Taylor in his bid for reelection. Truman's proposal, he boldly maintained throughout the campaign, was the fulfillment of the New Deal's belief in grassroots democracy as the basis for resource policy. His state had unfortunately joined in the assault on it, he lamented, at the behest of an odious private power monopoly. For a moment, even Republicans sensed a slight increase in support for the federal project. To head it off, they coupled Taylor's role in the Progressive party of 1948 with his belief in CVA as proof of his un-Americanism. The *Boise Idaho Statesman* almost daily held up this equation to demonstrate the "red record" of Taylor. Quite understandably, the senator hoped that the Truman Democrats would help him in this struggle for political survival. Chapman at least wrote privately in his behalf, but the president, perhaps recalling 1948, remained silent. Although the issue of CVA was not decisive in Taylor's defeat that November, Republicans jubilantly concluded that it was a measure of their power to block the proposal permanently.[37]

The Democrats lost half as many congressional seats in 1950 as they had in 1946, but that was enough to preclude the possibility of passing legislation for CVA. They had expected that the marked increase in party registration in Oregon, for example, would alter traditional Republican strength. But CVA was either too complicated or too abstract to affect the voting there. Both Republican Senator Wayne Morse and Governor Douglas McKay were only weakly opposed for reelection. Afterwards, the latter anounced that CVA was "a dead duck" for two years at least and maybe permanently. Democrats who had feared that the CVA matter was too hot to handle were visibly relieved when a procedural alternative was found. The so-called Weaver-Newell agreement between the Army Corps of Engineers and the Bureau of Reclamation seemed to be a response to the Langlie-McKay assertion that interagency administrative machinery was an adequate and desirable plan for the Columbia River basin. Although spokesmen for Truman's water policy denied that the agreement could permanently solve the region's future requirements, that arrangement was confirmed when Congress approved an interstate compact in July 1952.[38]

Morale was decidedly low in the Interior Department during the months after the elections of 1950. The sense of futility Krug had experienced before was now shared by his right-hand man. Davidson resigned in 1951, although he continued to advise the department on water and power policy. CVA opponents alleged that he resigned because he was disappointed that he would not be able to direct the new program. Interior officials wondered whether the Weaver-Newell agreement was the same sort of "bureaucratic sabotage" of presidential intentions that the Pick-Sloan accord had been a few years earlier. Straus's colleagues particularly feared that it was a green light for the Bureau of Reclamation's dominance of department policy.[39]

In retrospect, CVA seems to have been the victim of the Korean crisis. Once Truman made that foreign commitment, he viewed every aspect of the domestic economy through the glass of the war emergency. The months after June 1950 were no time for controversy

and experiment. Truman even withheld some of the recommendations of his own Water Resources Policy Commission, explaining to
chairman Cooke that they might arouse "such controversy and feeling
that it would prejudice the possibility of a fair hearing." Cooke objected, of course, and reminded his associates that a positive program
was needed, especially after the blocking of CVA. He sadly concluded,
however, that the administration had "got so involved—perhaps wisely
—in foreign affairs, that it has closed its eyes to the domestic situation."
The priority makers at the White House, he suspected, were responsible for the president's abrupt silence in face of continuing attacks on
his water and power programs.[40]

Had there been an overwhelming change of heart about CVA in
the West? Truman and his lieutenants had believed in a mandate of
1948 and had enjoyed a substantial swell of support among economic
organizations in the region. The Democrats had a majority of the
political control there and in Congress until 1951. But by that date
they found themselves harassed by their critics and deserted by
doubters within their own ranks. Most alarming was the thought
that the specter of "socialism," so effectively added to the other Republican charges about the direction of their administrations, would
be used in 1952 to expunge the upset of 1948.

Chapter Two

THE
LAND
GRABBERS

Julius Krug became secretary of the Interior in order to preside over the Truman administration's water and power programs, but he was faced with a significant challenge in the preservation of resources as well. The roots of that problem lay in the general public's overwhelming postwar desire for unencumbered economic development and in the political resurgence of those elements—Democrat and Republican—which had grown dissatisfied with Harold Ickes's resource policies. In Congress, they joined under the banner of economy to cut the budgets of the bureaus administering land and resource use and to halt any further centralization of administration in the Interior Department. In addition, just as the variety of opponents of CVA worked together, the spokesmen for stockmen, lumbering organizations, and extractive industries joined in tandem in order to modify regulations determining access to the public domain.

When the Taylor Grazing Act was adopted in the 1930s, the grazing organizations of the West had seemed cooperative and even anxious to have federal regulations that would bring order out of the chaos of conflicting interests. During the subsequent decade, however, they came to think of themselves much as the farming population did—as neglected stepchildren of the nation's economic policy makers. In May 1946 Ickes's hope for reorganization of the Interior Department was partly met when Truman created a Bureau of Land Management which absorbed the functions of the old Grazing Service and General Land Office. Stockmen were dubious about what seemed to be further centralization and bureaucracy. When Ickes resigned shortly thereafter, they became "more voracious"—in Chapman's words—in

seeking "vested rights and privileges." In November Republican
victories produced a favorable political climate. The department
was soon flooded with resolutions, complaints, and warnings from
stockmen's organizations. Some of these demanded "reasonable" access
to federal rangelands, and others protested the appointment of agents
not recommended by their own membership. Wherever the department's policies were under review—in congressional committees, at the
bureaus, or at conventions—spokesmen claimed that they were being
"crucified." Federal landlordism was an obstacle to western prosperity
generally, and grazing regulations were detrimental to their industry
specifically. The Truman administration, they charged, had no personal interest in their plight except to play politics with it. The time
had come, said Congressman Frank Barrett of Wyoming, to get
"proper justice" for the stockmen.[1]

With the legislative axes poised over the budget requests of both
the Bureau of Land Management and the Forest Service, the controversy ripped open the old sore of interdepartmental rivalry. Interior
officials sought the advice of professional foresters and were not
pleased when they suggested that the Agriculture Department assume
jurisdiction over grazing administration. Marion Clawson, director
of the Bureau of Land Management, instead seemed to be constructing
a greater centralization of land use policy in his own agency. It would
be based upon a total view of the ecological balance of human and
natural resources, rather than merely upholding particular economic
interests. Praise from preservationists for his intentions only damned
him more in the eyes of developers. Even Secretary Krug was disturbed. Feeling that the director was going too far, he informed all
his lieutenants that no suggestions should be made unless they were
first cleared with him and unless he was first convinced that they
would bring about real improvement. He thought that the department
had encountered enough criticism in the past "through dreamers going
off half cocked in this vital area of our domestic economy."[2]

The men at Interior were not all preservationists, but they welcomed
the assistance of preservation organizations in their defense against
the stockmen's pressures. With a total membership of over a million,
some dozen groups constituted a veritable lobby at the nation's Capitol.
Led by the Sierra Club, the Izaak Walton League, the Wilderness
Society, and the National Parks Association, they matched their opponents in self-righteous convictions about what constituted subversion of the public's true interest. Similarly, their rhetoric used

apocalyptic visions and absolutes. Developers eyeing the federal domain were branded as "land pirates" bent on a "great land grab." Although they were not solicitous of western economic interests as such, they expressed the old suspicion of monopoly as ultimately destructive of economic opportunity. They were especially sensitive on the subject of parkland and wildlife preservation, and threats in those areas prompted them to assume the function of publicity phalanx for the department.

Early in 1947 several western congressmen proposed that units of the national park system be opened to mineral exploration and lumbering. If the nation's primary goal was to build free enterprise as a bulwark against totalitarianism, they argued, these preserves were a luxury unless they served that purpose. In Florida, real estate promoters of the postwar boom demanded reduction in the size of Everglades National Park while oil operators asked for extension on their drilling leases within the preserve. Created in 1940, but not opened because of the war, the wilderness park seemed to local residents an unattractive wasteland, too harsh and isolated to bring in many tourist dollars. With the secretary distracted by the fight for CVA, Park Service director Newton Drury had to fend off these pressures. Fortunately, he had Truman's support. When the demands increased, the president made a special trip to Florida to dedicate the park. In his address, he firmly defended the national parks as an important resource.[3]

Another attack at the system came from Frank Barrett of Wyoming, the stockmen's friend. Because of the Republican victories in 1946, he became one of the most influential members of the House Public Lands Committee, while a fellow Wyomingite, Edward Robertson, exercised equal power on the Senate Interior Committee. Resuming Barrett's decade-long struggle to prevent the enlargement of Grand Teton National Park, they sponsored another bill to abolish the Jackson Hole addition. Under Secretary Oscar Chapman, who had guided the Park Service's proposal for years, welcomed the aid of the preservation organizations' publicity and the assistance of former director Horace Albright, who used his stature as a respected Republican businessman among his many old friends in the Congress. Joseph O'Mahoney, Wyoming's Democratic senator, painfully aware of the political impact of the issue at home, tried to sponsor a compromise. Parliamentary maneuvers by friends of the parks produced a substitute to the Barrett bill, however, and the enlargement was approved late in 1949. When Truman signed the measure early the following year, he could count it as one of his administration's few congressional victories in that era of bad feelings.[4]

During the same period, a new attack was made on Olympic National Park. Lumber companies, still smarting from the "Ickesian grab," asked legislators of both parties for redress. In March 1947 Senator Harry Cain sponsored a bill to redraw the park boundaries, explaining that all that would be necessary was the transfer of tracts in the park to the adjacent national forest. Democratic Congressman Henry Jackson thought that there were some areas that never should have been included in the preserve. Hoping to confine the inquiry to executive procedure rather than legislative action, Drury and Davidson went out to the peninsula, examined the portions sought by the lumbermen, and decided that no alterations were warranted. By thus responding to the demand at all, preservationists complained, they were suspect. The Sierra Club, apprehensively watching as Barrett took a subcommittee out to the parkland region, criticized Chapman for being too acquiescent. They were not relieved when he noted that any transfers would not constitute the "giving away" of park tracts. Interior was making no real effort to defend Olympic, they concluded, and had failed to avail itself of its best weapon: publicity. Krug answered these accusers, but privately commented that they were a "hair shirt that the National Parks Service has worn, perhaps for the Nation's sins against conservation" ever since the days of Stephen Mather.[5]

Official silence merely provoked louder noise from the watchdogs, however. In April 1947 former secretary Ickes learned from a Park Service officer that Drury had apparently capitulated to the pressures. The land pirates seemed to be "swarming all over the place, getting ready to grab everything in sight," he informed Irving Brant. Worst of all, Drury's office was about to surrender "all the gains we made during the Roosevelt years." Writing in his syndicated newspaper column, he publicly accused the department of doing an "Alphonse and Gaston" act for the benefit of lumber barons. The president, he implied, was acquiescing in the crime. His distortions may have represented resentment over Krug's development emphasis. Or he may have known that his successor had criticized past poor relations with westerners in Congress which had resulted in budget cuts. The secretaryship of the Interior, Ickes now wrote, was no place for a man "who won't fight or for a man with political ambitions." Then he turned on his former appointee, Newton Drury, with a vengeance. Dramatically but inaccurately he recounted the episode of the Sitka spruce crisis during the war years and claimed that the director had first revealed his villainy on that occasion by trying to destroy the inviolability of the national park system. Only his own prompt action, Ickes wrote with customary modesty, had prevented that disaster. Many preservationists, similarly mistaking diplomacy for duplicity, accepted Ickes's version of the incident because it seemed to explain their current fears about Drury. Brant wrote to advise the director that he was surrendering needlessly. The enemy's strength was exaggerated and, if he called upon preservation organizations, they could rout that enemy.[6]

Ickes transmitted his charges against Drury to Eleanor Roosevelt and other members of the old regime. Perhaps he was thinking of the effective maneuver used by his fellow Progressives in 1910, when they branded Interior Secretary Richard Ballinger with conspiring to dismantle the resource policies of Theodore Roosevelt. The new chain of collusion, he implied, was Drury to Krug to Truman. Mrs. Roosevelt, at least, was convinced. She protested to the latter two that Drury was "weak enough to be bowled over by the lumber interests." It was therefore essential that he "be changed and this be stopped since it can only be a precursor of many similar raids on national territory."[7]

Krug replied that Drury was the strongest defender of the park system and that he was personally watching the Olympic matter. (Privately, Brant was satisfied that at least Krug had the proper attitude on the subject.) After escorting fifteen congressmen to the park, Drury testified before their committee that boundary alterations were not wise. A short time later, the Park Service withdrew its report proposing possible transfers to the national forest, and Barrett discontinued hearings on the subject. The president had acted discreetly during the whole affair. In order to avoid further controversy, he had declined to discuss it publicly, but supported Krug and Drury without question. He consulted with his friend Governor Wallgren of Washington. The latter confirmed the wisdom of resisting the lumbermen. If any park tracts had to be transferred to the national forest, equal areas from that reserve should be added to Olympic, he proposed. Wallgren's tactic was not needed.[8]

In 1948 Krug advised the Senate Interior Committee that it would be futile to reopen the subject because no arrangement would ever be acceptable to all parties concerned. After Congressman Jackson withdrew his request for further investigation, Interior announced that it would recommend absolutely no future land transfers at Olympic. Krug expanded upon that emphasis by promising that as long as he was secretary of the Interior, there would be no boundary changes resulting in the reduction of any national park or monument. Republican Congressman Russell Mack of Washington continued to plead for the lumber interests of the peninsula, but the Park Service remained firm. "I don't think there is enough 'smoke' yet to drag out our big guns," one of Drury's aides told preservationists. Like other aspects of the "land grab," threats to the national parks did not die at this point in time; they merely lay waiting for a more favorable political climate. Unfortunately, the Olympic issue tarred Drury with suspicion that would persist for years. Albright had kindly reminded him that "Harold Ickes is a very ruthless fellow . . . I have known [that] for many years—and you have known it too." Most crusaders, however, were prone to measure the integrity of both friends and enemies against their own zeal.[9]

Developers and preservationists alike assumed that a Republican victory in 1948 would bring striking change in federal resource policy. Advocates of change would not only sit in executive offices but preside over congressional committees as well. The "land grab package" was apparently already made up, wrapped, and tied, as Bernard De Voto saw it. If the Republicans bought it, he thought there would be a scandal of greater dimensions than that of the Teapot Dome. He expected oil lands, grazing lands, and probably power and forest reservations to be "extinguished in the first session of Congress." One of the gang of land pirates would certainly become secretary of the Interior. The *Seattle Times* predicted an end to "the Ickes hangover" of the department and a "clean sweep" there. Oregon's Senator Guy Cordon and Colorado's Senator Eugene Millikan were said to be candidates for the post. The latter struck De Voto as especially dangerous because he was a very able politician. On the basis of his voting record on resource legislation, he would "make Albert Fall look like a piker." According to a prediction by Harry Polk, executive secretary of the National Reclamation Association, if Robert Taft was elected, the Interior appointment would go to Hugh Butler of Nebraska, chairman of the Interior committee. Polk's friend Robert Sawyer of Oregon was also mentioned in the speculation. At Thomas Dewey headquarters, Cordon's name was most frequently heard, but he privately indicated he could accomplish much more in the Congress.[10]

The Republican presidential nominee was no more satisfactory to preservationists than he had been to westerners concerned with water and power policy. Brant published an open letter asserting that a Dewey administration would encourage the work of Barrett, Robertson, and Cain. "It is no secret," he addressed the candidate, "that Barrett wants you to appoint a Secretary of the Interior who 'understands' the West just as he does (another Ballinger)." One Dewey adviser, Republican Governor Harold Stassen of Minnesota, had already "swallowed the Barrett bait." De Voto rejected Dewey's denial that he favored the "land grab" because it was couched "in words that made conservationists shudder." Ickes joined in by adding from his newspaper column that Republicans would make a terrible mistake if they appointed any westerner to Interior. The conservation movement in the United States was, "with rare exceptions," the work of men from east of the Mississippi River.[11]

President Truman devoted most of his campaign speeches in the West to the subject of water and power development, but when he reached Texas, he talked about Big Bend, newest of the national parks. That preserve could be completed, he said, only if Democrats were reelected because only their party believed in a system of parks for the enjoyment of all the people. Evidently, many preservationists agreed. After the upset in November, Brant rejoiced that Dewey would not be in the White House. In 1946 the journalist had thought that Governor Wallgren would be a fine successor for Ickes; now he thought that the Washingtonian's stand against the Olympic "pirates" made his selection for the post very likely. But Truman retained Krug whose record on park policy equalled Wallgren's.[12]

Even before the elections of 1948 turned back the potential "land grab," the friends of the national parks realized that there were other dangers to the system. Economic interests and their political errand boys were readily opposed in battle, but how were intradepartmental conflicts to be met? The first point of contention among Interior's bureaus arose when new statistics demanded immediate solutions to old problems. Once wartime restrictions on travel and supplies were lifted, Americans started to travel in great numbers. Facilities constructed during the 1930s were in need of repair and addition. There was also a pressing need for redrafting regulations concerning private concessions and fees.[13]

In January 1949 the president had asked his new Democratic Congress for appropriations for the improvement of the national parks, but the request was turned down. Drury was anxious to see the fulfillment of wartime plans for expansion of the system, but he did not want to bargain for favors. Arguing that "the dollar sign" should not bar access to the units even in inflationary times, he rejected demands to increase park entrance fees. Instead of increasing the Park Service budget, legislators referred to the poor facilities as part of their criticisms of the department's policies. Communities adjacent to the preserves, far more interested in roads and water storage, resented a program that seemed to be offering nothing more than "a series of views and natural spectacles . . . spread before elderly, eastern spinsters." Congress subsequently told Drury to confine his activities to improving existing accommodations and liberalizing concession contracts. With Davidson's support, however, the director decided to terminate monopolies among concessionaires and to discontinue using fees as a source of revenue. He hoped that facilities serving the public could eventually be owned and leased by the federal government, but it was not likely that that plan would be accepted in the midst of the oratory about "socialism" and "private enterprise" heard during those years.[14]

Although the secretary was firmly committed to the policy of maintaining the true wilderness qualities of the park system, some members of his department ignored the principle of park inviolability. The Bureau of Reclamation continued to pursue its surveys next to and within units of the park system. This procedure was allegedly followed without the personal knowledge of Michael Straus, the commissioner, but he invariably approved of the results. In 1948, for example, the agency recommended a project that would back up storage water into one of the valleys of Glacier National Park in Montana. Local citizens eagerly anticipated the benefits that would accrue from construction of a Glacier View Dam. Senator James Murray and the Montana Reclamation Association, enemies in the MVA fight, both endorsed the plan. Democratic Congressman Mike Mansfield of Montana quickly drafted legislation to authorize construction. Yet public opinion was divided on the issue in Montana and elsewhere in the West. As in so many other cases, opposition to it came from reclamationists in other states who were pressing their own schemes, as well as from preservationists. Drury objected immediately. There was little enough parkland left in the nation as things were, and the people should defend what they had. Others described Manfield's bill as "an effort to break established precedent." Reclamation and the Army Corps of Engineers agreed to concentrate their plans on other areas and promised to look for alternative sites. But Straus continued to withhold information about the bureau's surveys from his colleagues in the Park Service. Truman remained silent, as he had in the Olympic affair and for the same reason. Drury thought that his immediate superiors were remiss in not enforcing the statutory requirement for interbureau consultation in such cases.[15]

This same misunderstanding was at the center of the controversy that exploded over the Upper Colorado Basin project (UCB). Just as the CVA issue reached a point of stalemate, it was succeeded by discussion of the federal-state proposals for development of that vast, arid river valley. Far more costly and extensive than the Columbia plan, UCB would harness water courses stretching from Wyoming into New Mexico and draining parts of six states. The power potential of the basin had been examined by private and governmental technicians since the 1920s. At the end of World War II, it seemed desirable to bring new population and prosperity to that region by building a complex system of reservoirs for irrigation and hydro-electric dams. The deep, spectacular canyons throughout much of the basin were deemed perfect natural sites for these constructions. In the preliminary surveys, more than forty of them were designated as such. In 1946 the Interior Department appointed Harry Bashore, former commissioner of the Bureau of Reclamation, to act as its representative on the Upper Colorado River Commission formed by the governors of Colorado, Utah, Wyoming, New Mexico, and Arizona. President Truman pledged his support of the project during the 1948 campaign and warned westerners that Republicans would want to turn its dams over to private utilities. His administration welcomed the creation of an interstate compact in October and gave it official approval in April 1949.[16]

Unlike the projects that would have been part of CVA, those in the UCB plan would endanger over a dozen units of the national park system. The dilemma of priorities in resource policy had never been drawn so sharply. For the preservationists, it became a crisis many times more dangerous than the Hetch Hetchy fight thirty years earlier. The national monuments in the Upper Colorado basin were not as pastorally beautiful as the California valleys, but for purists there are no gradations in aesthetics—only varieties. Although the development of the arid basin was generally commendable, the scope and complexity of the proposal seemed to them overdrawn and based upon an assumption that there would be a great increase in population which would require reservoirs and power plants. There had been an influx of workers and farmers into the Rocky Mountain states after the war, but it was hardly sufficient to justify the utopian projections of the UCB proponents. Finally, preservationists were puzzled by the inconsistencies of westerners who denounced federal spending and dominance while demanding a billion-dollar federal project, and those who sought the expansion of agricultural areas while complaining about the growing farm surpluses of these years.

The knotty dilemma was embodied in a veritable microcosm called Dinosaur National Monument. Situated at the junction of the Green and Yampa rivers where northwestern Colorado adjoins Utah, its fantastically carved, vividly colored canyons offered the finest potential reservoirs that the Bureau of Reclamation had found in the whole region. It had not been made a national monument in order to preserve these attributes, however. When a large accumulation of prehistoric animal fossils was discovered there in 1915, eighty acres west of the canyon junction called Echo Park were withdrawn as a federal preserve. When Ickes expanded the national park system during the 1930s, he selected a dozen units in the Great Basin and approved the enlargement of Dinosaur by the addition of the adjacent canyons. The citizens of Vernal, Utah, the community nearest to it, supported the increase by petition and assumed that the larger monument would attract more visitors and more dollars. Some of them were interested in mining the possible phosphate deposits near the canyons, but the Park Service plan seemed to hold more immediate promise in those depression years. When Ickes approved the plan in 1936, he announced that the future development of potential mineral, water, and power resources would be determined by Congress, if and when it was economically feasible. The federal planners assumed that there would be a demand for mining and grazing access, rather than one for water and power development. In fact, the Utah Power Company had just withdrawn its application before the Federal Power Commission for use of water sources at that site.[17]

In 1936 the National Park Service announced that Dinosaur would be expanded by 200,000 acres. Tentatively renamed Green River National Monument to emphasize the attractions of the whole area, it would straddle the border of Utah and Colorado; the canyon portion was mainly in Colorado. Although the enlarged preserve was almost entirely in Utah, Governor Henry Blood and Senator William King of that state objected to the enlargement. They were already disturbed by Ickes's grandiose scheme to carve a large monument out of the southeast corner of their state. In the case of Dinosaur, therefore, they demanded that specific recognition of mineral and reservoir rights be put into the proclamation. Conrad Wirth, the Park Service's chief of land acquisition, concluded that there was no need to make any decision about reclamation or power use. Those subjects would "give relatively little difficulty" in the near future, he wrote. In order to meet protests from local stockmen who used the high plateau bordering the canyons, however, he agreed to adjust the boundaries. But the demand for either irrigation or power would not be great enough, he assumed, "to force the construction of reservoirs within the proposed monument, at least not for a great number of years." In time, Wirth would have good reason to realize how defective his crystal ball had been.[18]

In 1938 CCC workers were brought in to prepare access trails and visitor facilities. When the monument was ready to open, the Park Service tried to cultivate full understanding of the addition among the local people. In June regional supervisor David Madsen addressed citizens of Vernal, Utah, and Craig, Colorado, at each end of the preserve. Discussion thereafter ranged over the usual concerns of land taxes and use regulations and then focused on the possible future use of the canyon area, not for reservoirs but for grazing. Madsen's official report of the meetings did not say so then, but he later maintained that he had promised these assemblies that neither grazing nor power needs would be interfered with by the creation of the larger monument. At the time, the *Salt Lake Tribune* stated that the Park Service recognized both needs. It is possible, therefore, that Madsen did make the statement but did not report it to his superiors.[19]

After the Interior officials examined the statutory limitations affecting overlapping federal jurisdictions, they noted that the lands along the Green and Yampa rivers had been classified as potential reclamation sites when the first Reclamation Act was passed in 1904. Ickes secured an amendment to that law in August 1935 which excluded projects authorized by the Federal Power Act of 1920 from all national parks and monuments. The Park Service men were astonished to learn that even the Federal Power Commission was not aware of that exception and had issued permits affecting such preserves before and after the amendment. Therefore, they reasoned, any statutory recognition of reclamation development put into the proclamation would be null and void. Nevertheless, in order to prevent further delays they inserted a clause in that document stating that Brown's Park, a canyon north of Echo Park, which the Reclamation bureau was interested in, would be available for water development projects in the future. On July 14, 1938, President Roosevelt proclaimed the creation of the greatly enlarged national monument, still called Dinosaur.[20]

The wary antagonism that would later develop between the service and the bureau was not then in evidence. The park officials were well aware that their sister agency was conducting a survey of potential sites throughout the Upper Colorado River basin. The bureau tactfully hinted that the Park Service would have jurisdiction over wildlife protection and recreation in the event that any sites were developed after the war. Learning that survey crews were working near the boundaries of Dinosaur, the park officials asked the bureau for specific information. They were told that studies had not yet reached the point to warrant discussion about possible jurisdictional conflicts. For their part, they were confident that their position was firmly grounded in the exception stated by the amendment of 1935. Consequently, they did not hesitate to mollify local interests on the question of future development. When the Natural Resources Planning Commission met in Salt Lake City in June 1940, regional park superintendent Jesse Nusbaum told them that serious consideration would be given to modification of the boundaries of national monuments to meet the needs of river basin development "where it is logical to do so." Whenever recreational matters were under examination, he added, then interbureau agreements would be altered accordingly. Moreover, the Park Service assured Governor Herbert Maw of Utah that it had no desire to prohibit formulation of plans for future water and power development. Of course, it did not say that it would agree to the execution of any plans for that area.[21]

A month before Pearl Harbor, both bureaus tried to loosen the knotted question by consultations in Denver. Drafting a "memorandum of understanding," representatives of Reclamation and the Park Service noted the possibility that consideration of reclamation needs in Utah might call for a change in the status of national monuments to national recreation areas. Echo Park was not mentioned.

Commissioner John Page, a Coloradan, assumed that the service had no objection to this joint agreement to study further those reclamation needs. Park Service men assumed that necessary legislation for changing monument status would not be difficult to secure from Congress. On November 4, 1941, the memorandum was signed by Page and Park Service director Newton Drury.[22]

Wartime restrictions on travel reduced the total number of visitors to all parts of the national park system; during the war years few came to Dinosaur. A work party from Reclamation came there, however, and began drilling test holes inside the preserve—activities that aroused animated comment in nearby communities. Two sites were subsequently judged to be particularly desirable for reservoirs: Split Mountain, a canyon near the fossil beds, and Echo Park at the heart of the monument. In October 1943 Reclamation announced that it had withdrawn both places for potential projects.[23]

The Park Service naturally refused to be committed by the statement or to acknowledge that its jurisdiction over the area was thereby altered. The department solicitor assured park officials that the Reclamation withdrawals did not have the approval of the Federal Power Commission. They therefore decided to ignore them. Dinosaur's custodian, Dan Beard, however, urged them not to let the matter pass to future administrators for resolution. It was wrong, he wrote to his superiors, to assume that the postwar economic trend would move toward coal production of electric energy rather than water power. Utahans were already seeking federal support for projects in the basin. He did not believe Reclamation's assurance that Echo Park would not be needed for fifteen years, and maybe never needed. There was a very good chance that they would build a dam there, he thought, and "it is going to happen quicker than this Service has been led to believe." The park officials must not be lulled to sleep because the threat would persist. They were not alarmed, however. Drury jotted the word "thoughtful" on Beard's letter. The issue was too complicated and too theoretical to require immediate action. Moreover, the regional superintendent was told, "changing economic conditions and the growth of strong public opinion favoring the preservation of wilderness" like Dinosaur would settle the question properly.[24]

Businessmen from the mountain states meeting in Denver in 1943 were shocked to learn from reclamationists that the enlargement of the monument had jeopardized plans for "two of the finest dams in the nation." They immediately pressed their state officials to head off what seemed like another of Ickes's imperialistic moves, along with Jackson Hole and Escalante. Writing to the Park Service to protest, Maw of Utah argued that Congress, not mere bureaus, should determine the location of power projects and, in any case, the states should be consulted. Beard called on him soon afterwards. The two men agreed that Split Mountain was an integral part of the fossil area of the monument, but Maw would not give up his conviction that Echo Park should be dammed. Drury then wrote to the governor to remind him that the legal provisions of the 1938 proclamation mentioned only Brown's Park, but he added that the dam sites were by no means absolutely out of the picture. Privately, the director was confident that if Congress did ultimately approve of a resorvoir anywhere in the monument, its boundaries could be redrawn to preserve the principle of inviolability. As for the Bureau of Reclamation's surreptitious survey, park officials decided that it would be "the better part of wisdom to ignore the incident." Then, in a most prophetic afterthought, one of them wondered: "if we do, will the bird not come home to roost?"[25]

When the war was over, the Park Service began to bring together all its plans for expansion of the system—and ran right into the realization that Reclamation was as formidable an enemy as its traditional opponents, vested economic interests. Its special position enjoyed during the Ickes administration seemed to be in the process of an alarming erosion. While the service had been shunted off to Chicago during the war years, the bureau had remained in Washington, apparently whetting the interests of congressmen by leaking its survey reports on future water programs in their states. Then its publicity machinery was oiled by the talents of a new commissioner, Michael Straus. In 1947 Park Service abhorrence of assuming jurisdiction over reservoir recreation sites was overwhelmed when land management experts began to emphasize recreation as "a major area of social need, obligation and opportunity." When both agencies pressed Secretary Krug on the question, he disappointed them by suggesting they seek legislation to define jurisdictions. In the meantime, he said, each case should be decided on its own merits. Generally, the Park Service was to take over recreation sites with national significance while the bureau was to be in charge of those destined for local, limited use. Lake Mead, behind Hoover Dam, for example, was of national significance, but in the eyes of the men at the Park Service it attracted so many visitors that it seemed no better than a commercial play-ground. The National Park Advisory Board supported the secretary's decision because it assumed that most of the reservoir sites would be of local significance. The question of the site called Shadow Mountain Lake near Rocky Mountain Park was the first substantial setback for the Park Service's stand. Drury insisted that the reservoir was primarily local and therefore not part of his concern. Assistant Secretary Davidson (who may well have been the source of Krug's decision) bawled him out for his stubbornness. Deciding that the area might ease visitor pressures on the national park, Drury reluctantly agreed to assume jurisdiction. In April 1949 the secretary further favored Straus when he announced that the White House had agreed that the bureau should "expedite completion" of its plans for the Upper Colorado Basin project. A press release issued by Reclamation shortly afterward noted that the program would include a dam at Echo Park in Dinosaur National Monument.[26] The land grabbers had been held at bay, but now the watchdogs of federal resource policy thought they heard footsteps behind them. As Drury must have concluded, eternal vigilance at home was part of the price of maintaining the principle of the national park system.

Chapter Three

THE PARKS'
EVAPORATION
RATE

While the alarms and excursions over CVA were still sounding late in 1949, Julius Krug resigned as secretary of the Interior. There had been talk of his replacement after the campaign of 1948, an event in which he had been noticeably less active than his lieutenant, Under Secretary Oscar Chapman. By the following spring, he very rarely called on the president; by October there was a rumor of friction in the cabinet. Truman declined to answer press questions about it, but there may well have been a mutual feeling of disappointment between the two men after the long, futile CVA fight. Krug faced further wrangles over departmental reorganization and the proposal for an Upper Colorado Basin project. The act of resignation was a bit strained: he told the press of his decision before he told the White House. Truman accepted his resignation "reluctantly and with sincere regret." The rest of the president's letter contained a passage that may have been an allusion to the real reason for the parting: "the people of this entire nation have a stake in the steady development of our incalculable resources in the great western domain. It would be hazardous to the nation to accept the 'status quo.' As you wisely observe, hostility to change is too often inspired by narrow timidity and selfish fear." Perhaps it was a formal version of what he sometimes said in the vernacular: "If you can't take the heat, get out of the kitchen."[1]

The appointment of Chapman to the secretaryship was one of the most popular decisions of the Truman administration. The Coloradan embodied the continuity which many Democrats considered so vital to uphold the Roosevelt tradition. One person described the appointment as "a triumph of *our* New Deal," inferring that Truman had gone astray. Chapman, like Ickes, was a master of the procedures and problems of the department. Like his former chief, he too was an advocate of liberal causes. He had proved his talents as a salesman during the campaign of 1948; and some Democrats wondered what he might have been able to do had he held the full captaincy in the fight for CVA. In contrast to Ickes, however, Chapman was a "gentle crusader," whose genial manner had earned him friendships covering a wide spectrum, from Dorothy Lamour to Milton Eisenhower. All these qualities enabled him to obtain a greater degree of coordination among the department's bureaus than Krug's young efficiency men had achieved. He preferred to increase the permanent supervisory responsibility of his assistant secretaries rather than to rely on an under secretary. He was not wholly successful in this policy, however, because of the scarcity of career officials and the brevity of their stay with the department.[2]

There was, moreover, a certain lack of forcefulness in Chapman's approach to personnel problems, according to those closely associated with him. He had the right point of view, David Lilienthal believed, but was not vigorous enough in expressing his convictions. The necessary zeal may very well have been deflated by the bureaucratic inertia he had lived with for thirteen years. His acknowledged political skills, Newton Drury thought, merely increased his inclination toward deviousness. Chapman seemed susceptible to all kinds of pressures and "utterly impotent" in the hands of his subordinates. Drury privately considered him a man of "very limited mental capacity . . . more or less a conformist," tending to vacillate because he had no philosophy of his own to defend. In bitter recollection, the Park Service director noted that with a man like Chapman in charge, the "great Bureau of Reclamation was the—well, it was like the state of Prussia in the German empire, where everything was weighted in its favor."[3]

An unusual amount of public interest was focused on Chapman when he assumed the secretaryship. He was the first westerner to hold the office in sixteen years, and he would have the task of guiding Interior through the shoals of the continuing "land grab" by westerners in Congress. That crisis, according to his Colorado friend Arthur Carhart of the Izaak Walton League in Denver, was "nearing an explosive stage." Both developers and preservationists hoped Chapman's background would allow him to bring about a change in federal-state relations in resource policies. The expectations turned his ex-

amination by the Senate Interior Committee into a veritable love
feast. Many hearts were undoubtedly warmed by the nominee's
definition of conservation: "[It] does not mean, as many of our people
are prone to think, the locking up of some resource in order to keep
people from touching or using it. It means to develop the resource
in a wise way." The hearing concentrated on the touchy subject of
Indian policy, but Arthur Watkins of Utah raised the matter closest
to his heart, the UCB project. When he asked about the use of
Dinosaur as a reservoir, Chapman's reply was mollifying. Each case
had to be taken on its own merit, he said, and had to be weighed according to its bearing on the question of use "for the greatest benefit
of the greatest number of people." To illustrate his approach, he referred to the Big Thompson tunnel built through Rocky Mountain
National Park. As to the contentious subject of public opinion, Chapman said something most of the committee wanted to hear: "I think
you will find that the people who are farthest away are the loudest
supporting [the monument]." Watkins interjected his own corollary
to that: "People who know the least about it make the most noise."
Encouraged by the tone of the testimony, the senator pressed further
and asked the nominee how he would stand on the Dinosaur controversy. "I could not give you a decision on that this morning," Chapman
grinned, ". . . if my nomination depended upon it."[4]

However jubilant the developers may have been over Chapman's
remarks, the men at the Park Service must have realized that the
"bird" had at last "come home to roost." When Straus sent over a
spare park-ranger uniform someone had given him, Drury wondered
if it was symbolic of the "mortal remains of a ranger who tried to stop
construction of a dam." Preservationist cohorts decided that they were
"perilously close to losing [their] shirts." The Utah officials seized
the opportunity at once. Just in case Chapman might still try to be
neutral, Watkins brought in maps and statistics, and Governor J.
Bracken Lee forwarded dozens of civic and business resolutions demanding action on the basin project. The governors of the other
affected states telegraphed their hope that the use of Dinosaur would
be confirmed by the department. Those who were Republicans might
have enjoyed seeing the Democrats hoisted on the horns of the dilemma,
but in public remarks they insisted tactfully that partisan politics
were not involved.[5]

Secretary Chapman was painfully aware of the necessity for making
a decision on Dinosaur and of the equally essential task of determining

the public opinion on the policy of "greatest benefit of the greatest number." He was confronted with reports that fifty-six chambers of commerce in Utah and Colorado supported the reservoir; conferences called by Governor Lester Hunt of Wyoming were similarly resolved. At hearings held in Chapman's office in April 1950, developers pointed out that the Dinosaur site was economically and technically "necessary" and that there would be no damage to the fossil beds. As for the scenery, few had ever seen or used the preserve because of its rugged terrain and inaccessibility. At the same time, preservationists obtained reports from other engineers showing that an alternative dam site was available at Glen Canyon, across the southern border in Arizona. Privately they grumbled among themselves that even reclamationists described the UCB project as "thrown together in sort of a shotgun affair" by ambitious bureaucrats in Reclamation. If their opponents were correct in saying that the area was inaccessible, they told Chapman, that made the Parks Service's request for development funds even more pertinent. Using the figure of speech employed in past crises, they described approval of the dam in the monument as an opening wedge for dams in other units of the system.[6]

The preservationists appreciated the difficult position the secretary was in, but they found this case doubly dangerous. Brant sent Chapman his own analysis:

> [The Dinosaur issue is] one more move in the incessant drive to break down the national park system by subordinating all values not measurable in dollars. It also furnishes a serious indication that the Bureau of Reclamation—perhaps under the competitive pressure to which it is subjected by the Army Engineers—is reverting to the line of thinking from which it was happily redeemed during the 1930's. The Bureau of Reclamation, unlike some other government bureaus, bears no malice toward the park system. That increases rather than diminishes the danger. It is easier to cope with a deliberate attempt at destruction than one which merely represents lack of perception.

An outside threat, Brant observed, would enable the secretary to be a "clear cut champion of conservation," but what stand could he take in a struggle between his own bureaus? Director Drury reissued his 1946 compilation concerning recreational development of the parks and monuments in the Colorado River basin, one which emphasized human values over economic gain. But he must have known that it would not be read in the offices of the Bureau of Reclamation.[7]

Most Americans were shocked by the outbreak of war in Korea in June 1950, but preservationists were stunned also when Chapman made his decision on Dinosaur. Within a few days of President Truman's dispatch of United States forces, the Interior Department recommended congressional authorization of the UCB project, including the reservoir at Echo Park. The "demonstrated need for water" would be fulfilled, Chapman stated, but the decision in the case of Dinosaur would not be a precedent for "tampering with the inviolability of our national parks and monuments." His office was immediately flooded with messages of congratulations from communities and enterprisers in the basin states. Democratic Senator Elbert Thomas was particularly delighted and wrote: "I never doubted for a minute that Echo Park would be approved by you." The *Denver Post*'s coverage of the decision exemplified the attitude of westerners who considered parks as economic opportunities. With the cooperation of both the Bureau of Reclamation and the Park Service, it predicted, a multimillion dollar tourist facility would be built overlooking the man-made lake.[8]

The preservationists were incredulous. "I am very sorry," Horace Albright wrote to Bernard De Voto, "that my good friend, Oscar, has seen fit to give the green light to the Reclamation Service. In my judgment this was a very serious mistake on his part. Of course he still has an opportunity to find dissatisfaction with the plans or decide not to recommend legislation." De Voto was frankly surprised by the decision. Why did Chapman "yield to the pressure of the Bureau . . . and the western block in Congress?" Ickes had a ready answer: "I felt from the beginning that Chapman would decide in favor of the dam. His doing so is a powerful argument in favor of the theory that I have had for many years . . . that, other things being equal, a western man should not be appointed Secretary of the Interior." Arthur Carhart closely questioned his friend the secretary. The matter was now in the hands of Congress, Chapman replied, and if it did not recommend approval for the use of Dinosaur, he would not again support it. There was no reason to anticipate a precedent, he insisted. He would resign before he would let dam builders, lumbermen, or stockmen violate any unit of the park system.[9]

Carhart was one of several preservationists who feared that there was more than a coincidence in the joint announcements of Korea and Dinosaur. As he later expressed his conclusion, the secretary had been "stampeded" into approving the site in order to help gain

support for the president's action in foreign policy. Developers, moreover, interpreted the approval in the same way. During the next few
months they again demanded access to other federal preserves as part
of the economic mobilization. This time, however, the military administrators did not make their own demands. The Defense Department turned down a suggestion that Everglades National Park—considered a great wasteland by many—be used as a bombing range. The
Park Service was able to reject a request for another reservoir in
Capitol Reef National Monument, Utah, and announced that no grazing would be allowed in the units of the system for the duration of
the emergency. The pressures continued. For example, Congressman
Mike Mansfield of Montana maintained that the war made Glacier
View Dam all the more essential.[10]

During that tumultuous summer of 1950, the president's Commission
on Water Resource Policy traveled through the West taking opinions
and suggestions on desirable federal resource policy. Most of the
testimony offered to them came from developers, but a handful of
preservationists tried to get the commissioners to look at their subject
in a larger context. As an officer of the Sierra Club wrote: "aesthetic
values existing in outstanding scenic areas of the West are greater
than the values to be received from water development of every
stream and the production of the last possible kilowatt of electrical
energy. . . . It is our high belief that the government and the people
of the nation should never undertake so to state the issue in terms
of the dollar—unless the day should come when the nation is so
reduced in spirit that it must live on bread alone." Carhart summed
up the same admonition by flatly stating: "What happens [to the
national parks] determines how long we live as a nation." The Park
Service also reminded the commissioners of its basic beliefs. The
units of the system had to be kept free of water control structures
within them, and free of any outside which would affect their ecological
structure. Only in cases where the economic stability of the entire
nation, or its safety, required it, should there be any exception to the
well-established principle of inviolability.[11]

Although the touchy question of Dinosaur caused Chapman to
shy away from making other decisions on possible dams in the park
system, his associates were bolder. Paul Raver's Bonneville Power
Administration publicized the Glacier Dam project favorably, thereby
earning a word of caution from Assistant Secretary William Warne.
Commissioner Straus, however, was impressed with the increase in

demands for the structure. Referring to the previous decision to delay approval of the plan, he wrote Chapman with customary brashness: "I think the Department is wrong, and I am going to see that it is built—preferably by Reclamation." If his agency did not do so, it would be built by one with "less faith" in Interior policies, that is, by the Army Corps of Engineers. At this point Drury's analogy about the state of Prussia seemed confirmed.[12]

Secretary Chapman would never have yielded to pressures, the preservation organizations concluded, if public opinion had been sufficiently aroused. It was time, therefore, to "get strung out for a real fight." Congress could not be trusted to take an enlightened view of the issue; only a few eastern members would defend the parks. But if genuine public opinion were brought to bear on them, the legislators might be compelled to remove the Echo Park site from the UCB measure. A publicity campaign would also serve a second purpose. The complexity of the "great land grab" maneuvers of preceding years had divided the membership of preservation organizations to a dismaying degree. Contention over modification of federal regulation, the desirability of transferring bureaus and jurisdictions between departments, and the priority of development over the park principle had produced factions, resignations, and jealousies. Dinosaur provided a dramatically simple cause around which they could regroup their shattered ranks. They had worked in association with each other for decades, but had never really pooled all their talents and facilities.

Now a joint emergency committee was organized by the heads of a half dozen organizations. Presiding over its activities were David Brower of the Sierra Club, William Voigt of the Izaak Walton League, Howard Zahniser of the Wilderness Society, and Ira Gabrielson, formerly chief of the Fish and Wildlife Service in Ickes's Interior Department. It issued its own literature and encouraged each organization to produce additional material. Pamphlets, articles, speeches, and visual presentations were submitted to magazines and newspapers and to civic and commercial groups in communities across the nation. They were aimed toward the literate population in hopes that the word could be more readily transmitted to the policy makers in Congress and the administration. The burden of these polemics was tactfully more pro-park than it was anti-dam. They dissected the arguments of the developers, however, with precision. When, for example, Democratic Congresswoman Reva Bosone of Utah called the monument inaccessible, Bernard De Voto answered in his column in *Harper's* that all the western national parks since Yellowstone were at one time inaccessible and that was the reason for saving them rather than destroying them. The publicity arm of the Upper Colorado basin states, the Upper Colorado Development Commission, focused its own arguments on the engineering necessity of using Echo Park because of the minimal evaporation rate there. The preservationists easily found other engineers—most notably civil engineer Ulysses S. Grant III—who pointed out that the much touted advantage was actually one half of 1 percent over alternative sites. And so the war of words began, like the strophe and antistrophe of a righteously indignant Greek chorus.[13]

The effectiveness of the preservationists' first barrage could be measured by the increasingly harsh rhetoric coming from the basin states. The Chamber of Commerce of Vernal sniffed out conspiracy: the "absolute, notorious and unscrupulous" lies about evaporation rates were in fact part of the "hot air coming from the wind tunnels of the National Park Service." But the real power behind the scene were Californians, seeking to prevent use of upper Colorado River water before it reached their end of its run. The chamber called for state review of all national monuments; those where water was more important than scenery should be "released back to the people." The *Denver Post* charged that the entire preservationist attitude was unwestern. Replying to that canard, Utah-born De Voto wrote to publisher Palmer Hoyt in something of a drawl: "podner, as one Westerner to another, let me give you one small piece of advice before you start shooting again. Don't snoot those unfortunate [easterners] too loudly or too obnoxiously. You might make them so mad that they would stop paying for your water development."[14]

In spite of the vigor of their campaign, the monument's defenders privately shared a sense of gloom. De Voto was "extremely pessimistic" about the chance of blocking "these disastrously wasteful plans" in time. Their well-reasoned arguments presented to Chapman seemed useless. It was "casting pearls in a certain sense," Drury later commented. The secretary's replies were cordial, but they indicated that he had not changed his mind since the nomination hearings. For example, he reiterated that the combination of reservoirs proposed in the basin plan was "found to be more efficient in meeting the requirements of the Upper Basin States." There was no explanation of just how he meant to reconcile this preoccupation with efficiency and his resolve that the Dinosaur dam would not be an opening wedge. Instead, he repeated that the department's decision "should not be construed in any way as relaxing our standards for preservation of our heritage of natural wonders. . . . We will not recommend or agree to any invasion or depletion of those resources unless or until it is conclusively proved that the interests of the majority will be best served by such invasion and that satisfactory alternatives do not exist."[15]

Albright concluded that his friend was not "as good a fighter as Krug," while Voigt analyzed his behavior in detail: "Chapman is a smoothie and when politics comes in the door, conservation goes out the window. Political advantage carries tremendous weight with Oscar. [He would] push for the construction of as many of these [dams] as will, in his opinion, sustain or add to political advantage. Like a good politician, he will take orders as to one or another when he must. He will employ every stratagem possible . . . in order to magnify the significance, politically speaking, of a dam and reservoir proposal . . . and he has a formidable team of propagandists at his disposal."[16]

The preservationists' dismay quickly turned into paronoia, and that prejudice produced irresponsible behavior of the sort that had trapped zealots before them. In private communication, Drury informed De Voto that the secretary had ordered the Park Service to refrain from contributing to the publicity campaign in any manner. No such restraint was placed upon the Bureau of Reclamation whose agents remained in close communication with officials and businessmen of the basin states. The director consequently appreciated more fully the efforts of the park defenders and took them into his confidence. For example, he told De Voto that the Park Service had been "maneuvered into a fix" on the issue. Angered by the rule of silence, he asked park supervisors to defend the service's opposition to the dam before local groups. When he learned that their remarks were deleted from certain Utah newspaper accounts—while Reclamation's replies to De Voto's articles were widely reproduced—he went to his immediate superior, Warne, and protested. The assistant secretary promised to tell the men at the bureau to desist, but their statements continued and were repeated by state water and highway commissioners and army engineers. Drury thereupon made public allusion to his belief that bureaucrats were the main enemy of the parks. He also inferred that local potash developers were behind the scheme to use Dinosaur. As he recalled his actions, "I didn't think we should compromise at all," and so "I . . . made one or two statements which were true but perhaps not diplomatic." In an angry mood, he expressed himself freely at his next interview with his chief. When Chapman remarked that he had approved the reservoir at Echo Park because of the smaller evaporation rate there, Drury recalled a phrase he had used in his indignant correspondence on the subject and wondered aloud: "How about the evaporation rate of the national parks and monuments?"[17]

Like many genial personalities, Chapman was especially hurt by criticisms from his friends. Less than six months before this interview, he had given the director a raise in civil service rank, a gesture that Drury interpreted as "evidence of your estimate of the place of our Service in your Department." But now Drury seemed to have joined the zealots who were ignoring the realities of the moment and recklessly sacrificing the prestige of the department. The administration's prestige was also in danger of damage. Congresswoman Reva Bosone warned Chapman that Republicans were already claiming that the Democrats had no heart for reclamation. As Chapman saw it, he had listened to every argument and had made his decision on the basis of many considerations. His conclusion about Dinosaur was in keeping with the utilitarian expectations of most Americans and was certainly a fulfillment of the development emphasis of the Truman administration. Yet Drury and his associates were acting as if near treason was involved. The secretary was understandably miffed and uncharacteristically adamant. When the National Parks Advisory Board urged him to reconsider and rescind his decision because alternative sites to Dinosaur did exist, he was unmoved. Instead, he had Warne send out a request for unquestioning support of the decision by both bureaus.[18]

The preservationists quickly misinterpreted this action not as a plea for harmony, but as an intractable directive. Upset by the rumors about the interbureau squabble, Chapman lost a degree of confidence in Drury. In December 1950 he asked the director to take over the post of special assistant. Others could carry on in the Park Service, he explained, but Drury's knowledge of overlapping bureau jurisdictions was needed in a departmentwide capacity. Moreover, the change would give Associate Director Arthur Demaray a chance to serve as head of the Park Service as a mark of honor before his approaching retirement. Drury must have felt that the under secretaryship was the proper place for such a task. He may also have known that Chapman had tried to obtain Truman's approval of Assistant Secretary Davidson for that post, before appointing Richard Searles of Arizona. The director considered the secretary's offer for a few weeks, then replied that he would not accept the special assistantship. Communications between the two old colleagues became strikingly brief and official. Then, as if to open the floodgates of their feelings, they had a final, frank discussion. Chapman asked Drury if he had an offer of a job elsewhere. The director said he did not. In the exchange that followed, they expressed their private assessment of each other's conduct "up to and beyond the limits of discretion," as Drury later described it. Chapman said he thought Drury should resign, but the latter first sought Albright's advice as to whether or not to make a fight of it. Albright suggested that he avoid the bad publicity that would result from any public battle. Drury spent the Christmas holidays back in California, where he talked to his former associates in the Save the Redwoods League and with Governor Earl Warren. Then he asked Albright to tell Chapman that he would resign in two months. During that interval, Warren named him chief of the state division of parks and beaches.[19]

"I regret any damage to our cause," Drury told Charles Sauers, chairman of the Advisory Board, "but it was not of my doing. . . . The whole episode is deplorable but . . . the die is cast." If it was not of Drury's doing, his friends and critics asked, what had prompted Chapman to request his resignation? In later years, Drury asserted that the secretary had not been hostile to him, even though they differed over issues besides Dinosaur. As one familiar with California affairs, he had considered as unrealistic a move to turn redwood forests over to complete federal control, but Chapman did not hold that against him. Drury also later referred obliquely to other shadows in the background—to influence coming from "the top command" of the Democratic Party—though he volunteered no further details.[20]

One person who fit Drury's description was Harold Ickes. Although he reportedly had not really trusted Chapman after leaving the department in 1946, he subsequently resumed contact with his former lieutenant during the party crisis of 1948. Ickes also had an appointment with Truman on January 3, 1951, just before the final interview between Chapman and Drury. He had not hesitated to criticize these Interior officials in the columns he wrote for several newspapers and magazines. He was especially irritated when Drury failed to acknowledge his help in a current effort to make a national park out of the Calaveras Big Trees in California. When the director resigned, Ickes publicly praised Chapman for getting rid of him and added that he himself would have done so much earlier. Drury's record, he wrote, was a string of suspicious actions ranging from the wartime Olympic spruce incident to the issue of the redwoods. In the former case, Drury had not openly advocated commercial access to the park, Ickes noted, but "it was clear that this was in fact what he wanted us to do." Moreover, it was not Drury but Wirth and Gabrielson who headed the fight to save Dinosaur. Evidently Chapman had brought to Ickes's attention the 1941 memorandum of understanding between Drury and Page, although he refused to allow it to be made public. The secretary also told Ickes that the director had seemed ready "to walk out on him anytime he got a better private offer." Ickes concluded that Drury's claim of being fired over his stand on Echo Park was therefore nothing but a "pretense." He also criticized Governor Warren for giving the state job to Drury. Waldo Leland of the Advisory Board felt that Ickes's attack was most unjustified, but feared that any response would stir him up further. The *Washington Post* opined that Drury was dismissed because of his opposition to jurisdiction over reservoir recreation areas.[21]

The preservationists tried to penetrate the mysterious silence surrounding the affair. De Voto guessed that it was caused by the clash between the bureaus, not only over Dinosaur but over proposed dams in Kings Canyon and Glacier National parks. Sauers felt that Chapman should have first consulted the Advisory Board and complained that Drury was "so damn proper" about the whole thing. The "so-called confidential nature of the . . . situation," he wrote angrily, "makes me tired in both cheeks." There were many unanswered questions. Was the "trumped up post . . . with less rank and salary" a subterfuge? Was Chapman "preparing a program of appeasement and capitulation to the power, livestock, and land speculation interests?" Was he "in the hands of his 'Palace Guards'?" Did Straus really dominate the department? Had the Utah developers finally got Drury? Apparently the decision on Dinosaur was an opening wedge to much more than just the national parks. If it were, Sauers thought, then Chapman's action was "poor politics" indeed. "The millions of Americans who think and breathe conservation," he warned the secretary, would vote on the issue accordingly. The affair would "cause no end of trouble I hope."[22]

The preservationists next considered how to save the situation. Zahniser reportedly tried to get Truman to overrule the resignation, and Voigt, who assumed that Drury had been dismissed for "acting up over Dinosaur," asked for a statement from the White House. The president's assistants instead forwarded these letters to Chapman for reply; the secretary, however, preferred to use informal discussions. In them, he may have disclosed the substance of the harsh remarks made during the final interview. He may also have explained just who in the "top command" of the Democratic Party was behind the decision on Echo Park. Irving Brant was the most likely person to be told. Although he did not enjoy access to the president as much as he had in the Roosevelt years, he had warned Truman that there was "needless trouble" ahead for his administration. Chapman's actions would be "a black eye" and ultimately useless because preservationists would combine with private power interests to defeat UCB legislation. Truman replied that he found it "an interesting subject for discussion." He hoped to see the contested area personally sometime, but, for the moment, he said, "It has always been my opinion that food for coming generations is much more important than bones of the Mesozoic period."[23]

Sometime after this exchange, Chapman confided to Brant that the Dinosaur decision was in fact made at the direction of the president himself. Truman, he said, was responding to the urging of Democratic Senator Elbert Thomas of Utah who claimed that unimpeded adoption of the UCB project was essential to his election in 1950. Voigt also may have learned of the untouchable political basis for the affair, because he asked that his previous letter be "dropped in the nearest wastebasket and forgotten and forgiven." Unaware of the real reason behind Drury's misfortunes, Carhart decided that he had been "drygulched" and that an exposé was warranted. If he could "get the dope to do a punch, I'll punch," he promised. Leland tried to gather facts for an article in *National Parks* magazine, but all he could find were rumors. One of these alleged that Chapman had acted in order to build his own prominence and become Truman's running mate in 1952. Finally, De Voto concluded that the situation was so ugly that there was nothing anyone could do about it. Then Leland cleverly made the most of the upsetting climate by presenting a proposal to the secretary's office. "Yes, for God's sake," Assistant Secretary Dale Doty reportedly answered, "Anything to get us off the hook!"[24]

The officials at the Interior Department were receptive because they realized that the Drury affair had moved the upper and nether millstones of pressure from both camps markedly closer. As far as the public knew, the sanctity of the national parks was at the center of the matter. The former director himself sustained that belief in the months after his decision to resign. "No one knows better than I," he told a member of the Wilderness Society, "that the park ideal is not completely accepted." At the same time, advocates of the dam in Dinosaur asserted that the resignation had broken the ice jam of Park Service opposition to the UCB project. Straus, still insisting that he was "a genuine nature lover," admitted to friends that he had forced the issue because he was so sure of the paramount merit of resource use. The "current riots," he cautioned, would only make it more difficult for preservationists to get future legislation for parks and monuments "where they are fully warranted." Publicly, he derided the "museum and cemetery for Dinosaur bones" and told the press that Chapman was well aware of the meaning of the 1938 proclamation because he must have approved it while he was Ickes's assistant. J. W. Penfold, conservation director of the Denver headquarters of the Izaak Walton League, angrily denounced this statement as "inexcusable . . . pork baited misrepresentations" designed to excuse the secretary's actions.[25]

Drury said nothing about his former chief, but told the Sierra Club that Reclamation's aggression in the case of Dinosaur was a result of the inertial forces set in motion by the earlier order for Park Service administration of reservoir recreation sites. The Advisory Board concluded that this was at the heart of the controversy. The bargain they elicited from Chapman was consequently procedural rather than substantive. The secretary obtained a list from Straus of all reclamation surveys affecting wilderness areas and game refuges, in order to head off any future maneuvers. He also ordered that no further water studies be undertaken without his personal approval and announced that every area under the Park Service's jurisdiction would be protected from any adverse effect involved in reclamation or power plans of the department. In exchange for this new watchfulness, the preservationists agreed to let the Drury matter die.[26]

Other conditions contributed to the restoration of the preservationists' spirits. The legislation to authorize the UCB project bogged down in congressional wrangling over federal spending. Solons from the wealthier, urban states of the East and those protesting the high cost of farm subsidy and surpluses joined to oppose this and other water proposals. Even Governor J. Bracken Lee of Utah, an ultra-conservative in political economics, admitted that he too was hesitant to support the UCB because it would add to the "terrific" federal deficit. Legislators from the East, seeking to head off authorization of the project, found the preservationists' publicity useful ammunition. The Dinosaur issue, proponents of the plan quickly realized, was turning into a bottleneck. In their frustration, they fell among them-selves, arguing over details about future returns instead of obtaining the initial legislation. Several basin states—especially Colorado, Utah, and Wyoming—jockeyed for most favorable percentages in water to be delivered from the dams. The agrarian western half of Colorado, comparatively underpopulated and underdeveloped, feared that the eastern slope, with its cities and staple agriculture, would monopolize both water and power produced by the project. Echo Park, members of both sides suspected, was just a cover for these maneuvers.[27]

Secretary Chapman spent his last year and a half in office gradually restoring the authority which the Dinosaur controversy had under-mined during the first year and a half of his tenure. He seemed deter-mined to prove that the Park Service was not the adopted child of the department. His relations with the preservationists were substantially restored to harmony when he appointed Conrad Wirth as the new director of that agency. A landscape architect by profession and a disciple of Stephen Mather and Horace Albright, he had supervised the work of the CCC in the park system and had served as the bureau's expert on land acquisition since the days of Ickes. Drury considered him "a genius at organization," and he was undoubtedly as much a purist about preservation as his predecessor. The National Park Ad-visory Board particularly admired his skill in dealing with lobbyists and congressmen. All these talents would be needed to resolve the Dinosaur question, predicted one of its members, publisher Alfred Knopf of New York. Wirth immediately assumed an aggressive stance by undertaking to educate legislators about the service's plan for the Monument. Because it included development of facilities, preserva-tionists at first feared that Wirth's appointment was a mistake. Then they concluded that the development would be a useful tactic in garnering support for their cause. Wirth also contributed to their campaign by issuing a report on the commercial and bureaucratic threats to many other units in the park system. One of the most imaginative steps he took was to inaugurate a series of raft trips down the Green and Yampa rivers through the preserve in order to arouse the enthusiasm of prominent citizens. The exciting rides into the spectacular canyons would, he expected, convince people that Dinosaur was the only area in the system "that the public can get down into and see and enjoy" in that unique manner. "There is no more beautiful canyon in the country. We must keep it that way."[28]

Another ray of sunshine pierced the preservationists' gloomy skies in November 1951. Addressing a meeting of the National Audubon Society, Chapman announced that he favored a search for an alternative site to Echo Park. Afterwards, he appointed a task force of assistant secretaries to lead that search and, over the objections of the Bureau of Reclamation, asked Ulysses S. Grant III to contribute to its findings. The preservationists had urged him to modify his approval of UCB after the Drury affair, but he had waited for an opportune moment. The elections of 1950 provided a beginning for a new emphasis. Senator Thomas of Utah had been defeated for reelection and President Truman naturally had no wish to cater to the interests of the two Republican senators from that state. The administration's sense of obligation for UCB cooled down during the subsequent months just as it did for the CVA proposal. In California, Drury wondered if the secretary's change of heart was merely another indication of his tendency to bend to the winds of the moment. The *Denver Post* denounced it as a sign of weakness. But Democratic Senator Edwin Johnson of Colorado admitted that his support for the proposal was weakening too. Some developers in the basin states cried betrayal when he announced that he might join the preservationists' new demand to make Dinosaur a national park. When Straus learned of that move, he became worried and asked that a specific promise be inserted into the bill to include dam sites. The whole course of events upset the leaders of the UCB campaign. Wyoming's Senator Joseph O'Mahoney echoed a thousand earlier complaints when he charged that the Interior Department was not treating developers fairly or encouraging resource development. Chapman, he said, was not pushing a policy for the West.[29]

The secretary's task force found several alternative sites further down the Colorado River and specifically recommended raising the height of the proposed dam at Glen Canyon, Arizona. Basin state officials acidly inquired how the department could become convinced of something they had rejected the previous year. No new evidence had been offered, Senator Watkins told Chapman. If the Glen Canyon structure were enlarged, the impounded waters would back up and destroy Arches National Monument near Moab, Utah. The secretary replied that he would abide by his initial decision to use Echo Park unless alternatives were agreed upon. Privately, he knew he would not have to wrestle with the dilemma much longer.[30]

On that matter at least, the elections of November 1952 provided relief. Chapman spent the last weeks of his quarter century in government service in characteristically genial relationships with friends and foes alike. He talked with Republican members of the Senate Interior Committee about the outstanding problems which the new administration would face and invited his successor to briefings at the department. When he submitted his letter of resignation to the president in January 1953, he was one of the last of the top echelon New Dealers to leave office. He wrote that he was proud of the part he was privileged to play under Truman's leadership "in conserving and strengthening our natural and human resources." Perhaps thinking of the Drury and Dinosaur tribulations he added: "My task was made lighter by the abiding conviction that in times of stress I could always turn to you for advice and support." Then Oscar Chapman dropped the hot potato squarely in the lap of the Eisenhower administration.[31]

Chapter Four

THE WEST
&
THE MANDATE
FOR CHANGE

Positively stated, the issues of resources policy had helped swing the West to the Democrats in 1948. In 1952 these issues were viewed from a negative perspective and discussed as an example of what the incumbents had done and what the challengers would do if elected. The Republicans had several more effective themes on which to concentrate their rhetoric: the Cold War, Korea, internal security, federal spending, and the so-called Truman scandals. Although having less broad appeal, the controversies over water and power development reminded western voters of some of these larger issues. Cattlemen in Arizona and Texas, for example, demanded a thorough overhaul of the Forest Service. If the Republican presidential candidate properly recognized the interests of the mining industry as well, "the West will go to Eisenhower." The cry of "socialism" was ubiquitous that year, and the decisions and proposals of the Interior Department seemed to epitomize every pejorative sense of that word, including the innuendo of "communism." Although the label had been used to excess during the debate over CVA, many Republicans believed that it had served as the most convincing part of their criticism which had defeated that proposal. Now they remounted the weapon and armed it with scatter shot. "The fine hand of socialistic government appears to ride high in Interior," one wrote. A member of the nonpartisan League of Women Voters in Oregon testified that she was provoked into working for the Republican National Committee because of "the trend toward 'modified communism' in the Interior

Department." Even minor examples of public ownership were readily branded. In the Puget Sound area of Washington, resort owners declared that a local bond issue for a county park was "really a choice between a socialistic thing and free enterprise."[1]

Republicans in the Pacific Northwest began their attacks on the Interior Department early in the election year. Senator Harry Cain announced that a "grab" policy was already underway there. To prove it, he read from a letter written by Secretary Chapman to Governor Arthur Langlie in which the latter was asked to inform the department of any leases issued to private companies in the state's offshore area. Obviously, Cain charged, this was another example of "big brother" watching and scheming to deprive the states of their landed heritage. Similarly, just as the Democrats had tried to obtain federal dominance of water and power through the CVA, now they meant to secure it at Hells Canyon. Cain saw through such schemes: "the nationalization zealots in the Department of the Interior are . . . far too clever to tip their hand all at once. By slowly chewing up one State at a time, they are avoiding the explosion that would logically follow any attempt to swallow in one giant gulp the natural resources of all 48 States. . . . Their patience and skill would do credit to the masters of political corruption in the Kremlin."[2]

According to other commenators, Interior's policy should be one of disposition, not acquisition, and its guiding principle should be that of "returning" the public domain and its resources to the states. The president of the Oregon Woolgrowers Association specifically cited the department's Bureau of Land Management as the central obstacle to necessary development. "Let as much government as possible be given back to the States and local communities," he urged. "The public lands should be governed from within the states wherein they are situated. As much land as possible should go into private ownership and become tax paying to the county and state treasuries." A mining executive in Arizona was not sure that the laws had to be altered to effect a change in policy. "Maybe all we need is to have an intelligent, understanding, and forthright Secretary of the Interior, a man out of sympathy with the effort of the bureaucrats to regiment and socialize the mining industry." Lieutenant Governor Robert Smylie of Idaho thought that the gap between the department and local interests perhaps could better be closed by the establishment of an advisory committee composed of persons "whose business interests and experience qualified them to give unbiased and technically sound advice on Departmental problems, especially in the West."[3]

These ideas that land use policy could be redirected by political change were latter-day echoes of the grumbling raised against Ickes during the New Deal. The strong criticism of the Interior Department's water and power programs was an extension of the fight over regional valley authorities and federal reclamation regulations. Senator Arthur Watkins of Utah flatly stated that "nothing in the way of a national policy with respect to control of water and power sources" had been offered by the Democrats except schemes "to perpetuate government monopoly." In an ironic reversal of the situation in 1948, Montana Republicans denounced Truman's decision to stop all new reclamation projects because of the Korean emergency. In the meeting halls of reclamation organizations in the West, one of the main topics of gossip was the anticipated removal of Michael Straus as commissioner. A tough man should replace him, the developers decided, one who would unload political appointees and reduce the overexpanded publicity personnel of the bureau. In California, some water users prepared to break through the 160-acre limit regulation. In the Pacific Northwest, power users cast questioning looks at the Bonneville Power Administration which was "so big, so powerful and so capable of domination in relations with lesser utilities that real participation with local enterprises has never been achieved."[4]

Republicans eagerly transcribed the gist of these sentiments into the lands and resources planks of their party's platform that summer. The brief generalities of the 1948 statements were replaced by impassioned prose. In the management of lands and forests, they pledged "the elimination of arbitrary bureaucratic practices" and the adoption of legislation to protect users and the public interest against "corrupt or monopolistic exploitation and bureaucratic favoritism." In water and power policy, they favored "greater local participation in the operation, control, and eventual local ownership of reimbursable, federal-sponsored water projects. We vigorously oppose the efforts by this national Administration, in California and elsewhere, to undermine State control over water use, to acquire paramount water rights without just compensation, and to establish all-powerful Federal socialistic valley authorities. We favor restoration of the traditional Republican public land policy, which produced opportunity for ownership by citizens to promote the highest land use."[5]

Although the Democrats could have offered a critique of these assertions, citing Republican resource scandals of previous decades,

westerners were not interested in history lessons. Some of them, however, did detect an ominous sound in the phrases used in these planks.
Two staunchly Republican, development-oriented newspapers, the
Salt Lake Tribune and the *Denver Post,* feared that the language
could be construed as invitations to special interests to move in on
the public domain at the expense of the general public. The editors
suggested that an addendum should be attached to them, denominat-
ing the public interest as paramount to all others. This was the best
way to head off Democratic charges that the Republicans meant to
"turn the clock back."[6]

While the Democrats tried to raise the specter of what their opponents might do to resource policy if elected, the Republican presidential nominee delivered several speeches in the West which took
their departure point from the record of what the previous administrations had done. Instead of copying Truman's sharp-tongued ridicule,
Dwight Eisenhower couched his remarks in a tone of exasperation
overcome by determination. In Boise, he said that the federal government was so deeply involved in controlling water and power that it
did everything "but come in and wash the dishes for the housewife."
In Seattle and Sacramento, he drew upon ideas furnished by Governor
Langlie for his most memorable statement on the subject:

> The whole hog method is not the way to develop Western resources.
> These resources cannot be effectively developed without regard for
> local interests and local knowledge of local needs by bureaucrats 3000
> miles away in the nation's capital. Nor can it be done by the states
> alone. Nor can it be done by free enterprise alone. All have a share
> in the task. We need river basin development to the highest degree,
> but not at the expense of accepting super government in which the
> people in the region have no voice. . . . We want this to be done
> through partnership . . . bringing in the federal government not as a
> boss, not as your dictator, but as a friendly partner, ready to help out
> and get its long nose out of your business as quickly as that can be
> accomplished.

When he arrived in TVA country, Eisenhower admitted that for the
people of some areas, federal domination might be acceptable, but
that the government should never dictate to the residents of a river
valley what forms were more suitable to their needs and wishes. In
Spokane and Fargo, he dismissed the Democrats' predictions of a
construction drought after the Republicans took over. There were

reclamation projects built by Republicans, he noted, long before the New and Fair Deals, and there would be more built after those administrations had been forgotten everywhere but in the history books. In Portland and Fresno, he reiterated that the real purpose of development in water, forest, and land management could be restored if the government came to the West "as a partner, not as a patron or a boss."[7]

Eisenhower's prairie boyhood and folksy manner fit the western ideal far better than the urbane personality and eastern education projected by the Democratic presidential nominee, Governor Adlai Stevenson of Illinois. Because Stevenson was selected so late, Truman's resource advisers had only a few weeks to provide him with information on the subject. Western Democrats wondered if he could understand the details of water and power development, or even if he could be made to look sufficiently "outdoors-like" when he came to their region. Stevenson's efforts to satisfy these hopes were not much more successful than Thomas Dewey's had been. He assured a Wyoming audience that he had straddled the Continental Divide in that state when he was a boy, and he pointed out that federal projects had brought economic opportunities to Wyoming—but then seemed to let his focus slide away from the subject of resource policies: "You have seen power from Federal projects form the basis for greater farm output and new and expanded private businesses. . . . These are not the actions of an arbitrary bureaucracy, my friends, seeking any socialization of our economy. They are the actions of a sensible government interested in creating the conditions under which free enterprise can thrive. . . . I don't think the Republican Party can give you that kind of government. . . . [It has not] yet offered a single new idea for meeting any of the major issues ahead of this country." In Seattle a few days later, Stevenson unmindfully touched a sore point when he referred to eastern criticism of wasteful spending on fantastic projects in the Pacific Northwest, and then went on to list the bounty of dams built there by the Democrats. As Republicans gleefully noted, he made no mention of CVA, though he defended the efficiency of federal regional development and specifically supported the high dam at Hells Canyon. Inadvertently, he also agreed with his opponent that TVA was not necessarily the proper solution to the needs of other river basins.[8]

President Truman tried to carry some of Stevenson's campaign load, partly because his administration's record was the principal issue and partly because he enjoyed the fight. The controversy over ownership of possible oil deposits off the shores of several states—the so-called tidelands—became a favorite topic of Democratic oratory under his lead. For several years, westerners had supported a move to grant these offshore lands to the adjacent states. The subject was usually presented as a reassertion of both free enterprise and states' rights. Watkins of Utah even proposed the transfer of lands under navigable waters in landlocked states. Another Utah official painted an ominous picture: "The present National administration has opposed this measure on the same grounds they have used to extend their control to other areas . . . they have applied the principle of government ownership as practiced in socialist nations. . . . Unless we call a halt to this practice, the states will be stripped of all authority and the power of the Federal government will be oppressively overwhelming. That is what happened in Germany."[9]

Truman unequivocally defended federal jurisdiction over the off-shore areas; Stevenson repeated that stand during his campaign; and Senators O'Mahoney and Anderson unsuccessfully sought legislative confirmation of it. Harold Ickes entered the fray, denouncing the move before congressional committees and educators alike and calling the scheme "one of the most gigantic swindles in American History. . . . It is a bare-faced grab." When the land commissioners of the western states resolved in favor of state jurisdiction over the areas, Truman responded that state control would turn into a "giveaway." It seemed clear to Republicans that he would not hesitate to veto any grant to the states by Congress. They also spread the rumor that he was planning to secure federal control of the offshore tracts by making naval oil reserves out of them by executive proclamation. Senator Lyndon Johnson of Texas wrote to argue against any such tactic. It would be a meaningless temporary gesture, he told the president, and would result in division of opinion just when the Democratic party needed unity. Referring to Truman's preoccupation with the Korean crisis, he added that the action would also inhibit private oil production when the nation needed more for national security.[10]

Beginning in May and continuing through the weeks up to the election Truman took to the hustings with relish. In his characteristic free-swinging style he pointed to the machinations of the power lobby, "private rakeoffs" in transmission rates, and other echoes of his successful pitch in 1948. He dismissed Eisenhower's Boise speech, saying that Democrats "don't let propaganda about socialism scare us into failing to develop our resources." Indeed, that slogan about "creeping socialism" was actually "started by the private power monopoly." As to the Republican claim that they started reclamation programs, Truman agreed. But after Theodore Roosevelt left office, they had been dominated by men who opposed it. That party was "not one bit interested in these things," and if elected now, no more projects would be built. "If you want the Upper Colorado storage project," he told Coloradans, "you had better vote Democratic." At Grand Junction, he assured his listeners that Secretary Chapman was working hard to prevent the dam at Echo Park from harming the rest of the monument, then turned their attention away from the controversy with a joke: "I think that the Dinosaur National Monument . . . ought to be preserved. In fact it ought to be enlarged. After this election we will enlarge it to accommodate the dinosaur wing of the whole Republican Party. We will fill it up with the old Republican fossils. Then maybe we could change the name of it to the Republican National Dinosaur Monument."[11]

The officials of the Interior Department also helped make up for what the Democratic presidential candidate lacked in personal familiarity with resource issues. Secretary Chapman wrote the party's platform planks on the subject and was mentioned as a possible running mate to Stevenson, or as a member of a Stevenson cabinet. He also acted as legman and speechmaker in the West during the campaign. Commissioner Straus returned to that region to face decidedly mixed opinion about himself and his bureau. Reportedly "armed to the teeth" he tried to convince reclamationists that Republicans were controlled by water and power monopolists and were all budget cutters. Obviously, he hoped to repeat the successful tactic of 1948. Yet when Truman's own Bureau of the Budget sought cuts in several large projects and an increase in federal power rates, Democrats found themselves under the same guns they had used against their opponents four years earlier. Doubts about their stance as provider also arose because of the delays in the UCB project. Colorado Democrats hastened to warn the National Committee that that subject was the biggest issue of the campaign, but nothing was done beyond the brave rhetoric offered by the president there.[12]

Eisenhower's western advisers were far more accurate in their assessment of discontent and expectation in their region. Langlie, Thorton, Watkins, Cordon, and Barrett all presented insights into sensitive topics to the candidate's speech writers. Smylie of Idaho submitted surveys of the political situation in the western states to the general and to his chief campaign aide, Sherman Adams. Centralization was viewed as "a real threat" in the West, he wrote. Eisenhower must also face down the Democrats' allegations about Republican antipathy to resource development. Reclamation in Idaho, for example, was a Republican achievement. He must promise that projects in other states would not be abandoned. The party's criticism of Democratic policy did not mean opposition to federal development, but only to the way in which that policy was administered. Smylie explained that the people of the areas affected by the programs felt powerless against the influence of the so-called experts who made arbitrary decisions. Finally, he urged all party members to counter the two most common Democratic charges: that Republicans would destroy TVA, and that they would fire "sincere hardworking people" in the federal bureaus and agencies in the West in their pursuit of free enterprise and economy.[13]

Few of the other contests in the western states offered significant confrontations on the issue of resource policy, and fewer produced significant results. In Washington State, Arthur Langlie was challenged for reelection by Congressman Hugh Mitchell, author of the first CVA bill. The governor readily denounced federal domination and made moderate suggestions on equity and proper jurisdictions. His victory over his opponent was small, perhaps because of his heavy use of the issue of subversion. In Utah, where federal reclamation was "the life blood" of the area, Senator Watkins avoided demanding replacement of federal projects by private ones. Assured by him that a Republican regime would continue these constructions, the voters there rejected his opponent, Marriner Eccles, onetime New Deal economic adviser, and put Republicans into every seat on the state's congressional delegation for the first time in twenty-eight years. One of the losers was Congresswoman Reva Bosone who had stood with Watkins and Lee for the inclusion of Echo Park in the UCB project. Another congresswoman, Democrat Gracie Pfost of Idaho, was reelected although she had defended the federal high dam proposal for Hells Canyon. Another advocate of federal dams, Mike Mansfield of Montana, demonstrated that Democrats could stand against the Republican tide. His position on that resource issue helped him defeat Zales Ecton, the state's only Republican senator since 1912, in a constituency served by the huge federal dams at Libby, Fort Peck, and Hungry Horse.[14]

The Democratic administration took steps to secure its resource policies even before the Republican victory that November. Some of the advocates of public power urged Secretary Chapman to transfer the Hells Canyon plan from Reclamation to the Corps of Engineers in order to save it from the expected attack on Straus and his bureau. The president did not authorize that change, but did appoint Chapman's assistant, Dale Doty, to the Federal Power Commission which in the near future would be deciding on that and other regional projects. He had waited many months to fill the vacancy caused by Monrad Wallgren's resignation, he said, because he was anxious to find "a man . . . whose interest is in the consumer." Assistant Secretary William Warne also thought that the selection of his colleague would bring the commission and the Interior Department into a better relationship on policy matters. Truman sent a special economic report to Congress about the same time, repeating earlier appeals concerning the "utmost importance" of river basin development. In it he announced that the budget for 1953 would allot half of the total for water resources to multiple-purpose dams, including Hells Canyon, because of their potential contribution in national security emergencies such as the Korean conflict.[15]

Two weeks before leaving office, Truman made the most defiant gesture of all, seemingly confirming everything the Republicans had said about the Democratic bureaucrats. One of Washington's congressmen, Russell Mack, had been denouncing their centralist megalomania for several years. Since 1950 he assured the lumber companies in his district, the Olympic Peninsula, that further federal land acquisition would be halted by his fellow Republicans. Governor Langlie joined him in demanding immediate sustained yield logging within Olympic National Park. The *World*, organ of the milltown of Aberdeen, complained that the park could not be put "to any practical use" until the Park Service unlocked its great supply of timber there. The park was "so wild, its roads and trails so poor, that it is not even a tourist attraction to any thriving extent." The timber rotting within it was cited as proof that the Park Service was unable to manage the vast preserve. Adding to this commonsense reasoning, Mack pointed out that logging in the park would boost local payrolls. The subject started to heat up politically in 1952 when Congressman Henry Jackson challenged Senator Cain for the latter's seat. The challenger seemed embarrassed by the protests of local preservationists defending Olympic National Park and found it wiser to call for development of parks as well as dams. He defeated Cain by a margin no greater than Langlie's over Mitchell.[16]

Two weeks after the Republican victory in November 1952, Mack asked Langlie to invoke the "consultation" agreement of the original act creating the park. This understanding that state and federal officials would consult on future matters affecting the boundaries was a mere courtesy rather than a statutory requirement. By that time, the Park Service informed Secretary Chapman that about 47,000 acres of land had been acquired from the Forest Service transfers and purchases made during the war with the last of the WPA's funds. Most of these acres were contained in a strip of land along the Pacific Ocean, detached from the main body of the park. Preservationists who had fought for the creation of Olympic insisted that the strip be officially annexed to the park before the Democrats left office. They warned Chapman and Wirth of the mounting pressures from both private and state interests to transfer tracts back to the Olympic National Forest where they would be available to loggers. The people of the peninsula favored the addition, Irving Brant assured the president; he did not think that Eisenhower would revoke it. Truman agreed that it was an opportunity that could not be ignored. Early in December, he informed Langlie that the park would be enlarged by the addition of the ocean strip to within 1,692 acres of the total permitted by the act of 1938.

Congressman Mack tried to rally a public protest. Governor Langlie wrote to the president, insisting that there was "absolutely no justification" for the federal action at that time—a reference to the recent mandate against Truman and the Democrats. When reporters asked about the matter at the next White House press conference, Truman facetiously replied that he had never heard of Olympic, did not know where it was, and wondered if they were talking about Mount Rainier National Park. Langlie, soberminded and rather self-righteous, waved the president's letter before local newsmen as proof of the lie. The *Seattle Times* thereupon denounced the "lame duck scheme" as "one last New Deal blow to the economy of this state." Lumbermen confessed that the proclamation had caught them "somewhat flatfooted," but they tried to persuade their friends in Congress to do "some effective work in the brief time left." Walt Horan asked that the issuance of the order be delayed, but Jackson claimed that the matter was too complicated to be decided on in any other way.[17]

Brant sent his own draft of the proclamation to the White House in order to furnish good arguments for the addition. The ocean strip, he said, had been included in the original park proposal enacted in 1938 and was therefore not "suddenly cooked up without the knowledge of Congress." The president's resolve did not need bolstering, however, and he did not use the draft. In early January he announced that he regretted that the governor did not concur in the matter but noted that it was in keeping with the public interest and the original intention of Congress. He had accepted Brant's word that local opinion favored the enlargement. There was, in fact, a widespread expression of hard feelings about it on the peninsula—from lumber mill operators, real estate developers, and property owners.[18]

Harry Truman was in good company when he issued his proclamation. Theodore Roosevelt had created the original Mount Olympus National Monument two weeks before he left the presidency, while lumber interests were planning to block legislation for the preserve. He also withdrew dozens of potential water power sites from the public domain during those last days. His Democratic predecessor, Grover Cleveland, had ordered a large increase in the number and size of federal forest reserves just weeks before he was replaced by a Republican administration. Indeed, young Roosevelt himself had criticized that action because it did not have the consent of the western states. Truman's proclamation was unfortunate in one respect: it implied that resource policy could be redirected simply by the stroke of a presidential pen.

Redirection of national policies by new leadership was expected by the westerners who voted overwhelmingly for Republicans in local, state, and national offices. According to various commentators, that sweep was the result of a protest against years of bureaucratic dictatorship and a call for suspension of further federal land acquisition until a more liberal policy could be formulated. Eisenhower's election, one of Horan's constituents observed, was "so terribly necessary." With it, Smylie of Idaho claimed, "I think perhaps we have changed the course of history." Eisenhower could justly assume that he had been given a "mandate for change."[19]

Believing that they accurately read public opinion in that election, the president-elect and his advisers wanted to choose lieutenants whose records and philosophies reflected a commitment to the tenets of their crusade: pursuit of fiscal responsibility, decentralization of bureaucracy, and restoration of faith in local and private enterprise. The controversies over resource administration had focused an unusual amount of attention on the Interior Department during the preceding years. The distrust and discontent that had accumulated in the West would have to be met. The selection of a secretary of the Interior, therefore, would be a clear demonstration of Republican intention to fulfill the real desires of the region.

The Republicans were not merely making a gesture toward the West's traditional claim to the post, however. "Whatever the background of the nominee," the *Washington Post* stated, "the need for a man of incorruptibility is the greater because of the Eisenhower emphasis on local partnership." Pundit Raymond Moley explained that the new secretary need not be a westerner as long as he was "a true friend of the West and a servant of the whole nation." He had to be an experienced administrator, an enemy of corruption, and a friend of individual enterprise. What he must not be, the onetime New Deal "braintruster" added, was another Harold Ickes, the man who "stole the liberty of 2/3rds of the nation."[20]

Public and private speculation produced a score of names during the weeks following the election. Former President Hoover reportedly thought that the Interior post would be well filled by economic conservative J. Bracken Lee of Utah, or city planner Robert Moses of New York. The press listed three governors: Milward Simpson of Wyoming, Val Peterson of Nebraska, and Allan Shivers of Texas. Several Dakotans were also considered to be prospects. The names most frequently mentioned were those of Arthur Langlie and Dan Thorton. Washington's governor seemed to have an inside track because of his role during the Republican convention and campaign. Rumor insisted that he was actually offered the post. If so it must have been done orally because no documentary evidence has been found to confirm the offer. Just beginning his second, nonconsecutive term, he preferred to stay in the state. A second rumor suggested that he had promised his associates that he would do just that before the election. Colorful Coloradan Dan Thorton was also a member of the Eisenhower inner circle, but in contrast to the solemn Langlie, he was a hail-fellow whom some Republicans considered a bit of a clown. Denver preservationist Arthur Carhart gagged at the suggestion of his appointment. "YE GODS!" he exclaimed to Bernard De Voto, "He's an opportunist, showman, and . . . hasn't any concept of natural resource management except for his and pals' benefit—exploitation." There is no record that the position was offered to Thorton either.[21]

The National Reclamation Association tried to influence the choice of Interior secretary as it had in 1948. Its officers urged the members to support the nomination of Senator Guy Cordon of Oregon. Because of his knowledge of water and power legislation and his place on the Interior committee, he seemed to have a very good chance of getting the job. Two of the national committeemen from Oregon, Ralph Cake and Jess Gard, as well as Governor McKay, worked with Eisenhower's political advisers on Cordon's behalf. But the senator had not changed his ambitions since 1948. The "real fight on these socialistic measures," Moley agreed, was "in Congress." Few men there could match Cordon's ability "to discern the hidden enemy in innocent-looking bills." The senator did not act as if he had been approached on the subject of appointment and did not seem to know who would be selected. Perhaps it was he who suggested Douglas McKay's name to Cake. The committeeman, then traveling through the Pacific Northwest to collect names of nominees for federal jobs, apparently knew that Cordon would not be named. According to reclamationist Robert Sawyer, it was Cake who "without doubt" was responsible for the nomination of Douglas McKay as secretary of the Interior.[22]

Perhaps more than any of the others mentioned for the post, Oregon's governor was eminently available. Just finishing his second term in the statehouse, he did not have to give up a place of present or future influence. He was well known to the public and the party in the West because of his vocal leadership in the fight against CVA and his criticism of bureaucracy in federal resource administration. His entire career was the epitome of the Republican image of citizenship. Born to a poor family of immigrant Scots in 1893, he went to work at the age of thirteen, became a janitor and laundryman in order to pay his way through Oregon State College, and was elected president of his class and of the entire student body before he graduated. After being severely wounded in World War I, he returned home to become a salesman, first in insurance and then in automobiles. By the early 1930s, he had established his own dealership in Salem, the state capital. As the genial and energetic owner of "Doug McKay Chevrolet" (his first name was James, but he used his second name because he felt it had better advertising appeal), he was an indefatigable joiner of civic and commercial organizations and a recipient of awards and offices in all of them. During World War II, he volunteered for army service and reached the rank of major. Subsequently, he became commander of the state capital's American Legion post.

When the Republican party began its postwar return to power at the state level, McKay was one of its most successful members. In the midst of the New Deal's "honeymoon," he had been elected mayor of Salem and, in 1935, 1939, and 1947, accumulated the longest tenure in Oregon's history as a state senator. Although part of the Robert Taft wing of the party, he concluded that the Ohio senator could not win if nominated in 1952. With his friend Langlie, he became one of the first promoters of the Eisenhower boom. The general's military career particularly attracted veteran McKay, but he also admired the candidate's confidence in private enterprise and localism. Indeed, commentators described his respect for Eisenhower as something akin to hero worship. The president-elect did not know the governor and apparently had a personal leaning toward an unidentified Dakotan for the Interior post, but McKay had two other supporters who had access to the president-elect—Leonard Hall and Richard Nixon. Hall, chairman of the national committee, was undoubtedly impressed with the governor's party record. During the campaign, McKay had been the first Republican to give a red-carpet treatment to vice presidential candidate Nixon after his dramatic "Checkers speech." Nixon still remembered that courtesy ten years later.[23]

As governor, McKay had held a businessman's view of resource use. Private access and development of natural resources was the very basis of the state's economy. He did not approve of unwarranted control or abuse, of course, but promoted city-owned water projects and treatment of stream pollution. Consequently, he felt that his attitude on all resource issues was a middle road between the zeal of both extremes. As he explained in a speech to lumbermen in June 1951:

> If it pays to grow trees and there are men with the courage to risk their capital on such long-range crops, then I want to see tax paying land owners given the chance without having to hurdle unnecessary road blocks. As far as I know there is no secret formula which makes a tree grow faster on government land than on tax paying forest lands. I have no sympathy for those mistaken souls who preach that our forests should be socialized and turned over . . . for . . . stewardship. Neither have I any particular sympathy for the person who screams about free enterprise and the right of individuals to own forest land and then abuses that privilege or does nothing constructive.[24]

McKay's Chamber of Commerce audiences enjoyed his folksy phrases, platitudes, and humorous digressions. Along with many others of the time, he was prone to overuse the label "socialist," often in an inaccurate, even libelous application. Moreover, he had a dismaying tendency to "shoot from the hip" when harassed or angered in public—an affliction suffered by other members of the Eisenhower team.

When Eisenhower called and dropped the "bombshell," McKay was stunned by the invitation to join the cabinet but was reluctant to accept. He was looking forward to winding up his public career in the governorship and entering a quiet retirement at his comfortable home in Neskowin, overlooking the Pacific. Yet he was also immensely pleased to have a chance to express his loyalty to the new president and to his party. He accepted the offer because, as Mabel McKay explained, "You just can't say no to General Eisenhower."[25]

The letters of congratulation arriving at the governor's desk expressed satisfaction that a westerner had at last been chosen. Horace Albright sent the best wishes of a fellow businessman; Assistant Secretary Joel Wolfsohn decided that McKay had "a good feeling for conservation and the policies that we have been pushing"; Robert Sawyer thought that he would "team up in fine style" with Guy Cordon. One New York mining engineer wrote to say that the appointments of McKay and the rest of those joining Eisenhower had already produced "a new feeling among the men of the producing industries that America can now go forward into an era of the greatest and soundest prosperity we have ever known." According to the *Idaho Statesman*, it was "the best news for the Northwest in years and years." Under the new secretary, "there will be the long-needed cleansing of the Interior department. The fuzzy haired boys will be gone. So will their aims and ideas. The great Northwest's natural resources may now be developed under American principles, and through the cooperation of the states." The most gratifying expression of such expectation came from former presidential candidate Thomas Dewey: "I am looking forward with great happiness to the wonderful job I know you will do in slaying the Socialist dragon of the Interior Department."[26]

Naturally, preservationists and public power advocates were dubious. De Voto was glad that Thorton had not been chosen, but he admitted that he knew nothing about McKay. He was depressed by the selection of Ezra Benson of Utah as secretary of Agriculture. Like Governor Lee, Benson had the "wrong" attitude on public land use and, together with McKay, could do "much damage" to federal policies. Irving Brant quickly warned Truman that the Interior secretary-designate was already acting as if he were in office by supporting Cordon's attempt to block Truman's Olympic National Park addition. The most outspoken public criticism of the appointment came from Wayne Morse. A onetime state and party supporter of McKay, the Oregon senator had often joined in predictable criticism of Democratic resource policies. But since his bolt from the Republicans over the nomination of Eisenhower, he considered himself an independent defender of the people's interests. He now called the selection of McKay "very good for reactionary forces that are out to plunder the people"; the nominee was "a well-recognized stooge of the tidelands thieves, the private utility gang and other selfish interests which place materialistic values above human values." Privately, other commentators thought McKay might be worse than a blatant villain—he would be a compromiser who would trade off parts of the federal programs to oil and electric companies in order to help pay off the party's campaign debts.[27]

After a round of farewell parties and meetings with Eisenhower and his cabinet colleagues, McKay appeared before the Senate Interior Committee for examination. The members were in a cordial and solicitous mood, and the hearing was perfunctory. Chairman Hugh Butler of Nebraska, never doubting confirmation, had already submitted recommendations to McKay for staff appointments. The rest of the committeemen seemed favorable either because they were Republicans or because they were from the West. Newly seated Senator Henry Jackson of Washington was the only one who showed concern.[28]

McKay's performance was not impressive. He made no opening statement, replied laconically to questions, and seemed to resent being asked about his views on any resource subject. He said that he had been drafted for the job, had disposed of stock in a few utilities and extractive companies, and had sold his automotive business to his sons-in-law. The rest of his replies were as superficial as the questions. Describing himself as a believer in private enterprise and the rights of the states, he admitted that he opposed any further federal ownership of power projects such as CVA would have been. He assured the committee that he did not intend to turn TVA over to private operation and, although he sympathized with the social aims of that agency and the Rural Electrification Administration, he did not share their economic and political philosophy. (He did not object to this question about two agencies that were not within the jurisdiction of the Interior Department.) When asked how he felt about the proposed reorganization of executive bureaus which would deprive Interior of some of its jurisdiction, McKay deferred to Cordon who, he said, knew much more about these matters.

The only moment of tension came when Jackson asked him about water and power contracts between federal and private organizations. Rather than take a stand on the issue of public versus private electrical production and distribution, McKay merely agreed that the public interest should have priority wherever federally generated power was transmitted to consumers. Just at that point the hearing was adjourned. No one could conclude from the transcript whether the new secretary would "turn the clock back" or whether he would institute wide-ranging changes in resource policy. They could only note that businessman McKay was already acting as cagey as any bureaucrat.

The nominee's reticence and the absence of prolonged challenge distressed some observers. De Voto, who praised Jackson's aborted questioning, confessed that he found reading the transcript of the hearing a "hilarious, melancholy, and rather frightening experience." Another comment came later from veteran journalist Elmer Davis who attended the new secretary's first press conference. The room was filled with the largest crowd he had seen there "since Harold Ickes' thunderous farewell." With western governors and senators ranged on both sides of the rostrum, McKay introduced his staff members and then asked for questions. To the obvious embarrassment of many, he hesitated, stumbled, and frequently turned to his under secretary "to get him off the hook." Two reporters whispered that the new administrators looked like "a lot of private utility thieves" and Davis was reminded of "the kind of characters you see in a night club, sitting with their backs against the wall and drinking alone, but ready to move in fast if a customer squawks about the check." Reporting the scene to De Voto, he added uncharitably: "so far as I could gather virtually all of those present shared my opinion—viz. that this man does not know the lower outlet of his alimentary system from a hole in the ground."[29]

Chapter Five

DOUG McKAY
&
THE DRAGON
SLAYERS

The new secretary of the Interior was the object of heavy-handed prejudice on the part of political pundits long accustomed to the sophisticated procedures of veteran Democrats. Everything he did thereafter was viewed through that initial judgment. It is time for an accurate assessment of his record and an account of the factors that transformed him into a public "villain." An examination of evidence in official and personal sources establishes three conclusions: First, McKay carried a heavier burden of expectations than any of his predecessors in the twentieth century. Second, his own view of his role, and the determination of those he depended upon, rendered him impotent as a decision maker. Third, more so than any of his predecessors, this Interior secretary was subjected to a broadly based, well-organized campaign of criticism which succeeded in distorting his actions and in pulling him down. There had been other whipping boys in the recent history of the office; Ickes was the most obvious example. But McKay's enemies based their allegations on the assumption that he was in charge of resource policy. He was not in charge.

McKay did not take the post in order to advance personal beliefs or plans. He had no profound store of information or understanding upon which original programs could be based. His correspondence from relatives and close friends shows that he was exposed to little more than banal cant in his private thoughts. If he had any personal philosophy at all, he would have been the first to describe it as plain common sense. With the members of the Eisenhower administration and many Americans he shared a belief in the commonality of individual effort and success. Those who came to him with complex problems were dismayed or amused when he sometimes protested: "Well you know, I'm just a Chevrolet salesman." He was obviously dazzled by the propinquity of celebrities and intellectuals in the nation's capital, but he preferred to remain just as he had always been. The same consideration was the basis for his admiration of others. The president, as he told a friend back home, "is just like your next door neighbor. In all his success he hasn't lost the common touch."[1]

McKay's ordinariness made him one of the administration's most popular public speakers. On scores of trips to the West and Midwest, he explained in simple, homely remarks what the Eisenhower team was trying to do. Although he used statistics and facts furnished by his subordinates, McKay's main emphasis in these talks was that common sense, fairness, and material progress were the proper bases for policy. When he was interviewed on television, he seemed just as happy talking about his love of horseback riding as about power policy. These things gave the impression that he was an intellectual lightweight, but he was actually expressing his full trust in the judgment of the common citizen. The people's views, he believed, were far more worthy of government attention than the theories of any kind of an elite. Of course his definition of "the people" was based on the types he himself associated with. He had no patience with crusaders or demagogues. His beliefs were just as righteously held as theirs, but he was convinced that good citizens would recognize true value gradually without manipulation by zealots. In a revealing letter written before he was sworn in, he assured a friend: "Since the announcement of my appointment I have heard so many remarks as to my policies and who I am going to hire and fire it really makes me dizzy. You can be sure that I am not going in there with the idea of turning things upside down over night, as that isn't the way to reorganize a business or a government agency. . . . We need two terms to do the job thoroughly, and the only way we can get a second chance is to so conduct the affairs of government that the people will be satisfied with the results."[2]

The secretary said little in private communication. Although he was pleased to have the factual summaries of pending problems presented at the transition conferences in Chapman's office, he spoke very little there. Distrust of Democrats might have accounted for

that behavior, but he sat in "rarely broken silence" in the meetings
of the Eisenhower cabinet as well. As one of the keepers of the
conservative conscience—along with Ezra Benson and Commerce
Secretary Sinclair Weeks—he apparently felt that his presence contributed as much to the discussions as expressed opinions could. The
president and his advisers reportedly disdained the character of the
"true believer" they felt their opponents clung to, but they were
happy to have such unquestioning conformity from members of their
own administration. McKay's acquiescence and keen sense of loyalty
invariably earned their praise and the compliments of his relatives
and friends at home. His receptivity to advice in the form of information from others made him a thoroughly safe and reliable
subordinate and a predictable boss. These same characteristics, of
course, also made him a cipher as an executive. The flood of solicita-
tions and warnings that came from above and below overwhelmed
him within the first three months of his job. A month after he was
sworn in, he told a friend that it was "the toughest civilian job" he
had ever held and that the responsibilities were "tremendous." He
was already in deep water before the unusually strong pressure of
controversies bore down on him. As his predecessors could have testified, the secretaryship of the Interior was no job for a genial clerk.[3]

Fortunately, Douglas McKay was surrounded by men who knew
what to do. In keeping with Eisenhower's preference for a general
staff type of command, several White House aides served as liaison
men for Interior Department affairs. In these subjects and almost
everything else, the ultimate decision maker was Special Assistant
Sherman Adams. A onetime New England forester, he was familiar
with some problems of access and regulated use of resources, but
his personal attention in this case was warranted by the fact that
the Interior policy had been one of the principal targets for change.
Anyone with business at the White House quickly learned to "clear
it with Sherm." They found the "assistant president" laconic and
seemingly cold-blooded, but gave him their absolute trust because
Eisenhower relied upon him so completely. Howard Pyle, another
administrative assistant, also handled many of the problems facing
the Interior Department. A former governor of Arizona, he was fully
cognizant of the West's expectations and needs and was personally
anxious to make his fellow westerner's tenure a success. In time,
one of Adams's own aides, Fred Seaton of Nebraska, acted as liaison
man for the Interior officials in public and legislative relations.

Standing in the background was Joseph Dodge, director of the Bureau of the Budget. Charged with watching over the administration's fiscal responsibility, he shaped the actions of each department on the basis of costs involved in executive or legislative proposals. He approached that task with a healthy suspicion. At one point, for example, McKay supported an unauthorized addition to Interior's 1954 budget, suggesting that it might be a mistake to discontinue all new starts on reclamation projects. Dodge was unmoved. The request, he told Adams, was "at least a misinterpretation of what has been included, and at the very worst a move to force the administration's hand in this direction."[4]

The Eisenhower men also recognized the importance of providing Interior with a staff of assistants who had specific experience in resource problems. As was customary, the secretary-designate was encouraged to choose his own under secretary. The man selected was so strikingly talented that McKay ordered the waiving of F.B.I. clearance; his new lieutenant, Ralph Tudor, was sworn in three months later. Tudor was a former colonel in the Army Corps of Engineers, a district engineer in the states of the Pacific Northwest, and in later private practice builder of the gigantic Oakland-Bay Bridge in San Francisco. His accomplishments earned for him a host of admirers among business and political leaders of the coast states, including Robert Sawyer, Guy Cordon, and McKay.

Cordon may have been the first to urge his appointment; however, when Tudor called to congratulate the governor in December 1952 nothing was said to him about the possibility of such an appointment. When it was later proffered, the stunned engineer asked: "What is an under secretary?" The turmoil and publicity of office held no attraction for him, and he initially declined the post. Hard-headed, practical endeavors had always been his choice. During the CVA debate, for example, he was asked to lend his name to the opposition campaign. Though he abhorred the centralist program of the Democrats, he had replied: "I prefer to play the part of the engineer." But because he had been one of many who felt a need for business-like qualities in government, Republican leaders were able to appeal to his sense of dedication. Tudor finally agreed to serve for one year in order to oversee a reorganization of Interior's bureaus and to improve what he described as the department's past poor relations with Congress, other departments, and the public. Within a week after taking charge, he was handling a dozen pressing problems inherited from the Democrats and was launching the new Republican emphasis in resource policy. Privately, he showed the amateur's awe of famous associates and irritation with the way "we have at least a daily crisis." But his professional competence enabled him to retain a self-confidence that brushed aside objections and commanded the respect of Democrats as well as Republicans.[5]

Although McKay contributed suggestions for appointment of the two assistant secretaries in charge of water and land programs, the selections were the result of time-honored patronage. Some party members looked for the selection of "top flight Americans" for the lesser posts, men who would give "no quarter for commie ideas and infiltration." Raymond Moley, for example, was anxious to see the dislodging of "socialists" who were "pretty deeply embedded" among the Democratic holdovers in Interior. Another Republican wanted to see them replaced by what he called "white folks."[6]

Westerners were particularly concerned about the officer who would preside over water and power policy. Harry Polk, former executive secretary of the National Reclamation Association, wanted the post for himself. His friend Sawyer wrote on his behalf, but he did not get the job. "I think it would [have been] . . . a sincere personal pleasure," Polk wrote in disappointment, "to work with and for Doug McKay through the belief that he subscribed to and advocated the same principles of private initiative and states rights in which I so thoroughly believed." White House patronage advisers chose another Dakotan, however, former congressman and governor, Fred Aandahl. Long a member of the Missouri Basin Interagency Committee, he still opposed an MVA and described himself as an advocate of states' rights. Yet he favored large federal reclamation projects and the preference clause in transmission contracts. Although Aandahl was not an engineer, Tudor thought that he was "a cracker-jack." His selection also resolved a struggle for favor among Nebraska Republicans. Hugh Butler, as chairman of the Senate Interior Committee, had enough influence to block the reported ambitions of Governor Val Peterson for the post and to sponsor his own friend Clarence Davis.[7]

Davis, however, was appointed solicitor for the Interior Department, an office that would become increasingly important after reorganization plans were carried out. A former legal counsel for water and power users in Nebraska, the only state in which all utilities were publicly owned, Davis was "pretty lukewarm" about regional valley authorities and hoped that the states could assert their proper rights under the laws. A Republican of the Taft persuasion, he once asserted that he thought Senator Joseph McCarthy was doing more good for the country than the State Department was. His views were not necessarily shared by his colleagues at Interior, but his keen legal talents were welcome. "This guy is terrific," Tudor told his friends. Davis was ready with advice for his chief, even to the extent of suggesting what the secretary's "proposed feelings" should be on certain issues. Sometimes his suggestions seemed impolitic, as when he urged the elimination of almost 30,000 acres from Glacier Bay National Monument in Alaska. But he was clearly aware of the probable political repercussions of transferring these lands into agricultural production. McKay was impressed with Davis's conservatism, however, and gave him his full trust. The measure of that regard was expressed when he chose Davis to succeed Tudor as under secretary late in 1954.[8]

The second assistant secretaryship was filled through the influence of Arizona Republicans. That officer would preside over the Bureau of Land Management, the Park Service, and the Bureau of Indian Affairs. It was the latter agency that particularly irked the state's new senator, Barry Goldwater. The incumbent Democratic commissioner was "entirely too much on the New Deal side to take the risk of keeping," he thought. To see that the job was done properly, he recommended Orme Lewis of Phoenix, an attorney whose firm handled cases involving power line rights-of-way across the public domain, including Indian reservations. Lewis had in fact wanted to be undersecretary, but took the lesser post after Pyle joined the White House staff and Tudor was chosen by McKay. Apart from his role in the highly controversial attempt to terminate some reservations, Lewis was well regarded by Interior watchers. Idaho's Senator Henry Dworshak expressed the feelings of other westerners when he said he was glad that a westerner had taken over the Bureau of Land Management, but at the hearing on Lewis's nomination, none of the committee members asked him about his views on the national parks. In the course of his two-year tenure, however, he pleased Tudor by enforcing decentralization in the bureau, while satisfying preservationists by resisting pressures to open portions of the federal domain. Looking over his new colleagues, Tudor thought they were "a team that was going to go places." McKay treated them as a team, letting them make their own decisions.[9]

The change in personnel was the first business of these chief administrators at Interior. Shortly after his appointment, McKay had promised that he would not sweep the department clear of career professionals. Ira Gabrielson, former director of the wildlife bureau, and others had urged Eisenhower to retain these men, especially those in land use and conservation agencies. With McCarthyism at its height, however, Interior joined other departments in succumbing to the urge to purge itself. Walter Hallanan, Republican National Committee chairman, pleaded with McKay to break the dike of civil service protection, but few positions would have been affected even then. Tudor discovered that ninety-two places out of 375 were available for replacement, and he was able to fill only seventy-eight of these by the end of the first eighteen months. Worried that incumbents would hobble the determination of the department reorganizers, he meant to root them out. This meant overcoming the tenacity of engineers in the Bureau of Reclamation who were "fighting tooth and nail" against reorganization. But he was particularly interested in getting rid of those employees he described as "screwballs" and "rabid New Dealers."[10]

Using the McCarthy-like label "security risk," he publicly claimed to have found hundreds of incumbents who were "not necessarily communists" but "persons who did careless things for which they might be intimidated or blackmailed by communists." Privately, he noted that many of them merely seemed to undermine the department's promotion of free enterprise. It should be said in Tudor's defense that, administratively speaking, he was acting realistically. As President Eisenhower informed McKay in September 1953, top positions should be filled with people willing to carry out the policies of the administration. Even minor personnel should be watched closely, so that their actions would not become "an undesirable and unnecessary burden." Republican officials were also mindful of the political advantage of the purge. In the course of two years, the total number of department employees was reduced from 56,000 to 49,000 and the administration proudly announced that fact as part of its attempt to fulfill the 1952 promises about economy and bureaucracy.[11]

But those were small fry. Far more important was the replacement of men presiding over the bureaus of the Interior Department. That task was both facilitated and impeded by the preceding controversies over regional authorities, interagency compacts, preference clauses, acreage limitations, and land use jurisdictions. Attention from both Republicans and Democrats in the West was focused first on the commissionership of the Bureau of Reclamation. McKay had whetted their anticipation by remarking that the first thing he would do when he took office would be to fire the Democratic incumbent. Many of Straus's critics were disappointed when he "read the handwriting on the wall" and resigned rather than "wait for the executioner," as Tudor remarked. In February Straus urged the appointment of Milton Eisenhower, the president's brother, who was then chairman of the Hoover Commission's Task Force on Water and Power. The White House instead merely thanked Straus for staying on to be helpful in the transition. The outspoken Democrat, however, could not resist a parting shot. In his last official statement he warned that the department's reclamation program was in the "double jeopardy of a nose dive." Theretofore, it had prospered "as a bipartisan effort under the Square Deal, the New Deal and the Fair Deal." Now it was to be "consigned to the evolving philosophy of the BIG DEAL." As sort of a footnote on consistency in politics, Straus's assistant commissioner who had secured the support of congressmen by running errands for them, was not replaced for two more years.[12]

Howard Pyle of Arizona had hoped that the reclamation states could influence the selection of the new secretary of the Interior in order to guarantee a more acceptable water and power policy. Although Eisenhower assured him that McKay would cooperate with them in that matter, some reclamationists believed that the Oregon governor knew little about the controversies. They were happy to learn, however, that he was looking for a professional engineer for the post of commissioner rather than another political publicist, as they felt Straus had been. McKay stated that he wanted "an engineer with administrative experience who knows reclamation and who does not come from California." That bias prompted questions about Pyle's possible influence on the appointment. Perhaps McKay was considering the fact that he already had two Californians on his staff: Tudor and Felix Wormser, assistant secretary for mineral policy. Moreover, he apparently was discouraged from doing anything that would exacerbate the bitter feelings between Arizona and California concerning the long struggle over Colorado River use. He complained that "the California boys" were already criticizing him. So were the Arizonans. When Senator Goldwater heard that a Californian was being considered, he personally protested to Tudor and elicited a promise that it would not be done. Eisenhower told the press that

he knew nothing about the rumor. McKay also felt that Utah had
already received "too much consideration" in appointments and turned
down recommendations for George Clyde, Utah's chief water engineer and a leading proponent of the Upper Colorado Basin project.
After six months had passed with no appointment, some western
Republicans began to fear for their political futures.[13]

Tudor was not well acquainted with the names of engineers in
the field of irrigation, so it may have been Senator Eugene Millikan
of Colorado who suggested Wilbur Dexheimer of his state as commissioner. The Coloradan had begun his long career in government
by joining the bureau staff during the Hoover administration. Naturally, he did not share the feeling of some westerners that it was "the
most over-stuffed, inefficient and loosely organized" agency in the
federal structure. His appointment was supported by Senators Butler,
Goldwater, William Knowland and Thomas Kuchel of California. The
selection thus fulfilled McKay's promise to appoint a professional and
a career man; at the same time he avoided the California-Arizona
wrangle. A Coloradan would also be especially valuable in assisting
the administration in its plans for the Upper Colorado. Tudor immediately insisted that Dexheimer satisfy western demands for dismissal of bureau employees. The commissioner mollified many former
critics by firing 600 employees at the Sacramento office alone. (At
least former Senator Sheridan Downey and his friends must have
been pleased.) But Dexheimer's main contribution was his ability to
continue the great influence of the bureau in the department and in
the West and to defend its actions on the basis of practical engineering
rather than political theory.[14]

Other incumbent chiefs ignored the handwriting on the wall.
Marion Clawson, head of the Bureau of Land Management, was
one of these. As convinced a centralist and publicist as Straus, he
had done admirable work in coordinating the vexatious problems of
classification of the public domain lands according to potential use.
But the new Interior officials cared only that he opposed their plans
for reorganization and was issuing warnings about a Republican
"land grab." McKay also received confidential letters alleging that
Clawson was an advocate of "complete planned economy" and a
member of what seemed to be a communist cell in Utah. Late in
April he asked for the director's resignation. Clawson insisted that
he should stay on, but returned a lengthy letter critical of the Republican regime. "It took this Department fully 20 years to live down the

Interior Secretary Julius Krug (center) and Reclamation Commissioner Michael Straus (left) talk with a local user of a Boise Project reclamation canal.

President Harry Truman, C. Girard Davidson, assistant secretary of the interior, and Oscar Chapman, interior secretary.

Two of the best-informed Republican advocates of water resource development: Congressman Walt Horan of Washington and newspaper publisher-reclamationist Robert Sawyer of Oregon (below).

Interior Secretary Douglas McKay (center) and Undersecretary Ralph Tudor show President Dwight Eisenhower the sites of future water resources development.

Republican Senator Arthur Watkins of Utah (above) and David Brower, executive secretary of the Sierra Club: two of the principal antagonists in the struggle over legislation for an Upper Colorado Basin Project.

National Park Service directors Newton Drury and Conrad Wirth, defenders of the park principle of inviolability.

The Green River cutting into the Yampa Canyon in Dinosaur National Monument, center of the preservation-development controversies of the 1950s.

Senator Wayne Morse of Oregon, who discovered
in the resource controversies of the Eisenhower
years the means of political success for himself and
his adopted party.

dishonest acts of one of your predecessors," he instructed his superior. "Your words and deeds do not warrant the trust of conservationists," nor could they trust a department "where there is such grave danger of politically inspired administration." In forcing Clawson out, McKay unwittingly courted the fatal mistake of his predecessor, Richard Ballinger, whose removal of a subordinate in the land office set off a chain reaction that helped pull down the Taft administration. But preservationists like De Voto had no high regard for Clawson, except to support him as a service career man, and raised no public outcry.[15]

To fill his place, McKay took the advice of his old fellow warrior in the CVA fight, Governor Len Jordan of Idaho. Edward Woozley, that state's land commissioner, was described to him as "capable, imaginative, resolute" and as a man whose views about Interior's past practices coincided with those of the Eisenhower team. His credentials included support for the "restoration" of offshore oil lands to the states even though Idaho would not benefit from that decision. As director of BLM, Woozley became so enthusiastic about reorganizing the bureau that he turned down the chance to run for the governorship of Idaho in 1954.[16]

The sweepings of Tudor's broom especially alarmed those pres-ervationists who thought of the National Park Service as holy ground. The controversies of the Roosevelt and Truman years made it as much a target for change as the Reclamation Bureau. Horace Albright anticipated the mood of his fellow Republicans by calling at the White House and Interior Department early in March. He liked the new secretary "immensely," he wrote to Sawyer afterwards. The position of director, he told McKay, had never before been made the victim of political changeover, and the tradition of keeping the service above politics should be continued. While writing public praises of incum-bent Conrad Wirth, Albright waited in vain for an official statement of his retention. Howard Zahniser and other preservationists called at the White House to warn against throwing civil service career men "to the political wolves." No one was safe, they felt, if the present trend at Interior was continued. The only one not worried was Wirth himself. Privately, he assured friends that there would be no change. Undoubtedly aware of these anguished warnings, McKay had no personal desire to make a change in that office. As he later testified, he was very impressed with the director's grasp of detail. The decision to keep Wirth, moreover, would further demonstrate his intention of using experienced administrators.[17]

The purge at Interior was a lesser ingredient in the growing apprehension that the Eisenhower administration was about to dismantle federal resource conservation. The first step it took on the subject was ominous. In September 1952 Horace Albright, acting as president of Resources for the Future, Inc., had proposed a Mid-Century Conference on Natural Resources, and had asked both Stevenson and Eisenhower to endorse it. As president-elect, the latter agreed that it was "high time the Conservation Conference of 1908 should be reborn in a mid-century setting." He later appointed White House assistant Gabriel Hauge to act as liaison man for the meeting. Hauge thought that Albright was "a man to be trusted," but Sherman Adams was dubious about the proposal. There was a strong odor, he commented, of "ex-New Dealers, radicals, and planners" about the organization. He may have been referring to the fact that Resources for the Future, Inc., was a beneficiary of the Ford Foundation, or to the membership of Ickes's old loyalists, Straus and former Wyoming governor Leslie Miller, as well as Morris Cooke, chairman of Truman's water policy commission. Albright tried to overcome suspicion by naming Lewis Douglas, prominent businessman and former ambassador to Great Britain, as conference chairman and by drawing up a list of participants to show that many important business spokesmen would be present. Adams was able, however, to cancel plans to have the conference at the White House. Other Republicans shared his hostility. Veteran Oregon forester Stuart Moir, for example, felt that there would be no broad base of participants. The conference would be merely "a sounding board for the zealous 'do goods,'" and its resolutions would be cut and dried by "a few individuals who would like to see our natural resources socialized."[18]

McKay, significantly, thought otherwise. "In view of the importance of this subject in the Nation today," he wrote to the president's appointments secretary, "and in view of the attention given to it in the President's program, I believe it is important that the President plan at some time to meet with representatives of the 'conservation' organizations." Tudor advised his chief, however, that Albright was "a bit out of his field on this matter." The conference's council of sponsors was made up of "educators, labor leaders, etc. Not much business is represented." That was also the objection of the United States Chamber of Commerce which announced that it would boycott the meeting.[19]

Some members of the conference were not sorry to lose White

House sponsorship, because there would be "considerably less inclination to duck issues" then. Others were shocked, however, by Albright's efforts to increase business representation. "It is now ultimately clear," five organizations informed him as they withdrew from the plan, "that the very forces which oppose a sound resources program are in the Mid-Century Conference driver's seat."

Cooke joined them. "I think the membership of the various meetings, panels, etc. will be so stilted as to prevent the kind of thinking which is needed" in the field of water resource policy. Because of the classifications used for issuing invitations, there would be few in attendance who had "the capacity to make a real contribution to the advancement of the conservation cause," while "those who represent private, as contrasted with public, interests will be there in full force." Former President Truman, "very certain that every effort will be made to discredit the report of my Water Commission," was glad that Cooke decided to withdraw. The conference was postponed indefinitely. Eisenhower nevertheless made a public statement to Albright indicating that he still wanted to encourage the participation of such private organizations in resource problems and promised that the secretaries of Agriculture and Interior would help to prepare for a later meeting.[20]

As the months passed without any further action taken, conservationists feared that the president "as yet, knows nothing about the public lands problem"; Eleanor Roosevelt made the statement that Eisenhower was not even interested in conservation. Albright warned Hauge that "a general impression has spread across the country that this Administration is somehow or other going to weaken the conservation policies that have been built up to control our renewable and nonrenewable resources since the days of Theodore Roosevelt." The president should use the conference to emphasize Republican contributions to those policies. Eisenhower may have seen Albright's suggestion, but it was a memorandum from his budget director that he paid attention to. As far as Resources for the Future was concerned, Dodge wrote, "I have my fingers crossed; I still believe that its emphasis will be to the left, New Dealish, and Democratic, and that the forces really in control are not friends of the Republican Party."

Dodge thought there was something suspicious about the fact that the conference had failed to attract wider support, and he thought he knew why:

The hard core of conservationists, to a great extent, belong to those groups who think the government has to do everything. This has been their view from the beginning. Though most of the work of the country is done through business and industry and by the people through their own effort, in 50 years' time the conservationists have never been able to grasp this elementary point. As a consequence, their thinking and approach to problems lack imagination and vision. To them, boldness is to suggest that government "do it." . . . The professional conservationists seem to have a built-in anathema for business; they find it difficult to identify business with doing anything constructive in the way of conserving our resources. One of the reasons for this is that they put the emphasis on conservation rather than wise use.

An adherent of the pragmatic tradition of environmental use, Dodge hoped that if the president did address the meeting, he would emphasize how the nation should make use of its resources in the wisest way: "not how we lock them up, not how we save them, but *how we use them wisely.*" In order to "get dynamics into resource development," you had to get "government out and the people in." If that were done, conservationists would "stop quoting Theodore Roosevelt and start quoting Eisenhower." The conference finally met in December 1953, amidst increasing criticism of the administration's resource policies. Eisenhower decided that it would be wise to make only a few remarks at the opening luncheon meeting. The Republican leaders thereby missed a striking opportunity to affirm their purpose in the face of those controversies.[21]

If the purge was part of the political tradition, and the administration's reluctance to align itself quickly with outside organizations was understandable, the public had real grounds for profound suspicion during those first months. In that time, and for almost two years afterwards, a coterie of western Republicans in the Congress seemed intent upon reviving the "great land grab" of the preceding years. Realizing the likelihood of such an attempt, conservationists had held emergency meetings shortly after the election. When they learned of the new administration's cabinet appointments, their apprehension increased. De Voto, for example, noticed that Benson claimed to understand national forest policy because he had grazed stock in the reserves for many years. There was doubt for some months whether he would dismiss Richard McArdle, incumbent chief of the Forest Service. When he did not, De Voto was relieved but still worried after Benson had met with a deputation from Wyoming, the state most strongly opposed to federal resource regulations. One of the callers was former Congressman, now Senator-elect, Frank Barrett, the man whom De Voto described as having "carried the ball for the land grabbers" since 1946. Another was Congressman Lloyd Betsen of Texas, allegedly the spokesman for "the cowboy clique." The passing weeks brought more alarming signs. The move to change the Interior Department into a Department of Natural Resources, with BLM transferred to Agriculture, and the Forest Service switched to the new agency, De Voto decided, looked "so nice on paper" but was "so deadly dangerous." Everybody seemed to have "a special knife out for the Forest Service" and was now "whetting it expectantly."[22]

There seemed to be substantial grounds for such fears. The president's first budget request included a doubling of the appropriation for building access roads in the national forests. Shortly afterwards Congress granted offshore oil lands to the states, an action that Langlie described as an unequivocal repudiation of the Democratic administration's policy of encroachment. Even Republicans who had high hopes for their administration were worried. "We must keep our friends from going too far," an officer of the American Forestry Association wrote at the time. "I hope we can bring forth a broad, common sense program along the lines of the President's 'middle of the road' general policies." Albright expressed his concern in a letter to presidential adviser Nelson Rockefeller. If such things as the reorganization of Interior and Agriculture went through, he wrote, it might result in a repetition of the Republican reclamation gaff of 1948. Other party members were unafraid, however. Talk of transferring the national forests and those administered by Interior to state or private ownership appealed to some residents of land grant states where excessive amounts of land were held by the federal government. Robert Sawyer of Oregon, however, warned that the new regime was "not so firm in the saddle" yet that it could dismiss the protests that would arise if serious consideration were given to these proposals. For himself, he was willing to put up with "the Federal Government's foot" on the necks of the western states for four more years. If any controversies arose because of these attempts, and the administration was voted out of power in 1956, "there won't be any more Republican Party." Senator Cordon assured him that there was "no sentiment of consequence" behind these machinations.[23]

There was a determined group of men in Congress, however. The new session was only a few weeks old when Republicans and states'-rights Democrats joined to pass a measure awarding much of the offshore oil lands to the states. The White House men were apparently pleased because the issue had been one of the basic differences between Eisenhower and the Democrats during the campaign. The president characteristically had not tried to influence Congress but admitted that he had believed in state jurisdiction over the submerged lands "long before I was persuaded to go into politics." Now a principle had been upheld, many assumed, and could be followed through on. In March 1953 Barrett and Congressman Wesley D'Ewart of Montana, "probably the most powerful man" on the House Interior Committee according to Walt Horan, began rounding up support for several measures. Taking advantage of the long accumulation of western complaints and of the precedent set by offshore oil land legislation just adopted by the Republican Congress, their bills would transfer jurisdiction over grazing lands to state and private users. It was designed, they said, to encourage stockmen by enhancing their right to determine use regulations and to protect their actions from federal prosecution. The *Portland Oregonian,* undoubtedly Republican in loyalty, summed up these proposals quite differently:

> In brief, the bill would give ranchers a vested right to national forest grazing lands which now they use as a public privilege. The right would be perpetual, in virtually all cases. Grazing lands would become, in effect, a part of the rancher's property, without the cost of taxes and administration and for payment of a low fee. They could be sold with the home ranch to a new owner and handed down to descendants. Wealthy ranchers could buy other "base property" strategically located to give them a monopoly on all the grazing lands they could use. A reasonable supposition is that the result would be larger and larger ranches, and fewer smaller ranches.

It would be the realization of a dream of Farrington Carpenter. In fact, Ickes's onetime director of grazing served as one of the lobbyists for the Barrett-D'Ewart bills.[24]

The authors of the legislation insisted that their purpose was to bring legal sanction to use regulations theretofore decided by bureaucrats. D'Ewart, once a forest ranger, later argued that they believed "this is a government of law, not of executive administrative directive."

Their bills took the phrases of the 1952 party resources plank literally: they sought "the elimination of arbitrary bureaucratic practices" and the adoption of statutes "to define the rights of users" and protect them through "independent judicial review." To their dismay, however, they quickly learned that few of their fellow Republicans really felt obliged to fulfill that political promise. Unofficially, the Interior Department informed them that their bills went too far in granting grazing permit holders legal rights to public property. The sponsors revised part of their scheme, retitling it a Uniform Grazing and Tenancy Act, and hoped to demonstrate broader support by having Congressman Clifford Hope of Kansas and Senator George Aiken of Vermont act as new sponsors. Conservationists were not fooled by the ploy and continued to refer to the "Barrett bills" in their critical publicity. Even Aiken was loath to touch the proposals, going so far as to make public reference to a "great raid" coming to a head in Congress.[25]

In July, Barrett was approached by "a western fellow . . . someone high in the favor of the administration" and asked to hold his measure so that it could be incorporated into some larger program at a later date. This mystery visitor may have been Ralph Cake of Oregon, because the senator's supporters wondered if he was speaking for McKay. Adams, however, appeared to be receptive to what he called the "conservation bill." He talked to McKay, asked Dodge to help Agriculture revise its initial adverse report, and called a meeting at the White House. Present were Benson, McArdle and an assistant secretary, McKay and Orme Lewis, Barrett and D'Ewart. Barrett strongly objected to the suggestion that he backtrack just because of "agitation from the sportsmen's groups." Hauge promised to work out guarded language for incorporation into the president's next address to Congress, but McArdle continued to oppose the scheme.[26]

Those westerners who supported the Barrett bills expected the administration to recommend adoption of the legislation. One Oregon lawyer assured the senator that he could accomplish as much with his new range code as he had when fighting the Jackson Hole addition to Grand Teton National Park. But unlike the frustrating outcome of that crusade, "in this case we have a fair-minded President in the saddle." The two main national stockraisers associations supported the bill, but the men at the White House were cautioned that such publicized support was deceptive. The chairman of the House Interior Committee, Republican Congressman A. L. Miller of Nebraska,

advised the presidential assistants that it was such a highly controversial measure that it was bound to have "far reaching adverse
effects on the public interest." As a result, the White House men asked
McArdle to examine and revise Barrett's draft. The new Hope-Aiken
bill eliminated the unwise ownership provisions, but the critics of the
original extended their attacks to the new version anyhow. They said
it was just the same old measure "in camouflage." Observing that some
western newspapers opposed perpetuating the monopoly of large stock-
owners, De Voto was confident that he could "keep the bastids [sic]
off balance" by rallying opposition from all sources. He used his
column in *Harper's* to that end and wrote many letters to congressmen.
For example, he asked help from Thomas Dodd of Connecticut
because it was "the historic function of the East to prevent the West
from committing suicide." Western Democrats also took a second
look at the bills. Senator Lester Hunt of Wyoming announced that
most of his constituents were opposed to the Barrett bills. Senator
James Murray of Montana called it "another monumental giveaway."
Believing that the matter was in a very delicate state of balance,
the bill's author refused to sanction reply to these attacks.[27]

Surprisingly, the balance was soon upset by Secretary McKay himself. Harassed by reporters at a Denver airport, he replied to their
questions with characteristic impetuosity and said that he thought
the grazing measure was "lousy." Later, he admitted that it was
"just another case of . . . McKay opening his big mouth too casually."
Writing to Langlie, he added that he would hate to meet the bills'
sponsors "after dark. In fact, I don't want to meet them at all at the
moment." But when he wrote to D'Ewart, he denied that he had used
the word "lousy" and insisted that his department had not yet
reported against the measure. "I'm an old cowhand and I'm confident
we'll live up to the campaign pledge and do something for the cattleman but not at the expense of the rest of the people. There's to be no
giveaway program of public land," he promised. Unfortunately for
himself and the administration, McKay did not think it necessary to
say these words publicly.[28]

Some western Republicans who resented further federal acquisition
of lands were doubtful about the grazing proposals. Sawyer decided
that the bills were mainly for political purposes and had no chance
of adoption. Lobbyist Farrington Carpenter, on the other hand,
announced that the "hate campaign" of the "wildlifers" had "flivered
out." In terms of votes, it amounted to nothing, as was shown in

Barrett's own election the year before. Undaunted, the senator continued to reshape his measure to fit objections from the two departments and the White House through the congressional sessions of 1953 and 1954. It was obvious to everyone else, however, that the administration would not openly advocate reduction of federal jurisdiction over use of the public domain, however it might oppose increasing that control. McKay and Lewis emphasized administration by law, rather than by bureaucratic fiat; if the department permitted "selective disposal" of lands not needed by federal agencies, in no instance was that to be pursued on a large scale. Sawyer suggested that the secretary examine Louise Peffer's classic study, *The Closing of the Public Domain,* or make a strong public defense of the retention of federal ownership, but McKay did neither.[29]

Eisenhower's advisers preferred to let the issue recede. The president's message to Congress in January 1954 did not call for further revision of federal land use regulation. Instead his Commission on Intergovernmental Relations was asked to include the problem in its deliberations the following year. Its Committee on Natural Resources confined its investigation to correspondence and consultation, rather than public hearings. Although Thorton of Colorado was a member, the strongest statement in the group's subsequent report was the observation that "the national interest is not necessarily best promoted by federal action," and emphasis should therefore be placed on state and local initiative "wherever it may be expected to give satisfactory results." There was no suggestion for alteration of existing resource administration machinery except a recommendation for more frequent consultation with state governors. The expectations of 1952 concerning overhauling of federal land use policy were thus quietly sidetracked. Barrett persisted in his personal crusade, even when his colleagues asked for still further revisions and even after Republicans lost control of Congress in 1954. Arthur Watkins of Utah and Herman Welker of Idaho, concerned about water development programs, feared that the bills would damage consideration of more important legislation. There was no chance of their being adopted in the climate of Democratic domination and the publicity about "giveaways." As one of the Wyoming senator's supporters bitterly commented, they were the victims of "a very obvious political coup."[30]

If the grazing bills had not been proposed first and had not raised the outcries of the critics, McKay's Interior Department might have been able to establish a public image as defender of the national parks. Once the alarm was sounded, however, preservationists and Democrats quickly assumed that the "grab" was aimed at those preserves as well as other parts of the domain. Although Wirth had been retained as director of the National Park Service, many critics felt that more powerful malignant forces were at work in Congress and the White House. They would have shuddered had they seen Dodge's letter to McKay referring to a service booklet on the parks as "an expense which serves no need and can be eliminated." Although he opposed "commercial inroads" and urged protection of preserves by state legislation, McKay permitted his actual feelings to be influenced by his critics and by the statements of Republicans who were opposed to the federal preserves. Asked by an interviewer for a national magazine whether he believed the parks should be turned over to the states, he ambiguously replied: "Not necessarily." Wirth's influence on his attitude may have been enhanced by the publicity over the Barrett bills and other "giveaways," because the secretary began a series of visits to the national park system about that time. Reading statements drafted by the director, he invariably reaffirmed his department's commitment to the preservation of these units.[31]

During those same first months, a Western Conference of Park Concessionaires petitioned Interior for an end to the Krug policy of federal monopoly over commercial facilities in the parks. McKay admitted that he knew no more about the problem than what western complaints alleged; he turned to Wirth to handle negotiations. Drawing upon information compiled by Newton Drury's concessions advisory committee of 1945, the director decided that some change in policy was warranted. He agreed that private-federal sharing of concessions could be viewed as one aspect of the administration's emphasis on "partnership." But he also found widespread disagreement over contract terms and was well aware of preservationist wariness about damage to the parks by profit-oriented activities. His superior, Assistant Secretary Orme Lewis, made some tactless remarks while in the West, in which he claimed that De Voto, still a member of the National Parks Advisory Board, opposed tourist facilities. In fact, the journalist had long been an advocate of larger Park Service appropriations to meet the increase in visitor use.[32]

Barrett further blackened his own reputation among the friends of the parks in 1954 and 1955 by proposing two bills. One would permit Wyoming to tax property in the large parks within its boundaries;

it passed Congress but Eisenhower wisely vetoed this challenge to federal jurisdiction over the public domain. Another bill, which would require federal compensation of concessionaires in Yellowstone National Park, was not acted upon. The senator easily obtained the support of Governor Milward Simpson for a plan to transfer concession contracts to the states, but Albright sent McKay a lengthy argument against "this fantastic proposal." Indeed, the secretary had no personal wish to make such a radical departure from existing policy; perhaps he also knew that other states showed very little interest in the idea. Some concession contracts for Mount McKinley National Park in Alaska were revised experimentally, but they failed to satisfy anyone concerned and were discontinued after 1956. Wirth also declined to act on the suggestion by a department reorganizer that electric generator plants in the parks be turned over to private utility companies.[33]

The director's influence was far more significantly involved in McKay's record of resisting renewed demands for commercial access to the national parks. Because of the critics' campaign, that record warrants review. As early as March, the secretary indicated that he favored action by the Oregon legislature to prevent such "inroads" on "the areas which the people of Oregon so long treasured." A greater threat came from Washington State and was led, to the embarrassment of the administration, by some of the most prominent members of the Republican party there. Goaded by Truman's last-minute enlargement of Olympic National Park, they revived a plan for a much smaller preserve that Ickes and Roosevelt had rejected a dozen years earlier. Congressman Mack once again confidently assured his constituents that the "grandiose experiment in socializing the tourist resort industry" would be ended. Along with several colleagues, he asked Governor Langlie to receive suggestions officially for boundary changes and then submit these to the secretary of the Interior. The Congressmen intended later to draw up a bill incorporating the changes and obtain department approval. Naturally, they would depend upon Langlie's friendship with McKay and the men in the White House. Relishing the opportunity to redress the "injustice" imposed on his state by Ickes, Langlie established an Olympic National Park Review Committee. To head it, he appointed William Greeley, onetime chief of the Forest Service and for many years executive secretary of the Pacific Coast Lumbermen's Association. It was no coincidence that Greeley had been one of the strongest

opponents of creating the large park during the late 1930s. Another
member was the dean of the College of Forestry at Oregon State
College, McKay's alma mater. The Washingtonians overreached
themselves, however. Seeking to stir up widespread objection to the
"untouchable, holy shrine . . . this sacred cow in our land use economy,"
as Greeley called the park, they took testimony in the towns on the
peninsula. None of it was any more substantial than that taken in
1947 or earlier. After considering it, the committee split down the
middle on the question of what recommendation should be made.
Dean Gordon Marckworth of the University of Washington's College
of Forestry advised them not to bring any such divided report to the
Interior Department. Their letter to McKay, consequently, merely
asked him to make his own review of the boundary question.[34]

Understandably, the secretary turned to his director for advice.
Wirth probably drafted the letter sent in May 1953 to forester Moir,
one of the members of Greeley's association. It began by noting that
the subject of boundary changes had been thoroughly aired and that
the new hearings had produced no more information than those held
earlier. However firmly foresters believed that parts of the preserve
could be subjected to sustained yield logging, "a larger body of local
and national opinion . . . believes otherwise." If parks were used like
forests, McKay's text continued, their very purpose would be defeated
and the system would "cease to be the increasingly important and
economically valuable attractions which over 41,500,000 people took
pride in using last year." Olympic, being so new, was just beginning
to take "its rightful place in providing such use." In view of all these
things, he concluded, "it should be left alone." Then in a surprisingly
perceptive afterthought, he added: "You know this Administration is
being accused of being a 'give away' group already and if we start
reducing the size of our parks for the benefit of commercial lumbermen we certainly would be in for some unusual criticism."[35] Wirth
had probably used the last point to secure his chief's decision to
ignore the overture from the Washington committee. Once again, it
was unfortunate that McKay did not issue the letter through well-
publicized official channels. Like other members of the Eisenhower
administration, he preferred to deal with controversial matters as
quietly as possible. As a result, his admirable standards were
obscured by the mounting criticism of those who had already made
up their minds about the intentions of the Republican policy makers.

The same sort of opportunity was missed in McKay's response to renewed pressure to authorize Glacier View Dam in Montana. Albright had warned him early that the issue might prove to be "political TNT" for the department and the administration. Perhaps with that in mind, Assistant Secretary Aandahl informed his chief in July 1953 that neither the Bureau of Reclamation nor the Corps of Engineers thought that a dam adjacent to the boundary of Glacier National Park was necessary at that time. A short time later, McKay went out to the preserve to dedicate a 100,000 acre addition. Once again he defended the units of the system as possessing utilitarian qualities equal to any other possible use. In February of the following year, however, Senator Mike Mansfield reiterated his state's desire for the dam and asked the department to make a decision on its acceptability. The Park Service drafted a reply, and the technical staff reviewed and amended it to conform to previous opinions on the subject. McKay thereby indicated that he would not alter the opposition expressed by his predecessors. As a result, Reclamation announced that it would study two alternative sites. Albright was elated at the secretary's firmness on Olympic and Glacier and urged him to publicize both. McKay again preferred not to do so, and the rising storm over the Dinosaur decision effectively obscured these positive accomplishments.[36]

About the same time, McKay's men faced down continuing demands for the reduction of Everglades National Park. When the Park Service tried to acquire waterfront land to add to the preserve, it came up against the opposition of local real estate interests who were just as determined to lease 17,000 acres of nearby mangrove swampland. In addition, oil companies demanded a five-year extension on exploration leases due to expire in 1958. Although past drilling had yielded no commercially productive sites, they were still certain that oil was to be found there. To allay these pressures, Wirth went to Florida early in 1954, but his efforts to explain the park principle met a hostile reception. Local businessmen attacked his "arrogant impertinence" and denounced the "grandiose schemes of the bird watchers and politicians." His personal value to their state, the director was informed, was "WIRTHLESS." Their cause was taken up by Senator Everett Dirksen of Illinois. The park, he said, was a "frankenstein monster" from the days of New Deal colonialism, and further expansion of it was of such doubtful merit that he threatened to seek redress through congressional action. At that point, a man who could not be accused of favoring "colonialism" came to the state.

Assistant Secretary Lewis reminded Floridians that he was from Arizona where 72 percent of the land was under some form of federal jurisdiction. Although he looked with a "very jaundiced eye" upon further additions to federal preserves, he publicly defended Wirth and repeated that the department would uphold its previous plans for the Everglades.[37]

A few other incidents demonstrated the manner in which McKay's department defended the national parks. It is likely that the "give-away" charges steeled his hand. At the height of the charges in 1954, Governor Langlie called on him to urge permission for construction of a ski lift facility in Mount Rainier National Park. As the *Seattle Times* argued, many Washington residents felt that "One valley for skiers wouldn't hurt Rainier." McKay preferred to listen to the editor of another Pacific Northwest newspaper, i.e., Fred McNeil of the *Portland Oregonian*. After considering his comments and the recommendation of Wirth, the secretary decided that no permanent facilities would be permitted in the park. Although McKay's critics had publicized the threat, they failed to notice the outcome of the issue. Similarly, they blindly condemned him in the case of the Wichita Wildlife Refuge in Oklahoma. In 1954 the army sought to take over a portion of the preserve which they referred to as an otherwise useless land "of rocks and rattlesnakes." Because the secretary of the army, Robert Stevens, was a close friend, McKay hesitated to deny the application. The issue smoldered on for another year before preservationist criticism prompted McKay to send a special agent to the site. Harry Donohoe reported upon his return that the preserve was "uniquely valuable" as a wildlife refuge and was certainly not the kind of terrain the army needed. Their control of it, he believed, would be "a first bite" into Interior's system of preserves. By January 1956 a satisfactory agreement was reached between Interior and the army, although it was still described as a giveaway by McKay's critics for many months afterward.[38]

Because McKay failed to publicize his respectable record as a preservationist, the resultant vacuum of public awareness was filled by the hyperbole of the administration's critics. In private, however, some leading preservationists acknowledged the secretary's contribution to defending the preserve systems. William Voigt of the Council of Conservationists, for example, congratulated him on the Glacier and Everglades decisions and remarked that McKay was "another Secretary of the Interior who has presided over an increase in our . . . National Park System." The secretary's reply to this was almost a plea for understanding from his critics: "I am still not without hope that years from now when we can look back over the period of my stewardship . . . you will agree that I have pursued the course involving the wisest use of our natural resources for the benefit of the greatest number of people."[39]

The reorganization of the Interior Department constituted an important contribution to the improvement of land and resource administration. In brief, Under Secretary Tudor realigned responsibility and command within each bureau and instituted a coordinating agency, the Technical Review Section, to serve all of them. In order to study the problems involved in that task, he personally chose a team of private individuals especially qualified in the subjects handled by each agency. The idea was very close to the suggestion made by Robert Smylie of Idaho during the campaign of 1952; it was also an expression of the widely held Republican philosophy of increasing the influence of businessmen in government. Horace Albright, for example, who was president of the Potash Company of America, acted as one of the advisers on mineral resources policy. After these teams had examined the complex of problems and past programs, they uncovered a mess of antiquated procedures and uncompleted work. Under the new organizational plan, problems affecting more than one bureau were handled in such a way as to prevent duplication or autonomy. It was the most thorough renovation of the department since the early days of the New Deal, but McKay and Tudor would learn to their dismay that it was not a foolproof correction of the ways of bureaucrats.[40]

The most immediate dividend of the reorganization was "Mission 66." When Tudor began his work, Wirth asked him to scrutinize first the National Park Service. In that way, the director was able to present an exhaustive account of the subjective and procedural problems his agency had faced since the war. Among these was the alarmingly wide gap between facilities and users in the units of the park system. Newton Drury's requests for additional appropriations had been spurned by Congress, mainly for partisan reasons. Wirth therefore perceived that he could secure these funds by making Republican legislators and administrators aware of the terrible conditions and then turn the rescue actions to their political credit. Information gathered on concession contracts, entrance fees, roads, and buildings was contrasted with the startling visitor statistics and projections. The total number of Americans visiting units of the system had risen from 25 million to 50 million and was expected to reach 80 million within another decade. De Voto summed up the crisis in an ironically titled article in *Harper's*, "Let's Close the National Parks." The piece brought a flood of letters to the White House, where the president and his aides were already disturbed about the bad publicity the administration had earned in the Dinosaur issue. One of the letters—from John D. Rockefeller, Jr.—referred to the article. Without acknowledging De Voto's polemic, Eisenhower informed McKay that he was receiving letters from people genuinely concerned about the deterioration of the national parks. "I must admit to a very considerable ignorance in the field," he added, "but I am of the opinion that if we are actually neglecting them merely to save a relatively inconsequential amount of money, then we should take a second look." Such a sign of personal interest from the economy-minded chief executive was encouragement indeed.[41]

Armed with Wirth's report, McKay called on the president and received approval of an increase in the total acreage of the park system, including the addition of 271,000 acres of wilderness land in the Everglades. In the spring of 1955, the Park Service's estimates were examined by the Technical Review staff and confirmed by the Bureau of the Budget. A coordinated plan was then drawn up whereby expanded facilities in parks and recreational areas would make it possible for the system to accommodate 80 million visitors by 1966. It would be financed with funds over and above the service's annual budget. When Eisenhower was briefed on this plan, he reportedly said: "What have you been waiting for?" It was something of an echo of his laconic "Let's go" before D-Day. In January 1956 the Park Service and budget bureau made a joint presentation of "Mission 66" to the cabinet in what was later described as a perfect example of the secretariat's "radarscope" in action. Every stage of the plan had been procedurally coordinated so that one bureau would not "pull the rug out" from under another. That kind of conflict had contributed to the recent Dixon-Yates controversy. McKay next asked for a full public presidential endorsement of the plan, but Eisenhower preferred the secretary's suggestion that it be transmitted to Congress. In February the president told the legislators that he was deeply concerned about the "irreplaceable natural treasures" of the park system and asked for a special appropriation of over eight million dollars to launch the plan.[42]

Some development-minded Republicans sniffed suspiciously at "Mission 66." A constituent of Senator Henry Dworshak of Idaho warned him that it would mean expansion of the Park Service's jurisdiction at the expense of the national forests. Moreover, the fact that Democratic Senator Richard Neuberger of Oregon favored it turned it into "something off color." Preservationists were also dubious about the plan. Naturally they welcomed the publicity for the parks. The Sierra Club used the occasion to call for a "Scenic Resources Review." Most of the organizations joined forces at this same time to obtain legislation to establish a system of wilderness preserves. But preservationists wondered if "Mission 66" was a political smoke screen, designed to obscure the other resource decisions made by the Eisenhower administration and thereby save them from assaults during the coming elections of 1956. In view of the plan's preoccupation with more facilities, it might result in a great increase of commercial inroads inside the parks. Because of such doubts, the announcement of the plan did not alter preservationists' prejudice against McKay. They still believed that he regarded the parks as "glorified tourist resorts, playgrounds for the titillation and entertainment of the public: he does not see any deeper ideology." Unfortunately their suspicion eventually touched the person of Wirth himself. There was, a preservationist noted, "growing uneasiness, unrest, and distrust" among preservationists over possible danger to the park principle. The issue of expanding recreational facilities and preserves in the park system may have contributed to his awkward resignation in 1963.[43]

In view of all the rhetoric heard during these years, McKay's department made surprisingly slight progress in fulfilling western demands and expectations. True, it had purged and reorganized the bureaucracy, but it had also withheld support for reduction of federal jurisdiction over use of the public domain. Public realization of the fact that such a policy constituted a defense of conservation was, unfortunately, smothered by the publicity given to the administration's proposals and decisions on water and power development. On those subjects, Douglas McKay and his "dragon slayers" first fell into a pit and then were crushed by the dinosaur that fell on top of them.

Chapter Six

THE
PITFALLS
OF
PARTNERSHIP

The promise to modify twenty years of federal domination of water and power development was one of the most striking issues of the Republican campaign of 1952. The party's candidates had called for a reduction in government spending in all areas, foreign and domestic. At the same time, they had implied that they would dismantle federal bureaucracy and restore reliance upon local and private initiative. Dwight Eisenhower asserted that a power policy based upon "partnership" could fulfill these promises. He and his lieutenants did not conceive of that emphasis as a backward step, however, but as a restoration of balance and, indeed, a continuation of the real tradition of both parties. In his first message to Congress in February 1953, he evoked the memory of Theodore Roosevelt and then observed that a strong program in federal resource development could be timed "to assist in leveling off peaks and valleys in our economic life." Pending projects that have been soundly planned, he assured the nation, should be carried to completion and new ones planned for the future. But the best policy would not result "from exclusive dependence on Federal bureaucracy. It will involve a partnership of the States and local communities, private citizens, and the Federal Government, all working together [in] the development of the great river valleys of our Nation and the power they generate . . . in the expansion . . . of upstream storage." Later he added that the emphasis upon partnership would also make possible the best use of community and individual effort and be the true basis for fiscal soundness. Government's larger role would be to encourage and share responsibility for cooperation in water and power development.[1]

The president based his partnership emphasis upon his deeply held conviction that the government should do only those things which the states and the people could not do for themselves. He did not oppose comprehensive river basin development, therefore, but wanted it accomplished with the cooperation of the states and local interests. Because of the recent growth of the West, however, he sought a reexamination of the federal role in the interest of bringing about a better balanced program. Unfortunately, his administration chose to execute its new emphasis, not by formulating and publicizing a fully planned program, but by an initial phase of routine decisions on pending projects. Because of the decisive influence of the Bureau of the Budget, economy was the yardstick applied to every matter inherited from the Democrats and every proposal for a Republican water and power policy. The Bureau of Reclamation's appropriations, already cut by the Truman administration during the Korean conflict, were not to be enlarged for the forthcoming fiscal year. All new starts on projects were to be eliminated for 1954, and current construction would be slowed or stopped wherever it was not very far advanced. Even the projects of the Corps of Engineers were cut substantially below the 1953 level.[2]

Western Republicans were shocked. Reclamationist Robert Sawyer feared that McKay was in the hands of the party Old Guard, and Congressman Walt Horan wrote "This *isn't* good" at the bottom of a list of water projects that had been cut. In response to early complaints, the Interior officials noted that they were actually sustaining more projects than the Democrats had. More importantly, their plan to reorganize the Bureau of Reclamation would bring in engineering principles and an end to federal dominance over state and local enterprisers. Rather than sabotaging traditional policy, they pointed out that the Democrats' restrictions, such as the 160-acre limit, were discriminatory and futile as a means of breaking up large landholdings. By 1955 the president called attention to the fact that Reclamation's and the Corps's projects had increased from thirty-nine to fifty. The following year he signed a Small Reclamation Projects Act, enabling the federal government to join contracts with states, district associations, and other organizations to assist in project construction.[3]

In the area of electric power production, the Interior Department also announced no new starts for the next year and advised applicants that contracts would be made only where private and local organizations could not or would not handle the need themselves. Specifically, local companies would be encouraged to build mainstream projects wherever they were willing to do so. The federal government would go in only on those complex, regionwide programs such as the development of the Upper Colorado basin. It would also continue to handle nonrevenue producing activities like fish protection and recreation. All profit for construction and transmission, however, would go to private enterprisers. Because of the preceding struggle over CVA and because Douglas McKay was secretary of the Interior, the Eisenhower administration first intended to display its new emphasis in the Pacific Northwest.[4]

Acting to redeem that region from federal domination, the Interior officials assumed they could rely upon the existing interagency compacts and state-private working arrangements in Washington and Oregon. Drawing upon the advice of Governor Langlie, McKay's successor Paul Patterson, and Len Jordan, they indicated that the federal government must develop main stem power plants—that is, the existing units at Bonneville and Grand Coulee, while private enterprise should be allowed to build these units on tributaries such as the Snake River. But it would not be necessary for the government to carry the burden of building transmission lines any longer. If that task were handled by local effort, the region's power needs could be met without draining the federal treasury. McKay promised that his department would assist in restoring the tradition of "greater service to a greater number of people," even at the cost of diminishing its own control over power production.[5]

The Secretary was pleased with the president's "straight forward statement of policy" as the administration began its work. From such honest declarations he said, the public would readily recognize that "we are on the right track." Both men, however, let unguarded remarks distract public attention from their professed purpose. In March 1953 McKay told the Portland Chamber of Commerce: "The thing I want to say to you businessmen and women today is that we are in the saddle at the present moment as an administration representative of business and industry." Some reports of the remark turned it into: "We're here in the saddle as an Administration representing business and industry." Horseman McKay was using a figure of speech that was familiar to him, but his critics seized upon it as a naive admission that the Republicans were errand boys for the vested interests. The Republican National Committee would have to keep correcting the reported statement for years afterward. A few months later, McKay more tactfully cautioned another audience: "This is a businessman's administration, but let me warn you—business is on trial. The people can throw us out again. We must look for only fair profits. We must show statesmanship."[6]

During those same months, statesmanship did not appear to dominate the decisions of the Interior Department. In the absence of an overall program, the procedural actions taken there offered the only evidence of what partnership would actually mean. Unfortunately, the first of these actions burst like a bombshell on the public consciousness. Although officials had no wish to revive the bitterness of the past public versus private power debate, neither were they willing to let it intimidate them. In previous years, they had been opponents of CVA and viewed the proposal for a high multiple-purpose dam at Hells Canyon on the Snake as a potential part of federal regional domination. Moreover, their strict constructionist view of executive authority caused them to decide that the department had improperly opposed the Idaho Power Company's application to build an alternative set of three single purpose dams.[7]

As Tudor saw the situation, it was a matter of which plan was technically feasible and which would do the job with the least cost to government. McKay later claimed that he had an open mind on the question and had been far less hostile to the federal proposal than some of his fellow governors. Remembering the Truman administration's frustrating quest for authorization of CVA, he understandably doubted that Congress would approve the high dam within the foreseeable future. In view of the fact that the legislators were slashing his own department's budget, he now realized that it was not time to defy them "in order to justify cheap power to build up an empire," as Tudor put it. In May, therefore, Interior announced that it was withdrawing Chapman's "untenable" demand that the Federal Power Commission reject the IPC application. Tudor and McKay believed that they were being both realistic and fair. There was no point in playing the role of Don Quixote or courting prolonged adjudication which they could not possibly win. Moreover, Congress would be the ultimate judge of both alternatives to Snake River development.[8]

Idaho Republicans had expected McKay to demonstrate the courage of his convictions, but the withdrawal of department contention in the Hells Canyon case surprised advocates both of public power and of partnership. Few critics accepted Democratic claims that McKay was thereby paying off those who had obtained his appointment as secretary. But many wondered why he had acted so precipitously on such a significant matter and why he was willing to diminish further the leverage of his own department, already battered by budget slashers. Instead of Reclamation building the high dam, moreover, the Corps of Engineers would assist the IPC. Tudor replied that the Northwest could not depend on federal action alone, or it would have an increasing power shortage. The high dam was "over-planned" and "a white elephant"; the three dams would be built at no expense to the taxpayers and did not preclude later federal construction on the river. The policy makers had no answer for the obvious consequence of the withdrawal: the IPC, a monopoly, would thereby inherit development of the middle Snake River. Whatever the "emperor" said about his new clothes, it seemed that there was some difference between "private citizens" or "greater service to a greater number of people" and turning over this valuable public treasure to one company by default.[9]

The men in the Eisenhower administration expected that the decision to withdraw from the Hells Canyon case would be controversial. Adams noted that it was "unfortunate, but inevitable" that the merely procedural detail would be pictured as a symbol of gigantic implications. But he trusted Tudor's knowledge of engineering and McKay's representation of local preference. Asked for an opinion by the press corps, the president agreed that "the weight of the evidence presented is on the side of letting this thing be decided locally" and that mayors and "people like that" had told him they did not believe in the high dam. McKay took much criticism from "New Deal columnists," as he described his critics, but was sure that his position was right, that it was the middle-of-the-road course, and that it would be supported by the overwhelming majority of people once they had all the facts. One well-wisher referred to the announcement as "a much needed bench mark in getting the relations of the federal government with its citizens back into line with the original intent of Congress."[10] The secretary's confidence was also bolstered by Tudor's assurance that the power issue was not politically destructive in the Northwestern states.

The question growing in the public mind concerning the intention of the Eisenhower administration was further inflated by the president himself a few weeks after the Hells Canyon announcement. His advisers, perhaps recalling a term used by former President Hoover, had used the phrase "creeping socialism" in notes Eisenhower read from while speaking in the West in June. In the context of congressional cuts and department decisions, Democrats charged that the words revealed the true sentiment of the Republican policy makers. When he was asked by the press to give a concrete example of "creeping socialism," an old party bugaboo came to his mind: TVA. In private he was even more hostile. "By God, if ever we could do it, before we leave here, I'd like to see us *sell* the whole thing, but I suppose we can't go that far." Publicly Eisenhower tried again and again to clarify his opinion, but only got himself in deeper. The current demand for facilities expansion at TVA was typical, he said: "since the Federal Government had seized and was practicing a monopoly in power down there, it was impossible for that locality now to expand unless the Federal Government spends more money down there. . . . So we get this curious thing in socialistic theory: that we, all of us, provide cheap power for one region—apparently it is subsidized by taxes from all of us over the country. . . . Now, please understand me, I have stated a thousand times, I am not out to destroy TVA."[11]

Eisenhower's budget bureau had in fact advised him of its strong opposition to new generator plants at TVA. Tangled syntax aside, he was trying to say what that agency's memorandum had said: the federal government should not provide tax-free power for industry in competition with utilities there or in other areas of the country. The presidential assistants were clearly embarrassed by the gaff, though they could not of course criticize their chief. Instead, Gabriel Hauge suggested that the phrase was "unfortunate" because it echoed Old Guard Republican rhetoric. Eisenhower's "new look" warranted a new terminology such as "creeping centralism or creeping Big Government." Another aide issued a statement declaring that the president was not against TVA, but for "its ever increasing expansion." A month later, Eisenhower said that he opposed the expansion of TVA because he did not want it dependent upon "vagaries of the Federal Government." Many months later he reminded press correspondents: "Now, I never said that all of the TVA was—I said there were certain features of that development that were alarming from the viewpoint of my political philosophy but I never said that the whole thing was such a terrible example of socialism."[12]

Democrats were appalled by the incident. "Hello there, David,"

Harry Truman bantered with Lilienthal, "and how does it feel to be a creeping socialist? . . . Wasn't that the most nonsense you ever heard? It is like so many other things: Ike just doesn't know what he is talking about." David Lilienthal replied that it was certainly not in keeping with Eisenhower's "habitual moderation and open mindedness." His successor as director of TVA, Gordon Clapp, considered the statement "a shocking smear on one of the greatest American achievements of this century." Both men asked publisher Palmer Hoyt of the *Denver Post* to urge the president to visit the area of TVA himself. Governor Frank Clement of Tennessee feared that the remark was the opening gun of a plan to dismantle the federal program. His suggestion for the formation of a fact-finding committee was accepted by the White House, but its report was prejudged by the budget bureau as "very biased."[13]

The hue and cry over the danger to TVA did not fluster the director, Joseph Dodge, in the least. The critics raised "imaginary threats," he advised the president; there was no need for an official apology or backtracking on the "creeping socialism" statement. Moreover, it would be impolitic for any Republicans even to deny that the administration intended to sell TVA to private industry. As in the case of Tudor's reasoning about criticism of the Hells Canyon decision, Dodge felt that the Democrats would make the most of any statement. The Interior Department's stand, that "responsibility for supplying electric energy is primarily a local one," should be sustained. If it was, then "everything that has been lost politically as a result of an improper emphasis can be regained." The problem could be handled by an approach "that avoids hitting . . . frontally, turning [policy decisions] into great fields of controversy. . . . We won't solve this one by getting mad at anyone." Rather than making reference to the ideological contention of public versus private power, argument should always be made on the basis of the technical-cost point of view.[14]

The Eisenhower men also meant to bring their new emphasis to bear by personnel changes which would prepare the ground for a full program in the near future. They did not intend to rearrange the interstate, interagency status quo in the Columbia basin states. When Walt Horan again asked consideration of his Columbia Interstate Commission proposal, Tudor drafted a letter for McKay which put the congressman off. Like Hells Canyon, the Bonneville Power Administration (BPA) had been a potential unit in the Democrats' regional authority concept; it could just as readily be made to serve the partnership projects. Primary to that redirection was the removal of BPA's "bumptious" director, Paul Raver, and his "swollen bureaucracy." Chameleon-like, Raver seemed to assume the coloration of the new administration after the election of 1952. Because he agreed with Horan that local distributor utilities should be given "as free a hand as possible" in the development of transmission facilities, the congressman urged state Republicans to treat him respectfully. Idahoans, alarmed at these signs that the "Public Power Ox" was still alive and well, had to be assured by Senator Henry Dworshak that Raver was "scheduled for dismissal." But Tudor's well-used broom encountered an embarrassing obstacle: Secretary McKay himself. Aware that his chief thought highly of Raver, indeed thought that the incumbent could successfully bring a "fresh outlook" into his organization, Tudor had to bide his time for many months. In the meantime, he personally rejected the director's recommendation for a regional engineer advisory board and made private arrangements for transferring some of BPA's transmission lines to local operation. Convinced that Raver had gotten "too far out of line," he ordered the power administration to limit its sales of electricity. Interior was not trying to "emasculate" BPA, he assured a worried Oregonian, but merely promoting local utilities of any type.[15]

Early in 1954, the under secretary thought he found the man the administration needed: William Pearl, dean of engineering and acting president of Washington State College. Known locally as an adamant conservative, Pearl impressed Tudor as a "solid citizen" who would avoid controversy and make an excellent appearance. The appointment, he decided, would also put an end to the "radical propaganda going on." After a year in office, however, it was rumored that McKay was not pleased with Pearl and never had been, a report which led public power advocates to assume that Tudor had forced the selection. Ironically, although Democrats predicted that the new director would act as BPA's "executioner," by 1956 some Oregon Republicans were complaining that he had "naively strung along" with the enemy by appointing "ADA-Neuberger type Democrats" to key positions. Because those staff members resisted plans for "better management of projects," these Republicans demanded that Pearl be ousted.[16]

The replacement of Clapp as head of TVA was part of the same determination to apply the new emphasis in power policy through administrative procedure rather than a legislative program. The incumbent would not resign. Democrats and public power advocates praised him for "holding the fort" against Republican "wreckers and thieves." Clapp continued to argue for expansion of the TVA, and the White House men continued to ignore the request while they searched for his replacement. As the months passed, they were desperate enough to consider a multimillionaire butter and egg man, a heavy contributor to the party coffers who was undoubtedly free of "New Deal tendencies." If such an inexperienced man was chosen, Dodge urged, then he should be given a highly qualified technical assistant "to protect him against the overwhelming pressures of the old-line technical organizations with a completely different philosophy and objective." Republican Senator John Sherman Cooper of Kentucky warned that the appointment of this man would be a grievous mistake because it would provide Democrats with a fine opportunity to dramatize the old public power issue. Moreover, Senators Albert Gore of Tennessee and Wayne Morse of Oregon would try to block confirmation and would claim in the debate that the administration was surrendering to special interests. Cooper also admitted that he was concerned that these controversies would affect his campaign for reelection in 1954.[17]

Finally, in August 1954, the president announced the appointment of General H. D. Vogel as head of the TVA. A former Corps of Engineers officer, he had recently been chairman of an interagency commission for the Arkansas and Red River valleys. Eisenhower assured the press that no special interests had sponsored the nominee and that, as a competent engineer, Vogel would be the best judge of the question of TVA expansion. Lilienthal was not pleased with the idea of a Corps officer in the vital post, but hoped that Vogel would "succumb to the allure" of the valley administration. The latter humorously informed Lilienthal that "you people are considered a bunch of socialists down there," but seriously admitted that he would be going to Tennessee to "clean house." Vogel dependably favored the rhetoric of TVA's critics, but Sherman Adams kept him from direct association with any utility industries. In line with Dodge's advice, Vogel refused to ask for expansion of facilities until Congress appropriated the money for them. Realizing that the Democrats did not have enough support to obtain the funds, public power men decided they would have to compromise in some way with the Eisenhower administration.[18]

The administration had been in office almost a year before it began to shape a general policy for water and power development. The power policy makers had resented the outcry over Hells Canyon, but they were not shaken by it. Tudor noted that 78 percent of the nation's newspapers supported the partnership emphasis. Assistant Secretary Aandahl claimed that all sections of the country but one were in favor of the new direction; only a handful of Democrats from the Pacific Northwest seemed to continue their selfish opposition, he thought. Evidently he was referring to a joint letter sent by Morse, Murray, Mansfield, and other senators from the region to the president calling for a suspension of further administrative decisions until the Congress could properly express its own attitude on the subject.[19]

The publicity given to McKay's and Eisenhower's tactless figures of speech prompted the men in the White House to check all public statements in advance of delivery. They also redefined the "no new starts" position to exclude projects vital to national security. Although influential Republicans like Arthur Langlie and Paul Patterson privately worried about the "political dynamite" of water and power appropriation cuts, they were constrained to say so publicly. Many observers still admired the political philosophy behind partnership, and their letters of praise confirmed the determination of the policy makers. "We are all proud of what you are doing," a professor of forestry told McKay at the height of the protests from Pacific Northwest Democrats, "and you musn't get discouraged. For 20 years these spenders and pinks have been in office—they are going to fight like hell before they quit."[20]

At the end of 1953 the Bureau of the Budget sent an "administratively confidential" memorandum to the president, suggesting a line of argument which the administration should thereafter use to take the offensive against its critics. The mistakes of the past should be portrayed in the cold, clear light of their consequences. The big dam policy had been "spectacular but exceedingly costly," the projects weighed down by "marginal frills and uneconomic appendages which served to extend and perpetuate Federal activity." There could have been more emphasis on "upstream watershed development and less on mainstream storage"—a reference to the Upper Colorado basin proposal. Similarly, "bigger and better" reclamation projects had been authorized merely to meet "political demands." In place of such "opportunism," the partnership emphasis could be defended as a long-term plan, adequate enough to meet all the water and power needs of the nation, but fiscally sound and equitable in its arrangements.

The participation of private and local organizations was "not incon-sistent with furthering the interests of all the people."[21]

These were the arguments carried by spokesmen for the Interior Department, the White House, and the Republican party in statements and speeches before congressional committees, engineering and power organizations, and constituents. They seemed to promise the restora-tion of high principles and modern technical means to federal power policy and the replacement of the centralism of the preceding decades. As the Intergovernmental Relations subcommittee on national water policy put it, only by leaving power supply to local enterprise could the nation avoid transformation into "the complete welfare state." For a year and a half, these assurances continued until even Republi-cans like Horan realized that they were only assurances. Instead of McKay's "some new starts" promise, he learned that Tudor had blocked construction of new dams. Others called for congressional investigation of the department's behavior. No one wanted to return to "Trumanism," but the new direction was eroding the revulsion directed against that centralism in previous years. Even the National Reclamation Association split into factions over the subject of partner-ship's consequences.[22]

The Eisenhower men's emphasis upon procedural details was no match for the tactics of the administration's critics. Skillfully weaving together the facts about appropriation cuts, the Hells Canyon decision, the references to "creeping socialism" and business "in the saddle," they were able to fashion a whole cloth of doubt in the public mind. Beginning with the first actions taken by McKay's department, an increasing number of organizations and prominent people expressed their dismay and suspicion. Labor leaders in the Pacific Northwest warned that the secretary's attitude toward federal construction would be "a severe blow" to the industrial development of their region. Partnership was impractical, arbitrary, and resulted in less spending at a time when more was needed. Instead of additional facilities at TVA, Governor Clement complained to Senator Dworshak, there was to be "slow strangulation" of the program. Jolted by the decision to withdraw opposition to the Idaho Power Company's application for Hells Canyon, public power spokesmen denounced it as "the first step in the boldest giveaway program of all time." In a few short months, Senator Murray wrote, the new administration had eliminated or jeopardized many of the greatest gains in the field made during the past twenty years. Raising the specter of the 1930s, he charged that

private monopolies were out to decimate the federal river basin programs. Former reclamation commissioner Michael Straus described
the Democrats' years of constructive work as being "McKayed,
Barrettized . . . scuttled and sabotaged."[23]

While no immediate defense of partnership was issued from the
White House, Democratic cartoonists such as Herblock portrayed the
president as a grinning boob, mindlessly acquiescing in the dismantling
of federal dams by private utilities. When Eisenhower appointed
Jerome Kuykendall to be chairman of the Federal Power Commission,
some Democrats thought they spied evidence of a conspiracy. As a
member of the Washington State Public Service Commission, the man
had been the mainstay of Langlie's state-private power program. His
selection was considered "a severe blow" by public power advocates
in the Pacific Northwest. Undoubtedly selected on the governor's
recommendation, Kuykendall's agency rather than McKay's department, they feared, would determine the direction of the administration's power policy.[24]

The sequence of Republican actions and Democratic interpretations
in 1954 was even more convincing. Kuykendall's commission awarded
the Hells Canyon development contract to the Idaho Power Company
just as the critics had predicted. The administration's determination
to avoid a frontal approach to such problems as modifying TVA
contributed to the manner in which a transmission arrangement was
negotiated with Dixon-Yates. Like Hells Canyon, this attempt to
find an alternative to federal control seemed to guarantee private
monopoly of public resources. Moreover, the "influence peddling"
circumstances of the arrangement belied the Republican protestations
of cleaning up the Democratic "mess" in Washington. The Dixon-Yates
"deal" was exposed to the already suspicious public view in late
summer 1954 and stayed in the news for over a year. During that
time, the Democrats successfully exploited all these cases of "giveaway" in their campaign to regain control of Congress. Thereafter,
they called for investigations of monopoly in the power industry and
the Interior Department's action in the Hells Canyon case. They tried
again to obtain congressional authorization of the high federal dam
on the Snake. On the advice of Langlie, Patterson, and Smylie,
Interior countered these efforts with Reclamation-Army Engineer
publicity concerning the superior technical advantages of the IPC
project. It was in fact a significant inconsistency on McKay's part; he
had earlier asserted that engineering considerations should not be

paramount in the CVA issue. When the Democrats' proposal failed in August 1955, their captain, Senator Lyndon Johnson of Texas, promised to "take another healthy swing at it" the following year.[25]

The Eisenhower men's response to these events was amazingly myopic. It was as if they believed their own public relations press releases and the laudatory coverage by business and partisan periodicals. There were warnings enough from those who shared their partnership emphasis. One Oregon Republican official begged Adams to see to it that further policy decisions were made more palatable to the people of the region. A Salem friend of McKay suggested that the administration announce support of pending proposals if they could make no new starts. Langlie urged Adams to play down the private enterprise role and emphasize the engineering feasibility of approved projects. The governor's own promising beginnings in state-private power programs had bogged down by then—because of bad advice from his lieutenants, Horan claimed—and the Eisenhower administration thereby lost one of the few examples of local alternative to federal river valley development. Single purpose dams such as those at Hells Canyon were far more difficult to defend publicly, Pacific Northwest Republicans argued, than multi-purpose units. If the present and future power needs of the region could not be met through partnership as practiced thus far, then a resultant power shortage would have both economic and political consequences. Even Adams admitted that the new emphasis had not been effectively sold to the public because of poor coordination between federal and local participants. Tudor had a "terrifically difficult time" getting Interior's staff members to carry out their part of the procedure. Yet he continued to defend the diminution of the federal role in power development before and after he resigned late in 1954 to return to bridge building.[26]

The men at the White House were convinced that they read the signs of public opinion correctly. Early in 1954 Tudor showed his chief an opinion survey which concluded that power had improperly been made a political issue. In fact, it could not be counted on to deliver votes because the public was not sufficiently interested in it. Howard Pyle was told that the distortions by the Democrats were especially resented in Idaho and that the announcement of the Hells Canyon contract and the commencement of work there would bolster the Republican cause in forthcoming elections. In order to establish closer contact between policy makers and local views, McKay asked Idaho's Governor Len Jordan to take Orme Lewis's place as assistant secretary. That official declined, saying he could work better to build a sound water resources policy where he was. In other correspondence, however, McKay claimed that it was none of his business as to how the people of a state wished to distribute their power. This was the viewpoint expressed by the president who, characteristically, refused to comment on the "giveaway" charges. Other administration spokesmen merely upbraided their critics for creating confusion in the public mind. Instead of counterattacking, they announced that they would ask for 240 million dollars for six Bureau of Reclamation projects and 750 million for thirty Corps of Engineers projects for 1957. The partnership approach, President Eisenhower informed Congress early in 1956, "is producing encouraging results."[27]

Ever since the defeat of Truman's regional river valley authorities, the Republican opposition had prepared to establish a federal water and power program based on what they believed was public distrust of centralism and faith in private enterprise. The gradualist, procedural approach to initiating the new emphasis of partnership may have reflected the Eisenhower administration's overestimation of the strength of that public attitude and the duration it would last. The confidence and determination engendered by the "mandate for change" similarly caused the policy makers to underestimate the effectiveness of their critics' tactics of linking circumstantial evidence—the sequence of "giveaways." McKay and Tudor allowed their zeal for restoring a middle-of-the-road policy to obscure their recognition of how their decisions appeared to the public. Fiscal soundness and engineering feasibility were desirable, it appeared to many, but not if they resulted in fewer appropriations for water and power development and smaller units constructed. Partnership was the proper emphasis, but the most obvious examples of it in action were the Idaho Power Company's authorization to control the middle Snake and the near-miss confirmation of Dixon-Yates. Apart from these dubious attempts, it seemed that the administration had not proved the workability of its policy, no matter how desirable it was. Having convinced many citizens that partnership would not mean an abandonment of federal construction, the Eisenhower men had little more to point to after three years than the completion of projects begun by the Democrats. Naturally, they declined to notice the failure of their trust in local cooperation in the Pacific Northwest. The only program they could consider to be their own accomplishment was the Upper Colorado River storage plan, authorized by the Democratic Congress in April 1956. "This is what I like," the president said as he signed the bill. What he did not say then or later was that his policy makers had almost failed to get action on UCB because they had again overestimated the public's grasp of practical necessity and underestimated the publicity skills of those they dismissed as a handful of partisan fanatics.

Chapter Seven

JUST
A TINY
DINOSAUR

The controversy over storage reservoirs in Dinosaur National Monument drew more public attention to the resource policies of the Eisenhower administration than partnership or Hells Canyon. The latter issues were regional and technically complex. By contrast, the apparent threat to the national park system seemed a clear struggle between the forces of Light and Darkness, a simple choice on a subject that Americans everywhere could understand. The subject had grown heated during the Truman years; now it exploded into a blaze that singed an otherwise popular administration, undermined public trust in its resource policies, and contributed substantially to its first political setbacks.

When the Republicans took over in January 1953, they readily adopted the cause of the Upper Colorado River basin project recommended by the Democrats before them. The tone and intention of the "mandate for change," the determination to uphold local interests, remove bureaucratic delays, and encourage private enterprise—all the substance of the platform of 1952 appeared to be subsumed in the proposal. All, that is, except the call for economy in government spending. The possibility that UCB would ultimately cost more than a billion dollars was deemphasized, however, as the officials of Utah, Colorado, and the other basin states pressed the new administration for action. Their happy anticipation was increased by the presence of Ezra Benson of Utah, the secretary of agriculture, Dan Thorton of Colorado, a personal friend of the president, and Arthur Watkins, one of the administration's advisers on water and power problems. The Utah senator had talked with Eisenhower during the campaign, undoubtedly describing the project to him at that time. He probably pointed out that it would be neither a gift from the government nor the TVA variety of federal authority. If it was somewhat costly, the expenditure would directly benefit local business and agriculture. Moreover, it would go far in discrediting the Democrats' allegation that the Republican party was not the friend of the West as far as water and power development was concerned.[1]

The new secretary of the Interior was in a far more difficult position than his predecessor on the subject of UCB. McKay had neither Oscar Chapman's procedural experience nor his personal knowledge of the area affected by the proposal. He was more dependent upon the directives of the president's staff and the arguments presented to him by his subordinates in the department. Generally he liked a program that would bring prosperity to a commercially stagnant area. But he also learned two things about the problem. First, Republicans in Congress and the White House meant to obtain authorization of UCB, including the sites at Dinosaur. Second, the department had initially endorsed the entire plan and modified the endorsement only after preservationists raised a storm of publicity. Because of the suspicious timing of that turnabout, McKay assumed that it was no more serious than a tactic to embarrass the incoming Republican administration. Like many others, he was willing to use approval of UCB to transfer western gratitude to his party. Taken together, all these considerations enabled Interior's policy makers to rationalize their stand on the issue.

During the first months of McKay's tenure, senators, representatives, governors, and state engineers talked with him and with Reclamation Commissioner Wilbur Dexheimer. They asked no more than that these officials allow forces already at work in Congress to fulfill the administration's support for the UCB project. "Our concern at the moment," wrote J. Bracken Lee of Utah, "is simply to have the project authorized . . . I am not asking for appropriations in view of the present budget situation." Like the decision to keep hands off in the Hells Canyon case, such a neutral role coincided with the secretary's view of the department's proper behavior. Park Service Director Conrad Wirth issued an argument against the inclusion of Dinosaur, but he had to present that indirectly through the new chain of command. During the first two months, he sent to his immediate superiors, Orme Lewis and Fred Aandahl, photographs of the area, preservationists' statistics, and a letter from onetime Republican presidential candidate Alfred Landon of Kansas who had taken the raft trip through the canyons. McKay declined to respond until he had completed a new study of the UCB proposal. In the order of things at Interior, that meant that Under Secretary Tudor would handle the question of Dinosaur.[2]

Before becoming a bureaucrat himself, Tudor had not liked the UCB proposal; as a principal policy maker, however, he saw the larger purposes of the administration and decided that it would be an excellent chance to demonstrate the new emphasis upon practicality. Naturally he respected the surveys and conclusions of the engineers in the Bureau of Reclamation. As for the dire predictions of the "do-gooders," he had already made up his mind about them. Only twenty-five persons saw the inside of the preserve that year. Tudor's opinion was similar to the view expressed by one of his engineer friends from Oakland: "these professors who are nurtured with taxpayers' money lose sight of the fact that . . . when the resources of the Country are handicapped by a lot of theorists, the whole future of the Country is handicapped." Still busy with reorganizing the department, Tudor first spoke with his technical review chief, John Marr, and with fellow Californian Bestor Robinson of the National Parks Advisory Board. Although both men were in correspondence with the Sierra Club, neither had adopted its arguments. Marr was concerned mainly with the problem of resolving jurisdictional differences between Reclamation and the Park Service—the clash inherited from the Democratic regime; Bestor Robinson was convinced that public opinion supported the inclusion of the sites in Dinosaur. While rumors flew that the department was about to omit the dams in the preserve, Tudor was actually formulating a corollary of Chapman's final position. In July he told members of the Upper Colorado Development Commission that he would approve the project as proposed unless alternative sites to those in Dinosaur could be found elsewhere.[3]

Before the Sierra Club heard that announcement, they had considered Tudor to be "an exceptionally competent engineer" who had sensibly described the UCB project as "the damndest boondoggle I have ever seen." Afterwards, they grumbled that Washington gossip must be true: "Tudor makes the decisions while McKay is making speeches." Now they joined other preservation organizations sending protests to the department and the White House just as they had done when Chapman made his first stand. This time, however, they had far fewer personal contacts in the administration. Their letters were consequently channeled to subordinates and answered with form replies.

Disgruntled with the way the subject was again becoming controversial, Tudor took his aides' advice and decided to visit Dinosaur to give substance to his decision. Along with Wirth and Dexheimer, he flew to Colorado that fall and spent three days and two nights in the area. He saw Split Mountain and some of the interior of the preserve, but did not get into Echo Park. He also went a way along the Upper Colorado River by boat, but not as far as the possible alternative site at Glen Canyon, Arizona. The rocks there, he was sure, were "the same." The engineering advantages at Dinosaur were most impressive to him, of course. Wirth nevertheless felt that talks with Tudor during the trip were encouraging and therefore assumed that no early action would be taken. But the under secretary prepared a full recommendation for McKay upon his return. As remarks in his diary reveal, this man who disdained the political considerations used by Democrats did not hesitate to use them to bolster the Republican cause: "Politically . . . [the project] is extremely sound because we do want to back up the many statements that we have made that we are not closing out the Federal Government in those developments and this is certainly one that only the Federal Government can do."[4]

In May, McKay told the Advisory Board that he believed the statutory basis for the use of Dinosaur was clear in the proclamation of 1938. In December, after receiving Tudor's recommendation, he gave them the impression that he was reviewing his earlier opinion more objectively. Because he was still deliberating, he said that he had not yet prepared a department decision one way or the other. He was similarly noncommittal in public statements except to announce that no further arguments were being submitted to him. A few days later, without informing the board, he sent in Tudor's recommendation to the president, saying that the Interior Department endorsed the UCB project in its entirety. Referring to the controverted site at Echo Park, he employed his lieutenant's words to convey a tone of regret necessarily overcome by practicality: "It is a matter of personal opinion as to the extent of harm that may be created by this reservoir. My own feeling is that the alteration will be substantial and if conflicting interests did not exist, I would prefer to see the Monument remain in its natural state. However, I do feel that if the dam is built, the beauty of the park will be by no means destroyed and it will remain an area of great attraction to many people." The department had examined alternative sites, and the argument for raising the height of Glen Canyon dam had been rejected as too costly and impractical. No other site had the advantage of the deep, narrow canyons at Dinosaur, none could provide such a low evaporation rate, and none had such capacity to bolster generating units.[5]

Governor Ed Mecham of New Mexico pronounced the recommendation to be a courageous one "showing foresight based upon a complete understanding of the problems involved." The *New York Times* (forgetting Hetch Hetchy) thought it heard Theodore Roosevelt and Gifford Pinchot turning in their graves. Preservationists were stunned. Arthur Carhart of Denver was especially incensed over the way the secretary had ignored the Advisory Board. The recommendation, he protested in public and private letters, had obtusely dismissed the principle of park inviolability as "a matter of opinion." It failed to recognize the likelihood that this invasion would be used as a precedent by others, and it measured the value of the monument's beauty by the absence of commercialized attractions for tourists. He did not know who was behind this attempt to "jam the deal through" but he perceived that McKay's action had "precipitated the controversy that has been latent for some time. . . . Unquestionably this is the show-down."[6]

Shocked and angered, preservationist leaders first tried to work through their few Republican adherents who were close to the administration. Horace Albright was urged to use his access to the president who was then preparing his state of the union message. The former Park Service director did so and also called on McKay about the Echo Park issue. Engineer Ulysses Grant wrote to the White House to deny the technical feasibility claimed by the department's recommendation. Charles Sauers, former member of the Advisory Board, told Eisenhower that McKay's approval had been obtained by "a vociferous and tenacious but small group" in the basin states whose needs could in fact be met without using Dinosaur. Just as he had once warned Chapman, he again envisioned "hundreds of thousands" of conservation-minded citizens, "fanatic in their beliefs," who would vote their convictions. All these letters implied that the president must not permit his administration to be branded as anti-conservation. Eisenhower made no personal replies to them, and he made no reference to the subject in his message to

Congress in January 1954. When Alfred Knopf, a Republican and a member of the Advisory Board, wrote to ask for a restudy of the Dinosaur decision, however, the Bureau of the Budget drafted a letter to be sent out over the president's signature. Employing Tudor's language, it stated that the administration was still not convinced that the whole project was economically justified in view of its determination to cut spending. The effort to get at all the facts would continue, and preservationist views would be given full consideration. The official assurance was misleading. No members of the cabinet questioned economic justification or feasibility. Some monument defenders who were also Republican nevertheless concluded that the president had "but passing interest in conservation policy." His acceptance of the McKay-Tudor decision constituted "a picture of complete political ineptitude."[7]

Remembering the lessons learned during the Chapman years, and doubtlessly encouraged by the current wave of criticism directed against the Interior Department's power policy, the preservationists once again took up their most effective weapon—publicity. The 1950 network of preservation organization leaders was revived as the Council of Conservationists. Its public relations staff set out to reach even more widely and deeply into the public consciousness. They issued a "Dinosaur Journal," pamphlets, articles, books, and films and distributed them to civic and service clubs, to schools, and to citizens both prominent and obscure. Those newspapers that proudly bore the mantle of enlightened, independent journalism ran series of special features and editorials on the crusade to save Dinosaur. The drawings of Herblock were especially favored, but one by Carl Somdal was also widely reprinted. In it, an innocently smiling McKay pointed down to the small head of a dinosaur munching on trees in "Our National Park System" and assured a stunned Uncle Sam that "He's only tiny." Uncle Sam's eyes are raised, however, to the looming bulk of the beast, labeled "Future Demands," towering over the department's proposed dam in the monument.[8]

The preservationists' general purpose, of course, was to raise a "hullabaloo" with this publicity. Aware of the practical-mindedness of Americans, they tried—in Carhart's western lingo—to "really knock the props out from under the dammers by nullifying their 'economic necessity' palaver." Like politicians, they well understood how the cry of scandal would cast a long shadow over candidates in the approaching elections. If they could obtain some measure of attention, they calculated, Republicans might induce the administration to change its decision before November 1954. As Knopf said in his plea to the president: "I am concerned that if Interior continues on its present course, we Republicans will lose thousands of independent voters in a year when this might well result in control of both branches of the Congress going to the Democrats."[9]

The publicity campaign raised a veritable flood of protest letters addressed to Eisenhower, McKay, and members of Congress. About ten thousand of these arrived at the rate of hundreds a week for more than a year. The messages of most, of course, were read by no one but filing clerks. "Mechanized civilization," a constituent told Idaho Senator Henry Dworshak, "is creating its own downfall by taking away our last primeval wilderness. Vote down the dams." The letters sent to the Interior Department were duly filed at the Bureau of Reclamation where attention was instead focused on the president's official approval of the UCB recommendation. His March statement referred to the proposed reservoirs at Echo Park and Glen Canyon as "key units strategically located to provide the necessary storage of water and to make the plan work at its maximum efficiency." Eisenhower told the White House press corps that the project particularly appealed to him because it "seemed to be a completely integrated plan." Prompt congressional consideration was therefore fully warranted. None of the reporters present at that or any other presidential press conference asked about the publicity opposing the use of the monument sites, and Eisenhower volunteered no reference to the protests. In view of his strict rule concerning which questions he would answer, and his dislike of publicized contention, it is probable that his aides discouraged any reporter from asking about the subject of Dinosaur. Special Assistant Sherman Adams assured inquirers privately that the president was "thoroughly conversant" with the controversial aspects of the UCB project. But this statement was made only because Interior felt one was needed, and even then the White House assistants were determined to keep it "just as general as possible."[10]

Eisenhower's puzzling silence on this occasion lent credence to the allegation that was subsequently spread by preservationists and Democrats: the UCB approval was the president's payoff to Senator Arthur Watkins (perhaps it was an echo of Truman's intervention on behalf of Senator Elbert Thomas). The Utah senator's subcommittee began gathering evidence a few months after the UCB announcement concerning the questionable behavior of Senator Joseph McCarthy. That evidence would provide the Senate with grounds for bringing a motion of censure against him by the end of 1954. Eisenhower later praised Watkins's integrity and sense of justice in that episode. Years afterward, Watkins labeled the allegation of a deal as "outrageous." As he remembered the matter, he talked to the presidential nominee about the basin project during the campaign of 1952, but Eisenhower did not thereafter mention his personal view on it until after the censure was passed. Then he called Watkins to congratulate him and "coincidentally" agreed to put a request for UCB legislation into his state of the union message for January 1955. Those who ignored this chronology were prone to believe the accusation, but the record shows that the administration had approved the project and sought legislation for it almost a year before the McCarthy censure.[11]

Eisenhower doubtlessly agreed with McKay that the protests over Dinosaur, like the protests over partnership, were the effusions of the same "political extremists" who had attacked Republicans during the debate about CVA and Hells Canyon. The Interior secretary was nevertheless obliged to answer some of the letters pouring into his office. Selecting those from a few important people—Republicans, technical experts, professors, and spokesmen for organizations—he drew up a form which merely restated the department's recommendation. The basin would still be "rich in scenery" without Dinosaur, and the retention of Wirth as director of the Park Service was cited as proof that the department was committed to the principles of the national parks. If the whole project was "necessary," as the McKay letter claimed, some recipients must have wondered why Congress did not authorize it with alacrity. The Interior committees of both houses were besieged with protests, however, prolonging their deliberations toward election time. Out of the Ickesian past rose the figure of former Wyoming governor Leslie Miller, who called UCB "unfeasible and uneconomic." Senator Frank Barrett of Wyoming was encouraged, however, when budget director Joseph Dodge pronounced it "quite worth while." The solon decided that the Echo Park issue had to be met head on because without the dam there, "the whole thing won't be worth a thin dime."[12]

Tudor weathered the bombardment of protests in excellent spirits. "We are damned if we do and damned if we don't," he joked in his private correspondence. Even the Sierra Club had found out that the

local people "did not want to be saved, they wanted to be dammed."
He must have been amused by a note from Congressman William
Dawson of Utah which said: "I understand the Sahara Club took
the dude trip at low water and didn't get all the way through." In
serious replies, Tudor assured friends that the department's recommendation was "devoid of passion or politics." He and McKay were
"as opposed as anyone" to the general philosophy of building reservoirs in national parks but the solution had to be "for a specific
matter and not a general philosophy." No blanket guarantee would be
issued, however. He thought that the arguments of preservationist
William Voigt had considerable merit, but he decided that nothing
less than a complete denial of these areas to reclamation and other
purposes would satisfy the protesters. "There may be exceptions,
each one of which should be considered on its merits," he added.
Rather than future generations being affected, "we are the generation" rightfully concerned with the decision. The immediate water
and power needs of the region could not be ignored "in favor of a
principle of no alteration of park or monument boundaries."[13]

The development-minded residents of the Upper Colorado basin
set up machinery for a counterpublicity campaign, but their literature
was far less widely distributed than that of the preservationists. The
interstate commission sent out formal arguments, while a "Grass
Roots, Inc." office issued the "Colorado River News" and distributed
a film called "Birth of a Basin." These communications expressed
the traditional belief in use of resources as the basis for material
prosperity. American respect for the new technology of the postwar
period made the words "necessary" and "efficient" incontrovertible
keystones to the department's decision. The preservationist argument
alleging an erroneous evaporation rate estimate at Echo Park was
"not important." What was important, the *Denver Post* pointed out,
was that there was a crisis in the "conservation of the Colorado River
water." Any challenge to the feasibility of the Dinosaur sites would
reflect on the feasibility of the whole project. The publicity campaign
against them would consequently be "disastrous to the economic
welfare and growth of the Rocky Mountain west."[14]

Many westerners displayed a superficial grasp of the preservationists'
concern. Wesley D'Ewart of Montana, for example, decided that the
critics were the same people who had assaulted his grazing bills the
year before. Other developers assumed that their opponents were
trying to protect the dinosaur fossils in the monument. They repeatedly

promised that these relics would not be touched. Less than a tenth of the preserve would be inundated, they argued, and instead of the the inaccessible wilderness that few ever visited, the waters would provide recreation for thousands. Their inability to see more than that was best expressed by an Oregonian who carried out his own publicity campaign by sending out copies of a letter that chanted: "Hot rocks, billions and billions of tons of hot rocks, hot sage brush land, hot deserts, hot cliffs, miles and miles of them in every western state—every color of the rainbow. Why would a group of nature fanatics object to building dams to form cool, placid lakes among some of the hot rocks and making cool, green fields out of hot, semi-arid wasteland?" Why, asked others, deprive thousands of citizens of a chance for material betterment for the sake of saving "a bunch of bones"? As the Oregon man implied, sensible people knew that scenery was forested lakes and mountains, not "hot rocks."[15]

Many people were confused by the terms bantered back and forth in the controversy. Was Echo Park a national park? Was Dinosaur a national park? (Tudor called it Dinosaur Park in his diary.) Did the monument's name mean that fossils were its only attraction? Some dam proponents assumed that the preservationists were really trying to protect wildlife in the monument. Indeed, when President Eisenhower finally made public reference to the controversy two years later, he explained innocently that the Dinosaur site "was originally controversial because of the belief on the part of some conservationists we would destroy wildlife in one section of the area." Perhaps these people were thinking about the fossils that were in fact in one section of the preserve. (Truman had them in mind when he explained his opinion to Irving Brant in 1951.) It is impossible to tell, of course, whether these superficialities represented ignorance or strategy.[16]

The developers frequently expressed one firm conviction, however. They were certain that the "fanatics" were few in number, wealthy, idle residents of the East and of California. They were a mixture of easterners and midwesterners who opposed spending for reclamation because it would lessen their long hold over the West's economy. Above all, the controversy was a subterfuge used by Californians who did not want to share the water of the Colorado River. This California "conspiracy" was confirmed by the prominence of the Sierra Club in the campaign for Dinosaur. Both Democratic and Republican legislators from the basin states insisted that the conspiracy was real in their correspondence and speeches.[17]

The illustrated literature sent out by the preservationists belied the claim that there was no beauty in the rocky canyons of Dinosaur, but it did not appeal solely to the public's aesthetic judgment. Instead, it dwelled on the erroneous evaporation estimate to suggest that the alleged necessity for using the preserve was a false claim by the Bureau of Reclamation. The publicists used other means to educate. With the cooperation of local outdoor enthusiasts, they organized raft trips through the Echo Park canyon in order to elicit testimony from prominent citizens about the grandeur of the preserve. The success of this scheme was measurable in impressive statistics. While only 12,934 persons had visited the monument in 1950, and forty-seven had taken the trip by raft, in 1954 the visitors numbered 70,652, of which 912 rafted through the awesome canyons.[18]

The effectiveness of the publicity campaign was also measurable by the protests and personal innuendoes issued by their enemies. The *Denver Post* referred to the California-eastern conspiracy allegation so often they made it seem to be a fact. Indeed the *Post* also claimed that preservationist leader Bernard De Voto was being paid by California. The journalist was greatly amused by this. Yes, he facetiously reported to Carhart, he was paid the nice round sum of $122,614.52 for his efforts. Then he wrote to publisher Palmer Hoyt of the *Post* to point out that the "long-haired, arm chair" caricature of the conservationist was an "ancient line" that had been "played out." Moreover, the "for-God-sake-authorize-Echo Park-or-California-will-steal-our-water" appeal was a "cheap slur" on the motives of congressmen from many other states. This was not a local matter but a national crisis. The populous states were directly involved, he pointed out. "Massachusetts will pay a larger part of the cost of any dam in the project than Colorado will; so will Knopf's New York." De Voto warned that if the states of the Midwest or East found out that they had been misled or "required to pay for unnecessary, injudicious, or inferior works" for the sole benefit of the West, their disinclination toward this and any future project would get much worse. His prediction was correct. A few months later, Senator John F. Kennedy of Massachusetts questioned the expansion of costly water projects in the West which would help few and would be paid for by many who did not benefit. De Voto praised his stand and agreed: "The entire concept of reclamation needs a thorough overhauling."[19]

Most significantly, the publicity campaign caused the men in the Interior Department to reexamine the entire UCB proposal in order to be better fortified against criticism from every quarter. Citizens' letters could be ignored, but those coming from congressmen— especially from Republicans worried about the impact of the controversy on appropriations and elections—could not be brushed aside with form replies. John Saylor of Pennsylvania, for example, was consistently dubious about the billion-dollar project and about the "necessary" Echo Park site. As a member of the House Appropriations Committee, his outspoken opinions commanded the barest respect by the administrators. At one point in the controversy, McKay called him to offer assurance that the department's resource policy was a change for the better after the Democratic regimes. In reply, Saylor thought of a particularly embarrassing comparison: "I am sorry to notify you that as far as I am concerned, I can find no change whatsoever in the Bureau of Reclamation. The projects presented today are as fantastic, if not more so, as those presented by the Democrats . . . Dexheimer is continuing the strategy of Mr. Strauss [sic]."[20]

One thing disclosed by the process of reexamining UCB was the discomforting fact that even Tudor's reorganization efforts had not altered the inertial force of bureaucratic deviousness. The chain of circumstances began in February 1954, when Robinson of the Advisory Board recognized that the Echo Park controversy was "moving toward an ugly situation. It has been obvious from the beginning that a head-on collision would occur." The secretary's office should be prepared for it by drawing up a white paper or legal brief or by appointing some independent and competent engineer to analyze the evaporation rates at the several basin sites and report his findings directly to McKay. If Reclamation's figures were wrong, it would be better to admit it publicly than to embarrass the department further. Three weeks passed before McKay replied to Robinson's advice. When he did, he merely affirmed the overall validity of the initial UCB report and dismissed questions about evaporation rates as unimportant. Tudor had created the Technical Review Office to screen data on matters of larger policy precisely like the UCB proposal. Now its chief, John Marr, examined every technical and legal criticism of the plan. He concluded that if all ten dams were built in order to fulfill the states' obligations under the existing basin compact, there was indeed no alternative to Echo Park. A site near Moab, Utah, would provide almost as much storage capacity, but its annual evaporation rate would be greater. Of course, Marr pointed out, if ever a slightly smaller capacity was deemed acceptable, there were suitable alternatives to Dinosaur. At the same time, the Bureau of Reclamation admitted that its studies had predicted that it might be thirty years before the storage capacity of either the Echo Park or Glen Canyon dams would be needed to meet delivery commitments. Even at that future date, the requirement would be for power rather than reclamation. Assistant Secretary Aandahl still thought that Echo Park was feasible, but agreed that these alternative sites could possibly be incorporated into the program at a later date.[21]

Clearly, these subordinates were preparing the ground for a possible face-saving solution, but McKay and Tudor did not see it—or preferred not to see it. Refusing to alter their initial reasoning in order to take their subordinates' suggestions into account, they perversely made a final effort to convince the preservationists that there was nothing to fear. As the Sierra Club's David Brower recalled the meeting in McKay's office, the earnest secretary tried to illustrate his conviction that Echo Park dam would not set a precedent for invasion of the whole park system by striking his finger on the edge of his desk. Just because he might give somebody permission to do something on his desk, it would not mean that it could be done anywhere else in the room. Later, in an ill-timed announcement at the height of the publicity campaign, he said that Interior would soon ask Congress for twenty-one million dollars for development of Dinosaur National Monument. This was not the plan Wirth had drawn up during the Chapman years. Instead, it included a lodge overlooking the reservoir that would inundate all but the top of massive Steamboat Rock, the striking formation that was the preserve's landmark and symbol. The department would thus secure a storage unit big enough "to supply a city the size of Denver," yet "build roads and facilities to convert this wilderness into one of the greatest recreational areas of the nation." The unfortunate phrase warned preservationists that he clung to the traditional American view of the natural environment. Brower called that attitude "farmer psychology"—"land is only good to raise crops on; scenery and natural conditions mean nothing." As someone said of Cedar Breaks National Monument, it was "an awful place to lose a cow in."[22]

If Conrad Wirth had resigned at that point, many would have felt his action completely justified by McKay's behavior. For months he had been in the uncomfortable position of having to answer protest letters by quoting his chief's official recommendation of the UCB project. Undoubtedly recalling the fate of his predecessor, Newton

Drury, he instructed his Park Service employees not to question the decision publicly, and he avoided any appearance of collusion with preservationist organizations. Of course he hoped that their campaign would provide sufficient pressure on the department. His own letters to Assistant Secretary Orme Lewis, however, objected to McKay's statement that the reservoirs would not destroy the preserve's beauty. It was a blatant error, he said, and it would not go down well with the public. Wirth had sought the administration's support for a measure transforming the Dinosaur unit into a Green River Canyon National Park (the new name would convey recognition of its larger attractions). Just as the House Interior Committee was considering the proposal in January 1954, the controversy blasted his hopes. Now, like Drury in the Olympic National Park crisis of 1943, he feared that he would have to reduce the boundaries of the monument to their original small measurements around the fossil quarries in order to uphold the principle of park inviolability. He was not even sure he could succeed in that ploy. Dejectedly, he told Knopf that he had done everything he could to change the department's decision; nothing more could be done about it. He refused to make a martyr of himself by resigning, because the dammers would then have clear sailing.[23]

McKay's announcement of recreational development at Dinosaur disgusted the preservationists. "Isn't that something!" Carhart exclaimed. "You spend ten bucks per year on a national park for two decades, but if you wreck its value, then you spend $21 to fix it up so people will 'enjoy' the mess." One tenth of the sum sought by the secretary would have paid for the access roads needed to increase the volume of visitors whose absence Interior had cited as reason to denigrate the monument. Dinosaur was about to become "a future Coney Island," Carhart predicted sardonically, with "shooting galleries, doll racks, a Slide for Life, and the biggest merry-go-round in North America." His Denver colleague in the Izaak Walton League, J. W. Penfold, acidly inquired of the secretary whether twenty-one million dollars was the assessed price of the desecrated preserve.[24]

During the summer months of 1954, the Interior officials had a second chance to find their way out of the impasse over Dinosaur. Tudor had admitted to Wyoming Congressman William Harrison, chairman of the House Interior Committee, that Reclamation's evaporation estimate for Echo Park was in error. Like Senator Watkins, however, he hastened to point out that the scheme to raise Glen

Canyon's dam level would either flood out nearby Rainbow Bridge National Monument or require construction of a substantial coffer dam to protect it. Moreover, a committee was already being formed to make a national park out of Glen Canyon itself. The undersecretary was privately angry with Brower for raising the question of error in public instead of coming to him first. Yet when Brower had invited him and McKay to take a raft trip down the river to review the canyon's value, they had refused. Sherman Adams himself had forwarded the invitation to them with the rather suggestive notation that "no propaganda" was intended. McKay disdainfully replied that he "wouldn't dare go on this trip with the Sierra Club and listen to their propaganda on how we are destroying nature's grandeur in Echo Park." Tudor responded to the suggestion by repeating the statement he had made to Harrison about Glen Canyon.[25] (It was a true prophesy. A dozen years later, Brower and the Sierra Club would be sounding the alarm as the waters behind that dam came within a mile of the Rainbow Bridge preserve.)

The department took other steps to bolster its position. It succeeded in getting the White House to delay the report of the Hoover Task Force on Water Resources until 1955, because of the criticism of such projects as UCB set forth in its preliminary findings. Six months after Robinson made the suggestion, McKay hired two engineers to make an independent review of the basin plan and report directly to him. The Bureau of Reclamation had to scramble to come up with figures that would sustain its original recommendation. Commissioner Dexheimer somewhat sheepishly reported that his subordinates had not mentioned the discrepancies in evaporation rates because they had thought them "not of great import." He was personally sorry that this issue had since become "very detrimental to our reputation and to the . . . Project." With Aandahl, he reminded the secretary that the Interior committees of Congress had already decided that the higher dam at Glen Canyon was unacceptable as an alternative to Echo Park. They doubted that these same men could be influenced to change their minds.[26]

As the buck was passed around during these tense months, everybody's prestige was brought down a notch. To defend the Bureau of Reclamation's evaporation error, some Republicans shrugged "they're only human"—a show of tolerance that had never crossed party lines during the Truman administration of course. But McKay was reported to be "livid with anger" and Tudor "furious" over the matter.

In a letter reprimanding his subordinates, the secretary brushed aside
Dexheimer's concern for the bureau's reputation and pointed out that
its "inexcusable negligence" had brought ridicule on the whole department. Because of the national attention focused on it by the publicity
campaign, Interior had suffered "a severe blow to its prestige and
doubt had been cast on its integrity." After almost eight months of
the most extensive criticism, the officials decided that some underlings
had marred the department's public image. Still using the small end
of their telescope, neither McKay nor Tudor saw this as another
opportunity to revise their original recommendation.[27]

The determination of the policy makers at the White House did
not weaken during the last part of 1954. Just as they rejected their
opponents' ideas on power policy, so they avoided considering the
preservationists' ideas. Special counsel and appointments secretary
Bernard Shanley declined to set up an appointment for Saylor,
Zahniser, and Packard to see the president. Privately he sneered
that the raft trips through Dinosaur would be "fun for the few
aristocrats of the wilderness" but would never appeal to "American
tourists as a whole." Although he admitted that water and power
projects had been used as pork barrel legislation in previous (Democratic) administrations, Shanley believed that UCB was not that
kind of thing at all. The presidential aides could remain comfortably
adamant, but a severe drought in Colorado increased the pressure on
legislators. Perhaps the bottleneck should be broken by a basin-state
governors' suit before the Supreme Court. Horan of Washington
found it difficult to remain neutral on the issue, and feared that it would
jeopardize his own proposals for Columbia basin development. In
contrast to his caution, Idaho Congresswoman Gracie Pfost, defender
of the high dam at Hells Canyon, announced that Dinosaur was
"good for very little else" except a reservoir.[28]

The president remained silent. Was he "encapsulated" by his
advisers? De Voto decided he was either "lazy or ignorant." Eisenhower's behavior may be more accurately described as discreet. He
refused to comment on any criticism from the administration's
opponents. When he spoke in public, he was sensitive enough about
his delivery style to make no off-the-cuff additions to what his aides
had drafted for him to say. As a result, he sometimes seemed uncon-
scious of subtle ironies in certain remarks. In September 1954, for
example, he toured the reclamation states of the northern Great Plains
and there praised his Interior and Agriculture secretaries for sustaining

individual enterprise and stabilizing the stock industry. He did not see anything wrong in an echo of Defense Secretary Charles Wilson's famous gaff by saying: "What is good for the agriculture interests of the United States is good for all of us." Sherman Adams probably bolstered his characteristic abhorrence of controversy. One of the letters Adams received contained pertinent advice which he may have passed on to his chief:

> I really think it would be the best part of valor for the President to stay away from this Dinosaur issue for a while. At least until the Hoover task group on water resources makes its report so that he may have available to him other judgments than simply that of one bureau looking at its plans and pronouncing them good. . . . It is worth remembering that the combined population of Utah and Colorado . . . is barely equal to the number of people who visit Yellowstone and Yosemite every year. . . . I honestly believe that this fantastic plan will prove a booby trap for the "economy minded" administration.[29]

The policy makers entertained no second thoughts. Secretary McKay refused to have any more conversations with the preservationist leaders. When Zahniser sought an audience in March 1955, McKay told a staff member that the man already had received the "full treatment." When department officials met with legislators at the White House on the Echo Park problem, they pointedly neglected to invite Congressman Saylor, perhaps because they felt he had made a nuisance of himself on the matter. After "quite a hassle" he was finally admitted, but when he asked for a list of the thousands of people who had written protests about the McKay recommendation, the request was denied. Even after the arguments of the publicity campaign about Dinosaur contributed to the storm over Hells Canyon and Dixon-Yates, Adams still answered his critics by insisting that "no man has worked harder or more objectively on every phase of the proposed Colorado River Storage Project than has Secretary McKay. He and his team of department officials represent as highly qualified and as honorable officials as could possibly be found."[30]

The new Democratic Congress that had ridden back into power partly on the strength of the "giveaway" issues took up its work in January 1955. Dinosaur's defenders tried to bring together several blocks of opinion to prevent authorization of the UCB. Knopf sent copies of his company's handsomely illustrated book *This Is Dinosaur*, edited by Wallace Stegner, to every member of the legislature. He also sent some to the men at Interior. His covering letter to Assistant Secretary Lewis pointedly suggested that if he did not want to read it, he should at least look at the pictures; if Echo Park reservoir was built, the book would be a record of "what once was." Zahniser later claimed to have written most of the speeches delivered by congressional supporters of the preserve. More raft trips through the monument were organized for the legislators. Even newspapermen from the basin states took them, though they did not alter their editorial opinion.[31]

Preservationists warned developers that they would see their region's great project blocked if the Dinosaur site was kept in the bill. To Democrats of the area, De Voto stage-whispered that Interior obstinancy might be a deliberate attempt by the administration to sabotage the expensive measure. Pennsylvania's Saylor also hinted that Congress would block other appropriations for the Bureau of Reclamation. Seeking a larger audience, Governor Lee of Utah submitted an article ghosted by his state water engineers. John Fisher of *Harper's* rejected it and told him that the large tax-paying states did not believe in the soundness of the UCB project. Why should the government spend large sums to bring more western lands under cultivation when they already had such large farm surpluses? Would it not be cheaper to reclaim untilled lands in the Southeast? Why, if UCB was so important, were no alternatives to Echo Park submitted to avoid a legislative bottleneck? These same questions were raised on the floor of both houses of Congress and in its committee rooms.[32]

The developers tried to match their adversaries in appeals to congressmen. Members of the Upper Colorado Development Commission came to Washington to lobby for the Watkins bill. The Interior Department sent out copies of the promise in the 1938 proclamation to everyone who had written in to protest the use of Echo Park. In March the Congress of Industrial Organizations announced its full support of the UCB project because it would provide jobs and because it would lessen the control of private power monopolies in the region. Spirits were raised when the president made some off-the-record remarks to the press, denying that the proposal was unnecessarily costly and agreeing that opposition to it was the work of Californians. Sensing that the tide was turning in his favor, Watkins offered a palm branch to the preservationists. He was now and had always been a conservationist, he said. It was time that "the bitterness over these

controversial reclamation units should be abated and that reason and
fairness should be allowed to prevail."[33]

Reason and Fairness were trampled on the Senate floor by
Determination and Desperation. The men of the basin states were
determined not to let their cause be ruined by a "political hassle."
When the measure was reported out of committee favorably, however,
newly elected Democratic Senator Richard Neuberger of Oregon
moved an amendment to eliminate the dams in Dinosaur from the
authorization. Senators Wayne Morse of Oregon and Paul Douglas
of Illinois supported it—one saying that the federal project was too
badly needed to be stalled further, and the other accusing the
Republican administration of overdeveloping the Upper Colorado
instead of other rivers. In the House, Democrat Clair Engle of
California, chairman of the Interior Committee, seemed to confirm the
"conspiracy" theory by moving to omit the dam at Flaming Gorge,
Wyoming, but when the bill got to the Senate, Joseph O'Mahoney
guarded his state's interest by blocking the maneuver. Neuberger's
motion was then defeated 30 to 52, but he was pleased with the
unexpected size of the minority vote. Moments later, by a margin of
58 to 38, the Senate voted to authorize the UCB project. Democrat
Clinton Anderson of New Mexico, Truman's former Agriculture
secretary, cast his vote with the yeas. Most Republicans supported
it as an administration measure. They were joined by Democrats
from the basin states and by Democrats who wanted a continuation
of federal water programs. Neuberger himself was in the latter group.
Knopf chided him for voting for "the biggest boondoggle of all time,"
but the legislators' inconsistencies did not surprise the publisher. In
all his experience, though, he admitted that he had "never seen any
issue turn otherwise honorable men into such God damn liars."[34]

In defense of the senators it must be said that they did not vote
for or against the principle of the national parks, but on the basis
of several often conflicting interests. The dilemma many of them
faced was best illustrated by the actions of Edwin Johnson of
Colorado. A Democratic governor during the 1930s (though by no
means a New Dealer), he welcomed federal spending but resented
centralization of power in Washington. He was elected to the Senate
in 1942 and became an influential member of the Interior Committee
where he was one of the principal sponsors of the Upper Colorado
development program. When Republican ranks were weakened first
by Hugh Butler's death and then by Guy Cordon's defeat, Johnson

realized that these events damaged the chances of authorization for UCB. That same year, 1954, he ran for another term as governor against Eisenhower's friend Dan Thorton. Outflanking his opponent by promising to break the legislative bottleneck on the measure, he satisfied neither developers nor preservationists with specifics. When his friend Arthur Carhart objected to the vague remarks, the governor-elect explained that it was not the time "to come out slugging." Their cause was not lost, but it had to be handled delicately. In December, Johnson decided to drop his bombshell, which was nothing more than the idea of using Ladore Canyon as the alternative to Echo Park. Since that site was only a few miles to the north and still within the monument, the suggestion angered everyone. The *Denver Post* and the Chamber of Commerce at Grand Junction, Carhart noticed, began "hysterically shouting." A new organization of Utahans and Coloradans calling themselves "Aqualantes" was hastily formed and began collecting emergency funds by selling "sheriff" stars for a dollar each. Carhart remained calm, however. He told fellow preservationists to remember that "Ed Johnson is in politics," and his idea was no more than an attempt to get both sides to think about alternatives to Echo Park so that the UCB bill could be accepted.[35]

In a larger sense, Johnson's behavior was prompted by a fear that his state would not receive its proportionate share of water from the project. Other basin state leaders exhibited similar symptoms. Watkins, worried that the issues would further delay authorization, was furious with Johnson and exchanged "barbed language" with him at a governors meeting in January 1955. Simpson of Wyoming tried to bring the Coloradan back into the fold by approaching O'Mahoney, another "lion in politics" who had served with Johnson since the 1930s. Both men had made themselves the watchdogs of the Interior Department since that time. O'Mahoney, worried that his state would lose its smaller share of river water to southern neighbors, wrote an article for *Collier's* arguing that Echo Park dam was essential to the whole project. The mail he received about it, however, was disturbingly critical of his stand. "I own a share of Yellowstone," wrote one constituent, ". . . I do not want the Department of the Interior to cut down my tree in the [Olympic] National Park. . . . In the same token I do not want my part of Dinosaur flooded by water that will benefit some stranger in Utah." Another letter came from an army private serving in Korea who claimed that the sanctity of the monument was one of the things he was fighting for there. The cruelest comment made by the correspondents said that O'Mahoney's article sounded as if it were written by "Senator Claghorn"—the bombastic, banal politician caricatured on the Fred Allen radio program. Made more desperate by these responses opposing the UCB bill, O'Mahoney even urged Watkins to ask the president to revoke Dinosaur just as Mount Holy Cross National Monument in Colorado had recently been removed from the park system roster. Somewhat wistfully, Watkins replied that "it would be wonderful if we could clear this mess up" that way, but he doubted that any president, even one as popular as Ike, could "slip anything through unnoticed . . . at this time."[36]

Governor Johnson expressed his "farmer opinion" that an alternative site to Echo Park could be found, and a growing number of developers seemed ready to agree. In June, the House Interior Committee deleted that dam site from the UCB bill and then approved the measure by a vote of 20 to 6. Eastern and Californian members combined to defeat it on the floor, however. While Dexheimer was claiming that the Dinosaur issue was dead, basin state men feared that the whole project would die if the impasse continued. When a caucus of Republicans promised that Echo Park would not be included in the bill at the next session of Congress, Utahans urged them not to abandon the cause. Just at that time, the Hoover Commission Task Force on Water and Power issued its report. The document specifically referred to UCB as a glaring example of federal subsidy, poor administrative planning, and dubious potential management. With the pendulum apparently swinging further away from them, the developers decided they had better give up many parts of the proposal that they had considered essential.[37]

The plight of the Eisenhower administration at the end of summer 1955 was summed up in a Conrad cartoon. In it, golfers Ike, McKay, Dexheimer, and Congress trudge worriedly toward the next session saying: "we all need 'birdies' on this hole!" Feeling the shift in the situation, the preservationists concentrated their publicity on the economics of UCB, the aspect that particularly embarrassed Republicans and angered easterners. It would be sixteen times costlier than the assessed value of farm lands and buildings in the four basin states. The hope of growing "bananas on Pike's Peak" was exceeded in irrationality only by the "monstrous impertinence" of dams in Dinosaur. By this time, the developers were also using melodramatic language. Senator Watkins led the chambers of commerce of Vernal and Provo, Utah, into the national monument for an inspection tour. He pointed out the blowing sand, poor roads, a silted river, and minimally developed campgrounds. These were the things that the preservationists wanted to save, he jeered. As he threw out each barbed remark, he turned to the host superintendent and asked loudly: "Did you get that, Mr. Park Service?" There were too many monuments in the park system, he said as the party prepared to leave, and he meant to ask the president to take all of them out of the jurisdiction of the Park Service.[38]

The basin state leaders were far more receptive to compromise than their rhetoric implied. In September 1955 Governor Simpson called another meeting of the region's governors and extended the invitation to the congressional delegations of these states. Over forty persons convened at the Brown Palace Hotel in Denver on November 1. Simpson sent a proxy at the last minute, but Lee and Johnson were there, along with O'Mahoney, four of the five signers of the caucus resolution, representatives of the Upper Colorado River Commission, and Elmer Bennett, the Interior Department's legislative liaison man. They did not invite a man from the Park Service—for obvious reasons. Under the chairmanship of Anderson of New Mexico, the day-long meeting discussed the possibilities of designating the higher dam at Glen Canyon as an alternative to Echo Park. If that was done, however, they demanded that a just proportion of "anticipated power profits" from that unit be guaranteed in the measure. "That is all we could ask," Johnson said afterwards, "and all we have ever asked." Then they adopted a resolution which expressed their opposition to any bill that included only Glen Canyon, and another which specified that four dams should be named in the legislation, including the one at Flaming Gorge, Wyoming. On O'Mahoney's motion, the senators and congressmen present then joined in an agreement not to reinsert Echo Park into the Watkins bill. Colorado, they agreed, could choose a substitute for it at a later date. A few days after the meeting adjourned, Anderson, Dexheimer, and their staffs met to incorporate these provisions into the draft being prepared for the approaching session.[39]

Both sides were jubilant over the news of the Denver meeting. (The only note of sadness for the preservationists was occasioned by the death of crusader Bernard De Voto two weeks after the meeting.) Lee pledged his state's support and the "Aqualantes" sent letters of congratulations to O'Mahoney for his part in the settlement. Wirth was certain that the struggle was "pretty well over" and was encouraged that some members of Congress were now interested in the Park Service plan to develop the monument's facilities. Nobody left the battlefield, however. Final details and the budget for UCB still had to be decided upon. Even without Echo Park, the eastern objections to cost and practicality remained. Knopf remarked of the basin proponents—"these poor fish"—that they were still in danger of losing a lot that they could have had three years earlier "if they hadn't been so stupid about Dinosaur." As Senator Paul Douglas of Illinois later explained, all such projects were "extremely unpopular" among his constituents who could not understand the necessity of reclaiming high altitude lands at an estimated cost of $800 to $1,200 an acre.[40]

Ignoring past incidents of official coolness, Zahniser again called at the Interior Department to learn whether McKay would concur in the sense of the Denver resolutions. He once more asked that a definite statement be inserted in the administration's measure prohibiting any unit of the park system from ever being used for water projects in the future. In their mood of triumph, the preservationists may not have noticed the inconsistency of this demand. They had long argued that the proviso in the 1938 proclamation could not be considered binding on the action of future Congresses or presidents. Yet they now sought to create just such a restriction. McKay replied by a memo to his staff in which he said that the department would adhere to the Denver resolutions when they were put into the bill—"However, I do not care to comply with the second request." The Bureau of Reclamation examined the alternative that they could not find before, and Sherman Adams suddenly decided that the UCB project was fully feasible without Echo Park. In an expansive mood, the Interior secretary announced that as soon as the bill passed, the National Park Service's "Mission 66" program would be applied at Dinosaur. Somewhat lamely, he then asked the Sierra Club to support the "very worthwhile and needed" development of the Upper Colorado River basin.[41]

When the new session of Congress took up the bill in January 1956, there was another outburst of wrangling. The representatives of the basin states were divided by a demand from Johnson that Colorado have "simple justice" in the division of water supplied by the project, that is, slightly over half of the total volume. Lee called it an ultimatum, and the followers of both men agreed that if they were again stretched on the "gridiron of communal controversy," California would use the opportunity to kill the bill. Simpson nevertheless reopened wounds not yet healed by making a public promise that Echo Park had been "only temporarily forsaken." The pending measure was "a foot in the door until we can show necessity for the reservoir there in the future." Senator Barrett cast his familiar shadow across the scene by pointing out that the will of Congress and future generations could not be bound by the authorization bill. "The time will come," he predicted, "when the Recreationists will find that they have been working against their own interests in eliminating Echo Park Dam."[42]

Were the Denver resolutions "a meaningless sop"? Preservationists intended to find out and quickly sent a joint letter to O'Mahoney insisting that he insert Zahniser's prohibition clause into the bill. Because that detail had not been part of the compromise, the senator responded by accusing them of a breach of faith. Spokesmen for the basin states also decried the Advisory Board's support of the demand as the same sort of infidelity. In turn, the preservationists pointed to Simpson's statement as proof that the developers would ultimately betray their own pledge. Somewhat nervously, Colorado's delegation agreed to sponsor a bill to make Dinosaur a national park. By the end of February, this last-minute hysteria dissolved. On March 9 Echo Park dam was removed from the UCB authorization provisions, and the measure was adopted and signed by the president in April.[43] On March 9 Douglas McKay resigned as secretary of the Interior.

Chapter Eight

THE
GIVEAWAY
BRAND

Months before there was evidence that the Republican administration was bent on changing resource policy, Democrats made the subject a special target of their attacks. Their primary purpose was to regain control of Congress in the elections of 1954; consequently they felt there was no time to lose if they were to discredit their opponents by then. Federal resource policy had been their proud possession for twenty years. It had been a dueling ground during the Truman administration and one of the most striking choices involved in the 1952 campaign. Perhaps they hoped to repeat the Clark Clifford strategy of 1948: contrasting their party's record with the Republicans' performance. They had first leveled the "giveaway" charge during the debate over the offshore oil lands in 1951 and 1952. After passage of the bill "restoring" those lands to the states, and the Barrett proposals to do the same with grazing lands, they easily extended the charge to the Republican-dominated Congress. Interior's decision to withdraw from contention in the Hells Canyon application by the Idaho Power Company and its recommendation of dam sites in Dinosaur were successively described as proof that the department was set on a "giveaway" course. Because these actions were a clear departure from the legacy of Ickes, Krug, and Chapman and because the party in power still bore the stigma of past scandals in resource policy, Secretary McKay became the Democrats' carnival pitching-game clown. They joyously discovered that his name neatly rhymed with their catchword, and they made "Giveaway McKay" the butt of cartoons, anti-administration jokes, and Cassandra-like editorials in partisan journals. The secretary was at first indifferent to their shafts, but Tudor was angered by them. "If there was ever a 'giveaway' program in existence in this country," he noted in his diary, "it has been during the last twenty years when the regime here in Washington has been 'giving away' the assets of the country for the benefit of a few." By that he referred to the tendency toward centralism: "Actually, I wish they would realize that what we are doing is taking these things away from the bureaucrats and giving them back to the people."[1]

The administration's critics were unwilling to give McKay time to demonstrate what he was trying to do. He had been in office only a few weeks when they began discussing the need to stop him. During the first months of his tenure, Democratic National Committee Chairman Stephen Mitchell toured the Northwest to spread the alarm. "It's giveaway time in the City of Washington," he announced in Lewiston, Idaho. "It's Bank Night at the Department of the Interior." McKay had "made it pretty clear he's going to move at least some distance in the direction of giving the break to private power monopolies," and he meant to do it "without leaving any finger prints." It was a phenomenon not seen for many years, Mitchell reminded his audience. "It has been a long time since we had a Secretary of the Interior who does not consider it his duty to be spokesman for the people of the country." In Tacoma he ridiculed McKay's pledge that the administration would see to it that business "not become *too greedy* or *too anxious* to make an extra dollar." Just how greedy was "too greedy" and how greedy was "just greedy enough"?

President Eisenhower was under greater pressure from these selfish interests than any other chief executive had ever been. Mitchell hoped that his renowned conscience would prevail against them, but left doubt hanging heavily in the air. In time, Democrats would point to the president's silences on the controversial issues as proof of their caricature of him as a genial boob completely surrounded by men of selfish intent. In Cheyenne, Portland, and Helena, Montana, Mitchell quoted editorials from the *Denver Post,* until recently one of the West's chief celebrants of the Republican return to power. Now it was lamenting the new administration's "War against the West" and was describing McKay as a man "more willing to hand over his sword than fight the battles of the West." No westerner had ever said that about Ickes, Mitchell asserted, or about "that great champion of the West—Oscar Chapman!" Returning to party headquarters in Washington, he reported to his colleagues that he had received "tremendous response" to his speeches in the region. Westerners understood the cuts in reclamation and power budgets and the threats by private exploiters against the national forests and parks. He was sure that the West, like the South, realized it was sitting at the "second table" in the Eisenhower administration's kitchen.[2]

Democrats inflated their fright balloon in private correspondence as well. Questions received from constituents were answered with ominous-sounding comments. For example Senator Douglas admitted that Eisenhower was "a good man" but warned that he was "out to gut the public power program, turn the marketing of power, so far as is possible, over to private companies." Assuming that McKay was making resource policy, Douglas claimed that he was the source of the bad advice that made possible the "betrayals," "land grabs," and "giveaways." Senator Ernest Gruening, former governor of Alaska, confessed that he had initially thought that McKay would be sympathetic and understanding of the territory's resource problems. Now he claimed to speak for many other westerners when he rated the secretary's performance in federal-local relations as "the all-time low." Whatever anyone said about McKay, Gruening grimly concluded, "it was an understatement."[3]

By the middle of summer 1953 the men in the White House were getting mail warning that the "giveaway" label would plague Republicans in the elections of 1954 and 1956 unless an effort at counter-publicity was made. The public still associated the party with greed and corruption in the past, one loyalist pointed out, so "we better start selling ourselves." In March 1954, at the height of the protests over Dinosaur, Congressman Harris Ellsworth of Oregon informed Vice President Nixon that the political situation in his state was slipping. Unless something was done to stop "all of this loose talk on the part of our opponents," people would make up their minds on the basis of the propaganda. Another Oregonian told Senator Barrett that the "socialists" were rallying forces "in hopes that they can soon return to political power and take over the offensive where they left off." State party leader Wendell Wyatt had a more realistic explanation: "The people in the streets seem to associate dams with power, power with industry, industry with more people and more jobs and prosperity."[4]

In Washington State, Hells Canyon struck one of Walt Horan's constituents as the "big sell out by this administration" which was endangering the party and the congressman's own chances for reelection. "The Republican administration [has] sure slipped a long way out here. I have always voted that way but if this keeps up I will have to support those I am sure will support us out here." Horan pleaded for more time before judgment was rendered, but the threats continued. "Here is one Republican who will vote for a Democrat for Senator," a Wenatchee resident wrote, "if the present attitude toward public power continues in the governmental program." Reclamationist Robert Sawyer could not wait either. In the course of the first year of the Republican regime, he became so dissatisfied that he refused to send contributions to the party campaign chest. The Hoover Commission task force had urged the administration to go slowly, he complained, but "obviously no thought on this subject has entered the minds of any in the Executive Departments." The president too was either uninformed or had "very bad advice."[5]

The reasoning used by the Democratic publicists was far more accurate about public opinion than that of the Republicans. They correctly assumed that most people believed McKay was the real policy maker. They also realized that the expressions of discontent about bureaucracy were based upon impatience with any bureaucracy that was apparently unfair or did nothing to fulfill campaign promises. Republican performance in resource programs was one of the most widely discussed subjects of the 1954 political contests in the West. A recession had affected many of the extractive industries in the region, and there was a "brownout" and the threat of a power shortage in the Northwest. Finally, the decline in general employment seemed directly related to the "no new starts" policy in dam construction. One of the bitterest races turning on resource programs was the challenge by Montana's Congressman Wesley D'Ewart against Senator James Murray. The Republican defended his own decade-long record of land use legislation and argued that the Eisenhower-McKay policies were worthy of full support. Murray and his fellow partisans from the Northwest, D'Ewart maintained, had recklessly pasted the "give-away" label on "every constructive measure" proposed or adopted by the Congress and the Interior Department. In truth, the Democrats deserved that epithet. In the preceding period they had presided over a *"Giveaway* to foreign nations" and a *"Takeaway* from Americans." Republicans had given back to the people "the right to develop their resources and minerals in the traditional American way . . . the way that has made us the greatest country on earth." D'Ewart (or his campaign manager) also depended upon the effective methods of McCarthyism. They issued broadsides about "The Red Record and Communist Front Associations of James E. Murray" and a booklet titled "James E. Murray and the Red Web over Congress."[6]

Here and elsewhere, Republicans seemed to assume that voters were more concerned with images and ideologies than with the specifics of resource programs. The results of the contest did not clearly determine whether these tactics had lost their appeal or whether voters were thinking of D'Ewart's part in the controversial Barrett bills. He lost the election to Murray by 127 votes. At the same time, Joseph O'Mahoney, who had been a casualty in the Republican sweep of 1952, regained his Senate seat for the full term by defeating William Harrison, chairman of the House Interior Committee. The Eisenhower administration, he reiterated during the campaign, had sold Wyoming and the rest of the West short by its policies in water and power development.[7]

The Democrats' most dramatic victory in the campaign to return to power by exploiting the "giveaway" charge took place in Oregon. There, Senator Guy Gordon, principal adviser to the Republican administration on resource policy and successor to Hugh Butler as chairman of the Senate Interior Committee, was running for reelection. His challenger was Richard Neuberger, one of the fifteen Democratic members of the ninety-member senate in the traditionally Republican state. Neuberger, who was twenty-two years younger than Gordon, had already gained a measure of fame as one of the best informed journalists in the nation and was regarded as an authority on western political and economic questions. President Roosevelt had sent him a note of praise in 1941 for his defense of federal conservation, remarking that Oregon was fortunate in having his services.[8]

Never a preservationist in the purist sense, Neuberger was nevertheless a vigorous advocate of expanded federal direction of natural resources. He wrote and spoke in support of such programs as CVA not merely because he was a loyal Democrat, but because he believed that only through federal administration could the conflicting, sometimes irresponsible, economic interests of the West attain the highest degree of opportunity. Like Ickes, however, he viewed the national parks as equally valuable resources for the people. It was understandable that he would be an advocate of greater resource development in a state whose economy depended directly upon the extractive industries. His concern for forests and dams, moreover, reflected his sensitivity to the growing number of working men that had moved to the Pacific Northwest since World War II. Federally regulated use and construction, he argued in his writings, not only meant jobs and contracts but those programs prevented the people's treasures from going into the hands of a few monopolies. He had campaigned on these issues as candidate for Congress in 1952, but the promise of change by the Republicans had been too attractive that year and he lost the race.[9] After the Eisenhower administration unveiled its new emphasis in resource policy—an emphasis that seemed bent on diminishing federal supervision and favoring private interests—Neuberger became one of the most outspoken members of the phalanx of Democratic critics. If he did not coin the title "Giveaway McKay," he became the principal wielder of that brand.

In May 1953, about the time of the Hells Canyon decision, former Senator Clarence Dill of Washington State urged Neuberger to run for Cordon's seat. The issue of public versus private power, he argued, would be the decisive factor not only in Oregon but in the other states of the Pacific Northwest. When Neuberger agreed to enter the lists, Democrats and preservationists were jubilant. De Voto privately considered him not sufficiently "statesmanlike" on the economics of resource use, but agreed that his defeat of Cordon would be "a portent so terrific in national significance" that the circumstances of his serving in the Senate would raise his stature "out of all proportion to his abilities." Oregonians were "scared," he reasoned, and the state was harder hit by recession than any other. Even if the administration suddenly reversed its "no new starts" attitude, he thought Neuberger had something better than an even chance to win.[10]

The challenger's task was to translate the generalized sense of recession into rejection of Cordon as one of the architects of the Republican economic policies. Because the decisions of the Interior Department and the Congress seemed to reduce construction and development of resources, Neuberger's denunciations of McKay, or the "McKay-Cordon giveaways," were enhanced. Just as Democrats were doing on the national scene, so he could string together a chain of "proofs" to lead the voters to the desired conclusion. Cordon had been responsible for McKay's appointment, the sequence began; he had sponsored the forest land exchange legislation which contributed to the production and unemployment problems of the lumber industry; he had helped shape and continually defended the partnership power policy which in practice favored monopoly and cut down the number of dam construction projects in the state; he had contributed to the budget reductions for the bureaus in Agriculture and

Interior whose work was so important to the economy of Oregon. These points were made in speeches and spot radio statements. (Neuberger spent 85 percent of his campaign funds to buy radio time.) To assist in the significant battle, Truman's old warriors Chapman and Davidson stumped for Neuberger, while former Forest Service chief Lyle Watts of Portland described Cordon as "one of the worst foes of conservation." From a distance, party leader Adlai Stevenson issued a helpful warning about the growth of the power trust in the nation's economy. Finally, and most helpfully, Wayne Morse returned to the state to secure the adherence of his own supporters in both parties for Neuberger, his onetime law student and political protégé. By election day, few voters in the state were unaware of the issue of Republican resource policy.[11]

The members of the incumbent party recognized the importance of the contest; not only was Cordon's influence vital to the administration's programs, they said, but the presence of his opponent in the Senate would have a disastrous effect on those programs. Neuberger, moreover, was the epitome of the "fanatics" so abhorred by the men in the White House. But the Eisenhower men were confident that their chief's record would be acknowledged by the voters of Oregon. Public versus private power would not be a big campaign issue there, Tudor assured them. Neuberger was "talking too much and too early." McKay could not believe that there were not enough "dumb weak sisters" at home to fall into a trap "laid by the demagogues." Because of the way in which his name was abused in the state and in the nationally syndicated columns of Drew Pearson, the secretary meant to take an active part in the fight, but finally decided that he would not, perhaps because of advice from the White House. Instead, he merely answered some of the charges in private correspondence. He assured Horan, for example, that he had never intended to turn over the national parks to private interests, and "would never do so."[12]

The seemingly casual attitude shown toward the Oregon race by the president's advisers greatly disturbed local party leaders. Not until October did Eisenhower lend his popularity to Cordon's cause by a personal appearance. On his way to the West, he claimed that he had kept his 1952 promise by picking a cabinet "that would do its best and not be swayed too much just by the interests of any one group, class, or section." (Mitchell might have asked: "How much is *too* much?") When he came to the banks of the Columbia River to dedicate the new McNary Dam, he praised party candidates in Oregon and Washington and mentioned Cordon's name along with McKay's. Characteristically, he described the election of Republicans as being a recognition of that party's efforts to restore equity to national affairs. Other party stalwarts, like McKay, claimed that the election's larger significance was embodied in the Cordon-Neuberger struggle which would be "fought on the issue of collectivism on the one side versus Americanism on the other." That was the interpretation employed by most of the Oregon newspapers. Neuberger's defense of public power was a defense of socialism, his defense of the national parks was proof that he shared the "fanaticism" of the preservationists.[13]

In November, Neuberger won the seat in the Senate by a margin of 2,500 votes which, if distributed statistically, amounted to about one vote per precinct throughout the state. For the first time since 1917, Oregon had two Democratic senators. It seemed probable that 20 percent of the usually overwhelming Republican electorate crossed over to vote for the Democrat. The question was why did they? Richard Nixon and other administration leaders concluded that Cordon's defeat was not a warning. Oregon counties adjacent to Hells Canyon, though supporting Neuberger, also voted down measures which would have financed public power agreements. Morse nevertheless joyfully concluded that it was "a tremendous victory" for public power development in the Pacific Northwest. Other Democrats read the victory as a mandate on the Eisenhower partnership emphasis and a repudiation of McKay. The president was not amused when reporters asked him if the secretary of the Interior was going to resign because of the election. That persistent rumor was also heard later in the winter at hearings held by the Senate Irrigation and Reclamation subcommittee in Washington, Oregon, and Idaho. Ironically, both the White House and the victor agreed that the primary factor in the election had been organized labor's support of the Democrats. The Republicans considered it a case of CIO intimidation of its members, but the senator-elect viewed that support as proof that "the people . . . will vote for progressive and liberal policies when the opportunity is clearly presented to them."[14]

Local Republicans and advocates of private power development were so angered by the allegation that Neuberger's election was a repudiation of Eisenhower-McKay partnership policy that they ordered an in-depth study of the 1954 elections in the Pacific Northwest. The report, subsequently distributed by Spokane's Northwest Associated Businessmen, Inc., dealt with the election results of each of the candidates who had mentioned the subject of power policy in their campaigns.[15] It stated its conclusion at the start: "In the 1954 elections in the Pacific Northwest, a few candidates talked public power and won. A great many more talked public power and were defeated. Public power was also decisively beaten where it was a direct issue." The effort made by Oregonian Al Ullman was the most convincing example cited. An officer and moving force of the Northwest Public Power Association, he had led the fight against the Idaho Power Company's case at Hells Canyon. The vote that November, he insisted, would be a referendum on the administration's power policy. In his own try for the congressional seat of his district he stated: "a vote for my opponent is a vote for McKay." Former commissioner Michael Straus and liberal Democratic Senator Estes Kefauver came to the Snake River area to speak in Ullman's behalf. The incumbent Republican, Congressman Sam Coon, nevertheless carried most of the counties in the district by a clear margin.

In the adjoining congressional district, Harris Ellsworth, Cordon's colleague in the forest land transfer legislation and fellow defender of partnership, also won reelection by a healthy margin. Both Coon and Ellsworth had argued that partnership was working and pointed to the way in which three private utilities had furnished 273 million of the 310 million dollars involved in the construction of the John Day Dam. The Democratic candidate for governor had pursued the same course used by Neuberger, although he did not have the latter's mastery of the issue or his prominence. He pledged himself to prevent a "steal" of the "people's river" if elected but though he received a few more total votes than Neuberger, he lost the race. Referenda for bond issues to continue public power utilities failed in every county where they were proposed. "Whatever the last election proved or didn't prove," the *Gazette Times* of Heppner, Oregon, remarked, "it's impossible to find a mandate for socialism in it."

Democrats in Idaho naturally made the issue of power the center of their platform statements. Referring to the ubiquitous debate over the Hells Canyon case, their convention accused McKay of planning to turn over "our priceless heritage of valuable dam sites" to a private monopoly. Their candidate for governor favored the high federal dam plan because it would provide much greater opportunity for labor and business. Their Republican opponents hailed the partnership policy, opposed federal valley authorities, and supported the three single-purpose dams at Hells Canyon because they believed irrigation was the most important use for the river water. Senator Henry Dworshak, who maintained that these views had the full support of Idahoans, was challenged by former Senator Glen Taylor. As one of the foremost advocates of CVA and public power development and as a member of the ill-fated Progressive crusade of 1948, Taylor seemed to symbolize everything that the region had rejected in the recent past. Moreover, he was subjected to the same well-organized red baiting and smear tactics that he had encountered on that previous occasion. Dworshak was reelected by winning twice as many votes as his opponent. The Republican Party's gubernatorial candidate, Robert Smylie, attracted the personal assistance of men close to the Eisenhower administration, including Sherman Adams. Partly because Dworshak was talking power, Smylie played down that issue in his public statements and said that the number one issue facing the state was public education, not private versus public power. Partnership, he added, was a working solution to the many years of rancorous dispute on that choice. He was elected governor.

The only Democrat reelected in Idaho that November was Congresswoman Gracie Pfost. Nicknamed "Hell's Belle" because of her outspoken support for the high dam at Hells Canyon, she easily faced down a less colorful, less well-informed opponent, who charged that the federal dam would be "an indirect method" of setting up a CVA. Yet her own district gave Dworshak an even larger majority, indicating that the outcome was not determined only by her views on power policy. Wishful thinkers like De Voto nevertheless announced that her victory was "a complete repudiation of the administration's resources policy."

There were only a few races in Washington that year. In one of the congressional contests, Hugh Mitchell, architect of Truman's CVA bill, was defeated for reelection. In scattered campaigns for local offices, several Republicans who advocated cooperation between public utility districts and private service companies won out over men defending the Democratic record on power policy.

Elsewhere in the nation, however, Democratic use of the "giveaway" charge apparently contributed to one important victory for their party. Paul Douglas of Illinois bore down heavily on the economic consequences of the Eisenhower administration's executive and legislative decisions. Proper development and conservation of natural resources, he said specifically, was the incontestable property of the Democratic party. Partnership, like the offshore oil legislation, ignored the public's interest by allowing favored private enterprisers to monopolize the nation's resources. That kind of monopoly was not merely administrative, as was the "monopoly" Republicans alleged the federal government had, but brought profit to a few instead of the many. Similarly, he branded McKay's alteration of reclamation contract provisions as hypocritical federal interference. If that procedure were continued, he warned the secretary, "our historic reclamation policy" would be reversed. Douglas had also led the eastern opposition to the UCB project, combining in his person the roles of preservationist and taxpayer's champion. Helped in his campaign by a visit from Senator Morse, he employed frequent criticism of "the big 'giveaways' and the danger of government by the special interests." The latter charge was especially useful in appealing to organized labor, a primary source of his reelection victory that November.[16]

In a mood of triumph and determination, the new Democratic majority organized the Congress in January 1955. Those who had stressed resource policy in their campaigns joined veteran watchdogs of the "people's interests" to block or redirect the administration's proposals and to adopt their own program. Murray of Montana became the new chairman of the Senate Interior Committee and welcomed to it the junior senator from Oregon, Richard Neuberger, thereby fulfilling a long-held ambition on the part of the latter. Along with other authors of draft legislation, including Michael Straus, they proposed to secure authorization for several new multi-purpose dams in California, Idaho, and Montana. Although seeking larger appropriations for the Interior Department, Murray nevertheless remained critical of its "abandonment, liquidation or vilification over the past two years" of established federal policies. He also encouraged Straus to make another speaking tour in the West, urging him particularly to give "ulcers" to the National Reclamation Association. The Democratic majority welcomed the assistance of other publicists of their cause. Grateful for the campaign help given by former Forest Service executives Lyle Watts and Stuart Moir, Neuberger supported an increase in that agency's appropriations. He also joined Republican Thomas Kuchel in filing objection to the Interior Committee's approval of the UCB project, for which he received the heartfelt thanks of Horace Albright. Brower of the Sierra Club provided Douglas with information about the Bureau of Reclamation's ambitious and dangerous plans, which he described as "three times too much—30 years too soon." Even Republican pundit Raymond Moley denounced these "pig-in-a-poke" projects because they would restore the pork barrel of the New Deal days and undermine the Eisenhower administration's search for economy in government spending.[17]

"Much of the Democrats' publicity accompanying these legislative proposals indulged in time-worn stereotypes about the intrigues of special interests, prompting some observers to conclude that they produced more heat than light about resource problems. They should address themselves to the real need of creating a sense of responsibility for resource policy at the state and local level, one scholar commented. Other policy watchers, however, encouraged a prolongation of the innuendo campaign. Colorado's Carhart, declaring himself a Republican who was "angered sick" over the administration's actions, wanted the Democrats to make the most of its opponents' blunders. If successful, he predicted, they could transform the Eisenhower-McKay policies into the major campaign issue of 1956.[18]

Partly with that purpose in mind, Morse and Neuberger introduced a bill to authorize federal construction of the high multi-purpose dam at Hells Canyon and thereby reverse the 1953 decision of the Federal Power Commission. In reaction, the Eisenhower men adopted the Democrats' tactic and dispatched several speakers to the West to arouse public support for their decision. Clarence Davis, now under secretary of the Interior, proved to be particularly effective in the Northwest. Governors Langlie, Smylie, and Patterson also contributed their efforts to this countercrusade, describing the Morse-Neuberger move as nothing but "political hogwash." Public versus private power was not an issue, they insisted, and the previous elections had proved that it was not. Rather, the issue facing the people now was federal monopoly as against all other combinations of power developers.[19]

In September and October, Neuberger himself returned to Oregon for "ten dam nights" of debate in as many communities. His adversary was Congressman Sam Coon. Their discussions were focused on the John Day Dam as a demonstration of partnership and the actions of the Republican administration at Hells Canyon and the Upper Colorado River basin. The meetings received extensive coverage locally and comment nationally, thus keeping the topic of power policy in the public eye. Later, Neuberger reported that the people were very responsive to the "true story of who is blocking the federal program and what they stand to lose thereby." The publicity campaign had far less effect in Congress, however, where the Morse-Neuberger Hells Canyon measure was not acted upon.[20]

During these same months of 1955, the Democrats also continued their effort to undermine public confidence in Douglas McKay and perhaps force him out of the cabinet. The president, the woodworkers of eastern Washington resolved, should send him "down the road to political oblivion as he sooner or later surely will be." The senators knew that consummation was unlikely. The purpose of their rhetoric was to discredit him so that he would be an albatross which the president would have to carry through the campaign of 1956. There was "considerable evidence," they hinted, proving "tremendous influence" of private utilities in the administration and that McKay was one of the "partners in plunder." Obviously they were trying to find another Albert Fall and Teapot Dome; Morse indeed frequently employed that comparison in his public remarks. Senator Hubert Humphrey of Minnesota, urging prompt action on a wildlife refuge bill, claimed that the secretary was "notably lacking in any zeal to protect the public lands and refuges from encroachment." Others, displaying inconsistencies between McKay's official statements and his off-the-cuff remarks, referred to his "Jekyll and Hyde attitude" on these subjects.[21]

The extent of western disenchantment with McKay as a bringer of desired change was well expressed by the editorials appearing in the *Denver Post*. One of them was particularly exercised by the impasse over Hells Canyon and the Upper Colorado basin project: "The people of the United States need a Secretary of the Interior who will act boldly in the demonstrated public interest . . . one who will not retreat behind the fatuous doubletalk about 'socialism,' the preeminence of local interest or that frightfully abused phrase 'free enterprise' which is touchingly symbolized by what the late Mr. Ickes aptly described as the 'barefoot boys of Wall Street.' "[22]

McKay built up no special defense for himself or the department. A year later, he would ruefully conclude that he should have battled more actively against "these new deal, public power minded writers and politicians," and "rumor mongers" who had harassed him incessantly. "I just didn't have the time," he explained to Robert Sawyer, "personally to answer all the things thrown at me nor did I have the money in the Department to employ public information people to answer all of these charges." When he had tried to defend himself during the campaign of 1954, he merely stirred up "more emotion."[23]

To a great extent, however, the secretary was his own worst enemy. In October 1955, at the height of the publicity attending Neuberger's criticisms in Congress and the Coon debates, McKay showed his dismaying "talent for trouble" by naming Wesley D'Ewart as assistant secretary of the Interior in place of Orme Lewis. The new lieutenant would have supervision over the Bureau of Land Management and the National Park Service. McKay himself had referred to the D'Ewart-Barrett grazing proposal as "lousy" but later concluded that the Montana congressman was not personally responsible for the initial version of the measure. As a Republican, McKay had hoped for D'Ewart's victory over Murray in the Senate race of 1954 and was evidently not dismayed by the tactics used in that campaign. D'Ewart had subsequently been given an assistant secretaryship in the Department of Agriculture, with the task which the officeholder himself later described as that of "trouble shooter." Both Barrett and Benson supported McKay's desire to move him over to Interior, and so did Watkins of Utah and Senator Gordon Allott of Colorado. Sherman Adams at first did not agree. He considered former governor Len Jordan far more desirable in that vital policy position. The Idahoan, who had led the fights against CVA and for the private operation of Hells Canyon development, was then serving as a member of the Joint International Commission on the use of the Columbia River. Adams finally decided, however, that Jordan would be far more valuable to the administration if he stayed where he was. Because of D'Ewart's ten years of experience in resource legislation and because of his solicitude for local and private enterprise, Adams agreed to present the nomination to the president. Eisenhower, then confined to a Denver hospital after his heart attack, approved it for the interim period until the Senate could confirm it.[24]

The news of the appointment unleashed the greatest flood of public criticism against McKay since the decision to put dams in Dinosaur a year and a half earlier. The secretary's description of D'Ewart as "a man of very good judgment" seemed ill fitted to either the nominee or the man who chose him. Rumors claimed the incredibly mistaken selection had been secured by Adams at the bedside of the befuddled, sick president. Whatever the alleged reasoning behind it, the *Oregonian* sadly concluded, McKay had once again followed his "penchant for baring his neck on the political guillotine." "Doug Does It Again," exclaimed the *Denver Post;* he was truly the cabinet's "Mixed-Up Kid." If the Democrats were going to call McKay the "Giveaway King," it suggested, they ought to include the fact that he gave away political issues too.[25]

As usual, the Eisenhower men ignored the publicity. D'Ewart took up his duties while waiting for confirmation and was confident that he could serve the best interests of the department and the administration. He got on well with his new chief, noting later that "if you went up to him with some question that you should make the decision on, he just swept you off pretty quick . . . I like a department that's run that way." He also worked closely with Davis on the UCB program. Both of these men firmly believed that the federal government should recognize the "integrity of the state water laws . . . that it should be a matter of states rights." Although McKay was pleased with him as a conscientious worker, D'Ewart's attitudes continued to upset beehives of protest. The assistant secretary pursued the administration's desire to terminate Indian reservations and was puzzled when native Americans accused him of thereby helping private interests inherit their lands and resources. Why did the "do gooders" object to the proposed policy? "Everybody wants to be fair to the Indians," he later protested innocently. Similarly, he acted upon his conviction that the Davidson plan to have the Park Service own and lease its concessions was "Socialist." Because of these and other announcements, those who objected to his appointment were joined by many more who opposed his retention and their chorus of cries further stigmatized the department. His presence there seemed further confirmation of the Democrats' charge of a "giveaway" conspiracy.[26]

While the D'Ewart ball was still bouncing, the three-year long campaign to discredit McKay was capped by the explosion of the Al Sarena case.[27] That matter was another product of the tangle of legal ambiguities and questionable administrative procedures which had characterized resource policy throughout the nation's history. Similar morasses had contributed to the entrapment of Ballinger and Fall. A résumé of the case is warranted, because no other instance offered such dismaying proof that new brooms sweep superficially. Tudor's reorganization of Interior's procedures may have been an improvement, but the flaw involved in office and field personnel remained. No matter what the statutes said or what the policy makers intended, variation in execution was still possible.

After the war, the Al Sarena Company of Alabama became interested in possible mineral deposits in Oregon's Rogue River National Forest. In 1948 it applied to the Interior Department for exploration rights on twenty-three sites totaling 475 acres. It was encouraged to assume that customary procedure for patenting its claims would be waived. Two years later, however, the application was denied. With the assistance of Congressman Frank Boykin of Alabama, Al Sarena brought suit against Secretary Chapman to secure its claims. Because of the pending debate on the forest land transfer measure, the company assured the legislator that it did not care which department had jurisdiction because it was not interested in the timber standing on that acreage. Boykin thought that it was to the interest of the Interior Department to review the case in light of their jurisdictional dispute with Agriculture. In April 1950, however, the Forest Service sent over a protest to the Bureau of Land Management which asserted that a check of fifteen of the twenty-three sites in question produced such poor assays of mineral deposits that there was no reason to grant the claims. The next year, Interior's solicitor offered to hold the matter open pending hearings in the field, but the company remained strangely silent. Al Sarena's directors later testified that they believed the Chapman officials were purposely delaying the decision for political reasons. They were thinking about election results.

When McKay became secretary in 1953, he had no personal knowledge of the claims, but his assistants took them up with special zeal. The Bureau of Land Management, according to the head of the Oregon Geological and Mineral Department, had impeded confirmation of the claims by raising legal points pertaining to the timber on the lands. That complaint was sent to Congressman Ellsworth in the course of his work on the forest land transfer bill. It seemed the kind of bureaucratic inequity that the new administration was determined to bring to an end. As part of an effort to clear away 273 such cases pending before the land bureau, Solicitor Davis consulted with Ellsworth and worked out a novel procedure for reappraisal of the Al Sarena claims. By it, the Bureau of Mines (not usually involved in adjudicature) gave the company a chance to confirm its applications. At first rejecting the government's choice of three assayers, the Alabamians selected the services of a company from their own state, a company specializing in timber "cruising" for telephone poles. The newly run assays showed deposits of precious and nonprecious metals in excess of the samples taken by the Forest Service five years earlier.

The Interior Department did not notify the Forest Service of its review, even though it enjoyed much better relations with Agriculture than it had during the Democratic administrations. By failing to send such notification, Davis was technically guilty of ignoring a section of the 1946 statute requiring the bureaus of all departments working on the same matter to share their information with one another. Indeed, this was precisely the law mentioned in the Park Service's earlier complaints about the Bureau of Reclamation's surveys inside the units of the national park system. Davis later testified that he took these actions because he felt that it was wrong for any bureau to be prosecutor, judge, and jury all by itself. That same feeling was held by members of Tudor's team of reorganizers. Finally, after Ellsworth assured him of Al Sarena's reliability, Davis approved the patents at a fee of five dollars an acre in January 1954.

Local residents who were interested in the tracts were soon complaining that the out-of-state company was logging its sites. Eventually, the news reached Drew Pearson who quickly inserted it along with other allegations against the Eisenhower administration in his nationally syndicated column, "Washington Merry Go-Round." In October 1954 Oregon state senator Neuberger referred to the charge during his campaign criticism of Cordon's forest land transfer legislation. Only then did McKay learn of the case and of the decision by his subordinates. When Neuberger took his seat in the United States Senate, he immediately demanded an investigation of the Al Sarena case.

Republicans did not really worry until April 1955, when Pearson thought he found a "Dear Doug" letter involving the president in the affair. Oregon Republican committeemen quickly consulted with McKay, while party and White House officials predictably expressed their confidence in the secretary. The "Dear Doug" letter was not written by Eisenhower, they proved, and some of the photographs taken for Pearson were falsely labeled. The public was nevertheless advised by the Democrats to notice that not one cup of ore had been mined on the Al Sarena tract, but two million board feet of timber indisputably had been cut there. Morse's familiar rhetoric about McKay and Teapot Dome now seemed more than partisan oratory.[28]

The secretary of the Interior did not believe in ghosts, however, and refused to testify before the Senate investigating committee. In a letter to its chairman, Robert Kerr of Oklahoma, he wrote that he had played no personal part in the Al Sarena decision, had taken no action on it, and therefore could tell them nothing at all about it. Instead, Davis, now under secretary, presented them with a lengthy résumé of the case, defended his earlier solicitude for the claimants, and insisted that the department had no legal option but to approve the applications. Whether or not fraud had resulted, he insisted that all legal and customary safeguards had been applied at each step of the way. The presence of national forest timber on the land was not pertinent to the questions he had had to ask as solicitor. He believed that the whole subsequent controversy was based on a willful ignorance of the legal limitations involved. Many observers were unimpressed with this additional example of Interior's strict construction of its own jurisdictions. McKay, some concluded, was a "genial front man who did not know what was going on in the back room" where "earnest and capable men . . . knew precisely what they were doing." The same had been said about Taft and Harding. The secretary insisted that the record spoke for itself; now he was depicted as half-covered by a landslide of damning testimony.[29]

It was the Republicans' turn to cry "witch hunt." In a minority dissent to the committee's report, Senator Barry Goldwater described the Al Sarena charges as nothing more than innuendo and smear tactics. The *Chicago Tribune* said that the investigation was far more base than anything McCarthy had done because it was politically motivated. Davis's logical, responsible defense, the newspaper predicted, would make the whole scheme backfire. But the legalisms of the Interior officials could not distract public attention from the fraudulent consequences of their decisions. Added to the similarly questionable administrative procedures involved in Hells Canyon, Dinosaur, Dixon-Yates, and the D'Ewart appointment, Al Sarena was the proverbial "last straw" on the heap of doubts Democrats had raised in the public mind over the course of three years. Even the most partisan supporters of the president and his administration could see that these instances belied the Republicans' 1952 promise to bring an end to influence peddling and the "mess" in Washington. Speaking from a higher pedestal as defenders of the public interest, the Democratic majority of the Kerr committee warned any who were "dedicated to giving away the natural resources of our Nation" to hesitate before again misusing legal and administrative precepts to cover their machinations. It was hard to miss the implication that those so "dedicated" were Republicans.[30]

Chapter Nine

BATTLE
OF THE
CHAMPIONS

Douglas McKay had decided to resign before the Al Sarena investigation. There were occasional hints in his private correspondence and offhand comments that he meant to leave the cabinet at the end of the first term in January 1957. He wanted to retire to a quiet, nonpolitical existence back at his home in Neskowin, Oregon, where he could spend more time with his children and grandchildren. He was exhausted by three years of controversial decisions and partisan harassment. The sense of obligation to serve the president and the party which had caused him to accept the Interior post now seemed fulfilled. He did not think that the Eisenhower crusade was yet secure, however. Ever since November 1953 he had worried about the need for a second four years to accomplish the restoration of American traditions. If the Republicans lost the coming election in 1956, he predicted, "I feel sure we would be headed for socialism." During the Cordon-Neuberger campaign, friends had urged him to return to active politics by challenging Wayne Morse for the Senate seat two years hence. McKay replied that he would not do it and evidently promised his wife the same thing. But after another year and a half of taking punches from "this bunch of fair deal, new deal socialists," he began thinking about the possibility. The mere idea of beating Morse, the party turncoat and the administration's sharpest critic, was stimulating. Privately, he growled: "brother, how I would like to campaign against that guy."[1]

Morse's expected challenger was McKay's successor, Governor Paul Patterson. Some of the members of both state and national Republican committees feared, however, that he might not be sufficiently strong to defeat Morse. The local party was still rent by the disagreements of 1952 and 1954, while the Democrats had been actively soliciting voters among the newly arrived labor population. Suddenly, illness forced Patterson to withdraw his candidacy and a month later he was dead. The question of a replacement for the Senate race was now critical, and speculation about McKay increased. "Unless you run," friends again pressed him, "some of the lesser aspirants of the Republican Party might obtain the nomination." Shortly afterwards, one such candidate—"lesser" but more liberal—Paul Hitchcock, filed for the Republican primary. A public relations director for Portland's Lewis and Clark College, he had been assured that McKay would not enter the race. There was still no sign of interest in the secretary's statements. A "six year sentence" held no appeal, he wrote privately, and he would not have much influence as a freshman senator anyway. "I am still a Chevrolet dealer at heart," he admitted, and besides, "My wife won't let me." But the question of the Oregon party crisis obviously contributed to his personal tensions during the months of the Al Sarena investigation. Occasionally, he showed flashes of irritation and anger when friends questioned him about department policies. In late January 1956, he returned to Oregon for Patterson's funeral and was cornered by state party leaders who asked him to enter the Senate race. Members of the national committee urged him to do the same when he returned to Washington, D.C. When Secretary Benson was in Spokane a few days later, he told reporters that he thought McKay was the best possible choice to challenge Morse.[2]

The strident attacks by the Democrats, who were now sharpening their weapons for the upcoming election campaigns, acted like acid on McKay's determination. He was ready to do anything to help sustain public confidence in the Eisenhower administration. He certainly had personal reasons to seek vindication of his own policies. Once before, a secretary of the Interior from the Pacific Northwest— Richard Ballinger of Washington—had considered running for the Senate in order to do exactly that. Now as then, the opportunity was especially tempting because the opponent was a party defector and a critic of the incumbent administration. McKay, who had wanted the Cordon-Neuberger contest to be a demonstration of loyalty, realized that the Morse contest would provide an even more striking chance for Oregonians to prove their trust in the Eisenhower policies.[3]

Without telling the secretary, the men at the White House were already gathering opinions on the matter. They agreed that he had been "beaten down badly by the new Dealers" and had lost "considerable prestige" (McKay's description of himself). Even Benson had second thoughts about his earlier statement and decided that it would not be wise for his colleague to enter the campaign. Sherman Adams once more asked for Ralph Cake's opinion. The former national committeeman, now serving as political liaison for the executive staff, did not think that McKay could win. The rumor nevertheless reached Robert Sawyer that Cake had "turned the wheels" for the secretary's candidacy. Cake, Adams, and party chairman Leonard Hall, the story went, met together in late February and early March and made up their minds while McKay was telling the press, "Maybe a few new faces in the Cabinet wouldn't be such a bad idea." McKay's political friends in Oregon, one of his lieutenants remembered, then "put pressure on the White House." On March 7, a few days before the filing deadline in Oregon, Adams and Hall showed McKay a confidential poll taken by the national committee which concluded that he was the only man who could beat Morse. Wisely, they also showed it to his wife, Mabel. Adams promised both of them that there would be no other contenders for the primary nomination, even though he had been told by Cake and state chairman Wyatt that there would be others. He assured them, moreover, that the national party organization would finance both the primary and general campaigns. He undoubtedly added the argument that unless McKay ran, Morse would be reelected and the damage that "fanatic" would do thereafter would make McKay sorry for the rest of his life. It was the same appeal to his sense of duty that had overcome the governor's reluctance to join the cabinet in 1952. It worked again. The morning after the McKays saw the poll, Adams told the president that the secretary would make the race against Morse. Then he told McKay that Eisenhower was pleased by the decision. That same afternoon, the McKays were on a flight to Portland to file before the deadline of the following day.[4]

In retrospect it is difficult to understand the reasoning of the Eisenhower men; it must have been even more difficult for McKay to comprehend at the time. When he arrived at his Portland hotel the next morning, he learned that the field was not clear for him in the Republican primary. What must have been even more alarming to him was the realization that there had been no working communication between the leaders of the state party factions, the Oregon committeemen, and the Republicans at the nation's capital. Wyatt tried to dissuade him from filing, but McKay called Adams long distance. He suggested a retraction of the official announcement of his intention—Mrs. McKay had urged him to demand it—but Adams pointed out that the president would be greatly embarrassed by it and Democrats would take comfort in the confusion. The secretary acquiesced and, predictably, Oregon Democrats accused the White House of throwing him "to the wolves." Wyatt, together with state committeeman Elmo Smith who had conducted McKay's gubernatorial campaigns, vehemently protested to Adams and Hall and demanded to see the poll they had shown the McKays. They were formally advised, however, that the national committee declined to release that document to anyone.[5]

Several other party candidates withdrew from the primary after McKay's arrival, but many Oregon Republicans planned to rally behind Hitchcock, partly out of disgust with this "dictation from Washington, D.C." Their choice for the Senate race had a good record on resource conservation and no stigma attached to him on the subject. He was more attractive locally, moreover, while the secretary had been isolated from the state's problems for three years. The situation cast the actions of Adams and Hall into sharp relief. It appeared that they were trying to kill two birds with one stone: removing the embarrassment of McKay from the administration's neck and slaying the Morse dragon as well. Told of the local dismay, President Eisenhower said it was all a misunderstanding. Admitting that he had not understood the Oregon situation, he tried to smooth ruffled feelings with a private letter to Hitchcock, wishing both candidates a well-waged fight. For McKay, however, he issued a public statement commending him for responding to the call "like a champion" and expecting him to add "a great deal to the working strength we need and must have" to carry out the administration's programs. Thus the second crusade of "dragon slayer" Douglas McKay was shakily launched.[6]

Democrats were amused to see their opponents stumbling over their own feet. They jeered at the decision "superimposed . . . by fiat" and rhetorically asked how Republicans could now talk about the "so-called dictatorship" of Franklin Roosevelt. The most thoughtful comments on McKay's resignation did not repeat the Democrats' accusations of corruption, however, but generally agreed that the action was "no loss to the President or the Country." From the time he had entered the cabinet, the *Denver Post* lamented, he had "flopped futilely around like a Columbia River Chinook salmon on the cannery floor." Even when he had been correct in principle, he was "terribly inept in proving he was right." Whether justly or not, he let himself be identified with "retrenchment, retreat and apology." Under him the Interior Department, that "great western agency," had opposed "legitimate public works which contributed to Western prosperity and national security" during the preceding two decades. The editor concluded that McKay was one of several members of the administration who could not discriminate between "what was good for the West and what was good for the Republican Party." The secretary also received an unkind letter from a self-proclaimed loyal Republican who was "delighted" to see him enter the primary. "This should give my fellow conservationists in Oregon . . . the opportunity to retire to oblivion the greatest 'give away Secretary' the Department has had at least since the late Albert Fall." Morse's phrase was catching on.[7]

The Oregon primary, McKay found, was "a rugged race." He could not bear to criticize his opponent, so he dwelled on principles and abstractions which he thought he could defend better than the other contenders. His ability to do so was acknowledged in congratulatory letters from Attorney General Herbert Brownell, former budget bureau director Joseph Dodge, Senator Goldwater, Herbert Hoover, and radio pundit Paul Harvey. Restore "integrity" to Oregon, they urged, and strengthen "real Americanism" there. The *Idaho Statesman* struck the same note. Everyone who believed "in the American gospel of self-help and freedom of opportunity" would welcome "such an able champion of their cause," one who would seriously challenge the man "so flagrantly opposed to these concepts." Upon launching his campaign, McKay called the election a "showdown" on the question of "whether the President's program is to be jeopardized in the future, as it has been in the past, by those seeking personal gratification and notoriety at the expense of the national welfare." Public versus private power, he insisted, was not at issue. That was a phony part of the "slick propaganda technique I like to call the 'big doubt.'" The innuendo crept a little closer to the McCarthy style: Morse was a man whose ideas were "foreign to our historic traditions and beliefs."[8]

McKay drew upon Eisenhower's popularity in his speeches. The only real issue in the election, he said repeatedly, was: "Do you like Eisenhower or do you like Wayne Morse?" Hitchcock, ignored by his opponent and deprived of official party backing after he remained in the race, did well for practically an unknown amateur. At election time, about 60 percent of the eligible voters turned out to cast a quarter of a million ballots. McKay won, but his margin was only about 24,000. It was hardly a forecast for a mandate in November. Afterward, the winner confessed to Adams that he expected the job of beating Morse would be easier than this awkward primary had been.[9]

In Oregon and across the nation, the Democrats were happier than the Republicans over the outcome. For over a year they had considered Oregon "the most important battleground," as Lyndon Johnson called it. Almost as if they had written the scenario, their *bête noire* now crouched in the arena of a full election campaign, facing their champion gladiator. Their members immediately used their congressional privileges to ridicule the Republicans. Puckish Senator Hubert Humphrey read into the *Congressional Record:*

> Ike loves the name of Doug McKay,
> It rhymes so well with giveaway;
> To elect Wayne Morse would be a sad frustration
> To the Cadillac boys in the Administration.

Their speakers at the national convention in Chicago that August dramatically acknowledged the significance of the state contest. Delivering one of the principal addresses there, Senator Morse declared that his onetime party members had betrayed the principles of Theodore Roosevelt and Gifford Pinchot. He mentioned a warning by Roosevelt that water resources should not "be given away to private individuals," and he informed the audience that Pinchot's widow had endorsed his candidacy. Conservation and resource development, he concluded, were the key issues in the 1956 campaign. From the same rostrum a few days later, former President Truman rated it the "number 1" issue:

> For three and one-half years the Eisenhower Administration has been using every trick and device to pry our water power and our forests, our parks and oil resources out of the hands of the people and put them into the pockets of a few selfish corporations and individuals. . . . If these people are left in control for another four years, our country will have lost its last chance to make the fullest use of its streams and forests, its mountains and plains. Another four years of the Eisenhower Administration and there will not be another dam site left for the people. Now, there is not an "N" in that word. That is a dam site.[10]

The Democrats in Oregon did not talk about abstractions. Instead, they waved the still unresolved implications of the Al Sarena case like "a red rag" before the voters. By the end of the first month of the campaign, McKay admitted to Adams that that issue was hurting him more than any other. The Democrats also made the most of a strike at McKay Chevrolet in Salem. Their publicity, aimed at the already distressed laboring segment of the population, ignored the fact that the secretary had sold his financial and managerial connection in the company to his sons-in-law when he entered the cabinet. Paul Butler, the new chairman of the Democratic National Committee, charged McKay with "union busting," while appropriate cartoons and comments were inserted into local union newsheets. The political action committee of the AFL-CIO also contributed speakers and an unknown amount of money to the campaign.[11]

McKay's friends advised him to take the offensive from the beginning. "This is not a fireside chat but a battle," one wrote. He must avoid the mistake made by Cordon in 1954 and not merely dwell on his opponent's ideology or personality. McKay did not follow this good advice. He was convinced that the voters were just as preoccupied with high ideals as he was and answered Morse's detailed accusations about resource policy with definitions of intentions. As a result, the suspicions concerning possible conspiracy were not dispelled. Some observers concluded that there must be fire in the smoke of the "giveaway" charges. Similarly, McKay's response suggested that he either did not or could not understand the consequences of his department's policies. His image of integrity was also marred when Oregon Republican headquarters distributed a selective compilation of Morse's record, including a photograph cropped without permission from *Life* magazine. The picture showed the senator speaking to an apparently empty chamber as if his colleagues considered him a pariah.[12]

McKay's performance during his campaign differed little from his behavior as a cabinet member. He wanted to show that he was neither a sophisticate nor a snob, but just a hard-working, highly principled businessman. He refused to meet Morse in television debate, preferring to make a few formal appearances by himself. The impression he gave then and in other talks was a genial but unassertive one. He seemed almost too tired for combat, his friends told him. Advised by the White House that all party candidates should concentrate their efforts in marginal areas, rather than cities, McKay toured the many small communities in the state and spent most of his time with civic and business organizations—groups that were most likely to favor him anyhow. When he did go to factories in the urban areas, he told the workers that he had not gone "high hat" on them and then warned them that their unions were abject tools of the labor bosses. Some of his adherents were similarly tactless. The dean of forestry at Oregon State College referred to preservationist critics as "the daffodil wing of nature lovers," a sexual innuendo of the type used against Stevenson in 1952. McKay's demonstrated talent for shooting from the hip also backfired on him. A Democratic "fact sheet" tellingly lined up his pronouncements over the years to show them amusingly inconsistent or inane. The candidate's readiness to label his critics as "socialists" almost provoked a fight with a student on a college campus. These incidents of "unfavorable publicity," as his staff labeled them, helped to dull the shine on his armor.[13]

McKay and his supporters were counting heavily upon the Eisenhower coattails. They soon found out that aid from the White House was agonizingly late and little. Adams's promise of financial help from the national committee proved to be a hollow one. Mabel McKay, working as hard as her husband during these months, complained in no uncertain words to Adams and Hall that they had let the Oregon Republicans down. Their neglect may have been the result of frayed nerves and tensions at the White House during these hectic months of the Suez crisis. Risking further charges of interference, however, the administration dispatched a series of prestigious speakers to the state. In order to demonstrate their stated belief that the election of McKay was second in importance only to the reelection of the president, Vice President Richard Nixon, Secretary Ezra Benson, and Senator William Knowland of California came to praise him. On the specific issues of resource policy, McKay's actions were defended by Howard Pyle of the White House staff and the new secretary of the Interior, Fred Seaton. They denied the allegations of "giveaway" in the matters of Hells Canyon, wildlife refuges, and Al Sarena, emphasized the legal limitations involved in policy decisions, and reiterated that federal action by itself was no solution to power shortages. But the speaker who was needed most did not appear until the middle of October. Months earlier, Eisenhower had assured McKay that he was not forgetting his struggle, but he made an Oregon visit merely part of his own campaign swing through the West. On the way, he inaugurated the Upper Colorado project with a speech at Glen Canyon, extolling it as "a good example of one phase of the partnership principle." In Portland, he made only two references to his former Interior secretary, neither of them very useful. McKay, he said, possessed traits he himself regarded highly: "plain, ordinary integrity—intellectual honesty—honesty with people . . . I was with [him] under these special conditions . . . and I shall always testify to this: Douglas McKay has never pulled his punches on what he believed." A few days later, he added, "It is fun to work with him. It is valuable to work with him."[14]

The man who McKay had called the principal issue of the campaign announced at the outset that the real issue was "the protection of the people's heritage in Oregon's tremendous natural resources and the protection of those resources against the giveaway program of the present administration." Morse and his supporters expected that his opponent would be "extremely vulnerable" on those subjects. Aided by the writings and speeches of Neuberger, they pounded away on the past and potential errors of commission and omission made by Republican resource policy makers. Forester Watts once again took charge of a special committee exposing the sagging condition of the state's lumber industry. (His group was far more aggressive than the dubiously named "Conservationists for McKay.") Former Interior secretary Chapman, now a member of the Democratic National Committee strategy board, and "Jebby" Davidson lent their assistance to Morse as they had to Neuberger. Davidson was also running for a place as state member of the national committee. The most effective advantage enjoyed by the senator was his six-year-old personal organization which included a large following of independents and liberal Republicans.[15]

Morse's performance as a candidate was every bit as self-righteous as McKay's was and he sometimes outdid his opponent in expressing platitudes and trivialities. In contrast to folksy McKay, however, he had a hypnotically attractive delivery that he used effectively in frequent radio and television talks. Just as important, he seemed so much better informed, the master of examples and statistics concerning local problems and the actions of the Republican Congress. He focused the voters' attention on the way in which these factors affected the average man by producing tight credit, mounting unemployment, power shortages, and favoritism of a few enterprisers. As Republicans noted, Morse seemed to relegate the power issue to second place. "He has a new crusade," Pyle informed Adams, ". . . the small mill and timber operator who, I am advised, has been placed in considerable jeopardy" by federal restrictions on storage containers. In fact, Morse put that and all other economic hardships together and explained them as the consequence of Republican cutbacks in spending and construction. The only thriving enterprises in the region, he pointed out, were those monopolies favored by the partnership policy. At last, on November 4, the two champions of principle and the public interest made their final comments. (McKay's was characteristically tactless: "There are more good people in Oregon than bums.") Then they cast their ballots with the other voters.[16]

The overwhelming majority of Americans voted for Dwight Eisenhower and so did the majority of Oregonians. Yet the Democrats' equation of local economic dislocation and the administration's policies proved to have been excellent strategy. Their candidates won three out of four contested congressional races. Both Ellsworth and Coon, successful defenders of partnership two years earlier, were defeated. A Democrat won the governorship, though by a narrow margin; Democrats gained a safe majority in the assembly and an even match in the state senate. Douglas McKay was confident until the last hours that he would win the seat in the United States Senate, but knew that he had lost before he went to bed on election night. Wayne Morse received 54.3 percent of the over 700,000 votes cast in that race, 50,000 more than Neuberger had obtained two years earlier. He took almost every county—and almost won the remaining seven that went to McKay. The latter wryly noted, however, that he won in Morse's home precinct as well as his own.[17]

It was the most dramatic victory for the Democrats in the entire election. But it was more than that. Although Eisenhower's policies had been sustained, they insisted that "Eisenhowerism" had been clearly rejected in the contests for control of Congress. In view of the emphasis put on the Oregon Senate race by both parties, McKay's defeat looked like an undeniable proof of that claim. Naturally, the men at the White House did not agree. "You put up a wonderful fight," the president told his fallen champion, "one which in almost any other circumstance would have assured you overwhelming support." For that effort, done "cleanly and hard and for all you have done—for me and for the Party—you have my lasting and heartfelt appreciation." Wilton "Jerry" Persons, Eisenhower's assistant, wrote less formally. The loss was one of the greatest personal disappointments he had ever suffered, he told McKay. "The failure of the people of Oregon to recognize the wonderful job you have done for them and for the entire country is something which I just can't understand." Some Oregonians thought they understood all too well. "When they sent him back here," one reminded the men at the White House, "it was as if we had to make a Senator of him whether we wanted to or not . . . we rebelled." State chairman Wyatt resisted the great temptation to say "I told you so" and merely repeated that same interpretation. Another Oregonian added the warning that if the party was going to continue such interference, "the grave for the G.O.P. will go deeper with each future election."[18]

Mere factionalism did not give Morse his victory over McKay, of course. The senator had more money to spend, had a better organization, enjoyed the spotlight of national publicity, and had a very visible record as one of the watchdogs of the public interest. By implication, voters doubted that McKay could be any more effective in the Senate than he had been as secretary. A former Oregon governor, Republican Charles Sprague, decided that the defeat was based on McKay's "failure or inability to interpret to the administration the instinct for conservation held throughout the country." Yet most Oregonians, like most Americans, were conservationists only in a vaguely moral and materialistic way. They were proud of the protected parts of their land, but directly dependent upon use of its resources.[19]

More accurately, it can be said that the Democrats harvested seeds of the suspicion that the administration's policies were neither protecting nor equitably developing those resources. The economic downturn in the state was the overwhelming factor, however. The price of wheat had dropped, construction on reclamation and flood control projects had slowed, conditions in the lumbermills and forests had worsened. Even with an Oregon businessman at the helm of the Interior Department, water and power development in the state was at a level far below the record of previous Democratic administrations. During the Roosevelt and Truman eras, a large number of construction workers and contractors had come to participate in building these federal projects and the local facilities engendered by them. This working population, McKay agreed, was the primary factor in his defeat. "I guess we have too many industries," he explained to Edgar Eisenhower, the president's elder brother who lived in Tacoma, Washington. "Now we are paying the penalty by becoming a New Deal state." The influx of labor unions had strengthened Democratic support and widened the voter's receptivity to what Republicans called "socialism." The AFL-CIO committee on political action and its "army of outside labor organizers," McKay's friends believed, could be given "the lion's share of the credit" for Morse's victory.[20]

Could the success of the Democrats elsewhere be similarly explained? They obviously had been unable to make Adlai Stevenson look any more "western" in 1956 than he had looked in 1952. His campaign references to the "giveaways" were not couched in Truman-like phrases of indignation, but sounded like mere echoes of the criticisms which Senate Democrats had been making for three years. The Republicans had tried to deemphasize the resource issue by removing the platform planks of four years earlier and substituting a brief praise of their actions in that field as "one of the brightest areas of achievement and progress." Indeed, they accused the Democratic Congress of shelving part of the UCB project without mentioning that the shelved part was the dam in Dinosaur National Monument. Their administration also had insured for future generations access to the kind of wilderness environment known to the pioneers—perhaps a reference to "Mission 66." Eisenhower issued attestations to his "deep and lifelong interest" in conservation. Perhaps because his aides calculated that the issue might affect the election, he made public a last-minute response to a letter from Horace Albright which defended the party's past contributions to that policy. "I was brought up close to the soil of the State of Kansas," he said, "and my boyhood experiences taught me many of the principles of true conservation." The president was satisfied that plain statements made without exaggeration would offset the melodramatic effusions of polemicists. Of course, few voters believed that he was personally involved in any of the "giveaways" described by the Democrats.[21]

At the state level, Democratic victories in the West seemed to confirm their interpretation of the elections as a rejection of Republican resource policies. In Colorado, Dan Thorton failed to win a United States Senate seat, and in Montana, Wesley D'Ewart was defeated in a bid for the gubernatorial nomination. Republican Stalwart Herman Welker of Idaho naturally defended the Hells Canyon decision and opposed the federal high dam legislation proposed by the Democrats. Described by members of his own party as a lazy and undependable candidate, he was defeated by vigorous, articulate Frank Church who tellingly dissected inconsistencies and deviousness in the Hells Canyon matter. That same November, indefatigable Gracie Pfost was reelected to a third term in Congress. Spokane newspapers were appalled when Congressman Walt Horan supported Neuberger's bill for the high dam. One editor who admired him personally warned that no Democratic or independent votes could be won over by that stand, nor any from apathetic Republicans. "Don't sacrifice a GOP seat and House seniority on a damfool proposition like the Hells Canyon bill this year." The prediction was evidently wrong because Horan was endorsed by some Democrats and won reelection.[22]

The contest that appeared to be almost as significant as the McKay-Morse battle was the attempt by Washington Governor Arthur Langlie to win the seat in the Senate held by Democrat Warren Magnuson. Like his Oregon friend, Langlie found himself in a particularly uncomfortable situation. He had support from predictable segments of voters: those who hoped he would help turn back the "socialist philosophy" of increasing federal land ownership, aides who urged him to seek a central course "between the extreme of ultra conservation and those who would go overboard on industrial development," and other well-wishers who lamented the way in which he would have to bear "burdens not of your own making" in defending McKay's resource policies. Even Horan, his friend and colleague in the fight against CVA, felt that Langlie's public opposition to the federal plan for Hells Canyon and his failure to provide "adroit leadership" in a state partnership program would contribute to his defeat. The governor had been debating these issues with Magnuson since 1955, but polls taken at that time indicated that he did not have nearly as much support as the senator, whose seniority and defense of the interests of labor and the consumer were highly regarded. Washington Republicans advised the men in the White House of this fact, but they applied the same reasoning to Langlie as they had used in the case of McKay. Because party leaders indicated that the president would like him to contest the Senate seat, the governor agreed to try.[23]

Like McKay, Langlie faced factionalism within the Republican ranks when those in the eastern part of the state, traditionally conservative in persuasion, expressed resentment over his connection with the Eisenhower wing of the party. Almost as much as McKay, Langlie also ran into the full force of the Democrats' "giveaway" campaign. It did no good for him to trim his sails. Asked about his earlier advocacy of ski facilities in Mount Rainier National Park, he unctuously replied that they were not desirable "unless it can be demonstrated that wise conservation is absolutely protected . . . I would certainly not want to disturb the status quo." Some voters were not convinced by the rhetoric. "Governor Langlie does not represent us," one of them informed Horan, ". . . in fact we feel that he wants to cut up our Olympic National Forest and hand over all our timber, water and other natural resources to private industries. We feel that all our natural resources are God given and should be developed for the good of all of the people for this, and future generations. . . . P.S. This is not Socialism, it is Christian." As they had done for McKay, Seaton and Eisenhower came to Washington late in the campaign and defended Langlie's views and his sincerity. A large majority of the voters there decided that Magnuson had more to offer.[24]

After his defeat, Langlie ruefully recalled the precampaign polls which indicated that partnership was not yet accepted in the state. It was, he admitted, a "pretty difficult bill of goods to sell." It was a sound idea, but it had not been clarified or extended enough to encompass the region's power needs for the next decade. The average citizen, moreover, still did not understand the problems involved in favoring the Bureau of Reclamation over the Army Corps of Engineers in construction of power projects. One of Horan's constituents even doubted that there was any comprehension at the grassroots level of the highly publicized Hells Canyon controversy. He claimed that Senators Jackson and Magnuson had been elected handily by referring to the issue dramatically, but "more frequently than not" the voters had "no idea who was building Hells Canyon, where it was located and only a vague memory that they had heard something of a controversy over the project."

This cynical assessment seemed confirmed by a survey conducted in the western part of Washington by the Elmo Roper organization. Those questioned had indicated that they favored partnership to either government domination or private monopoly by three to one yet had voted Democratic by nearly the same margin. The Washington Water Power Company of eastern Washington took another sample and reported that only one third of the voters questioned in both Columbia River states could correctly identify the position of Eisenhower or Stevenson on water power policy. Fewer than one third knew Magnuson's position on that subject, and no more than 16 percent claimed that the issue had influenced their decision in the Senate race.[25]

Republicans in the Pacific Northwest and at the White House spent several months at this postmortem task. It was "realistically evident," the *Idaho Statesman* asserted, that election setbacks in Oregon, Washington, Idaho, Montana, and Colorado necessitated an administration reappraisal of its resource policies. Bitterly, it added that the paper could not continue to fight for irrigation in Idaho if the voters themselves had "thrown in the sponge" and elected Democrats. Wyatt of Oregon disagreed completely with the assumption that the power issue was the cause of party defeats. The issue of public or private power was so old in the Northwest, he told Adams, that "it is virtually dead and I do not believe that the High Hells Canyon decision or any other over-all policy of this Administration had any effect on the outcome of the election. Certainly the effect was negligible, if felt at all."[26]

At the White House, Howard Pyle tried to resolve the question once and for all. A public relations firm was hired to take a poll among voters in Oregon. Their subsequent report confirmed the other claims that no one really knew what partnership was or what had been accomplished under it. Less than half the voters questioned were able to define Morse's position on that subject, and only 22 percent knew McKay's. While most of them wanted less federal domination in power administration, most of them also voted for Morse. Indeed, in the county adjacent to Hells Canyon they voted heavily Democratic for every office on the ticket and gave a majority to Eisenhower at the same time.[27]

Republicans evidently did not consider the implication of these polls as they reflected on their beliefs in the grass roots. They were sufficiently satisfied that labor unions, not partnership, had caused voters to reject their candidates in the West. Their thoughts were well expressed by a letter received from a supporter in the Pacific Northwest: "Please! Do not 'revise' your policies on natural resources. They were sound, businesslike, and will produce the greatest good for all the people. We are working together and only need a little more time to prove that Partnership will work." When asked earlier by the press corps what he thought the influence of the power issue had been on the primary elections, Eisenhower replied that he had no opinion. His own overwhelming victory in November, his lieutenants believed, proved that Americans had not accepted the innuendos of the "giveaway" campaign. McKay had lost because Oregon had become "a New Deal state," not because he had a bad record as secretary of the Interior.[28]

In retrospect, however, the Eisenhower administration's political reasoning in 1956 must be described as myopic. The Republicans had encouraged public trust in their good intentions and had assumed that the people would express their satisfaction with the gradual, practical fulfillment of those promises. Yet they chose as their principal spokesman for resource policies a man who was unable to sell the partnership emphasis because of his own shortcomings and because of the limitations placed on his department by the policy makers at the White House. They had underestimated the depth and potential impact of the charges leveled against him and had overestimated the effectiveness of the president's personal integrity on local opinion. Perhaps they had not yet come down from the lofty heights of self-righteousness caused by the mandate of 1952. But their miscalculation had had cruel results in the West. Oregon Republican Charles Sprague said that the whole sad story of McKay's crusade reminded him of a joke. A man was hanging from a window in a burning building while his friends on the ground shouted up at him: "Jump! We gotta blanket, we'll catch you!" It was funny. "You know those guys didn't have no blanket."[29]

Epilogue

RIGHT MAN
ON THE
LID?

After Douglas McKay resigned as secretary of the Interior, the White House men quietly but pointedly hung a sign on the department policies reading: "under new management." They had to tread carefully in choosing a successor and do nothing that would lend credence to the Democratic charge that McKay had been "thrown to the wolves" in Oregon in order to remove the "giveaway" stigma from the administration. Nor could they appear to bow to their critics by appointing a man whose views would be a marked change from the partnership emphasis. As the president told the press in June 1956, their paramount purpose was to find a man who would be "the most effective in the position." The West once again asserted its traditional claim on the secretaryship of the Interior Department. Milward Simpson of Wyoming asked McKay to press that demand before he left office, and thirteen senators petitioned the president to recognize it. The usual newspaper speculation mentioned the governors of Wyoming, Montana, and even Oregon again. Langlie, the odds-on favorite in 1952, would have been a likely selection had he not already agreed to run for the Senate. Even the suggestion upset local preservationists who remembered his part in the Olympic National Park boundary review three years earlier. "How could such a biased man become the head of the National Park Service as Secretary of the Interior?" one wondered. "Everything the people of this area and the nation have fought for for so many years would be jeopardized." Former Idaho governor Len Jordan was also a possible choice, but his ties with the Hells Canyon issue made some state Republicans believe the choice would be "in the nature of a red flag in a bull's face."[1]

McKay wanted Under Secretary Clarence Davis to succeed him. The Nebraskan's familiarity with the matters being considered by the department and his outspoken defense of the administration's resource policies, the retiring secretary believed, made that choice most desirable. It also could demonstrate the White House's confidence in McKay's conduct of those policies. Because of Davis's part in the Al Sarena case, it would have been surprising indeed if he had been named to the post. McKay was able to round up support for his candidacy from a few party stalwarts, senators, and members of bar associations—but noticeably not from Nebraskans close to the White House. The latter, Ralph Tudor grumbled, were trying to make Davis look like a conservative and a reactionary and were evidently successful at convincing Sherman Adams of that image. Moreover, Civil Defense Administrator Val Peterson, former governor of that state, was reportedly again seeking the appointment. Tudor tried to drum up opposition to him from California Republicans. McKay sadly concluded that the selection of Davis did not seem to be "in the cards."[2]

Eisenhower had to assure the press that he was personally spending "days and nights" on the problem. Several difficulties were involved in getting "exactly the right man for such a post." In the careful deliberations at the White House it became clear that Pyle favored Davis but that Adams argued for "a complete change of management" at Interior. Pyle was worried about the way Davis's rejection would reflect on McKay's campaign for the Senate. "If I were the opposition," he explained to Adams, "I would move quickly to describe this as a repudiation of everything Doug has stood for." Indeed, that is how several Democratic newspapers referred to the matter.[3]

Perhaps the discussion about Nebraskans brought the president's thoughts around to Fred Seaton, Adams's assistant and White House liaison man for Interior affairs. Implying that he had found his "most effective" man, Eisenhower announced that Seaton would become the new secretary of the Interior. Owner of a chain of newspapers in Nebraska and surrounding states, Seaton had served briefly as senator in 1952, earning the praise of colleagues including Democrat Paul Douglas of Illinois. He joined the Eisenhower team as assistant secretary of state and then, in February 1955, became special assistant to Adams. In that place he was soon recognized as one of the "practical politicians" who were "running the White House." Adams considered him the "best member of his crew," according to other aides, and had mixed feelings about losing his assistant. Younger than McKay and as handsome as the latter was homely, he was as big and congenial as Julius Krug. His talents as a liaison man for the department had earned McKay's gratitude during the tense months of controversy over the UCB legislation and the D'Ewart nomination. After he took over the Interior command, he had gone out to the Pacific Northwest to defend his predecessor's policies. Democrats and some of McKay's adherents were nevertheless doubtful that he would continue the course set by McKay.[4]

Seaton had the difficult task of satisfying both the Democrats who would determine resource legislation during his tenure as secretary and his own party members who had defended the Eisenhower-McKay emphasis during the preceding three years. The first step in that undertaking was to satisfy the Senate Interior Committee at its hearings on the nomination. Chairman James Murray showed him every courtesy and encouraged him to present his own defense. Both Richard Neuberger and Joseph O'Mahoney questioned him closely about his attitude toward Hells Canyon, but Seaton would not let them intimidate him. He indicated that he was "absolutely" in favor of the public preference clause in power contracts and by no means opposed to public power wherever the local populace wanted it to go. He was, however, wary of the philosophy that the federal government should undertake all power development. Quite wisely, the committee members also wanted to know who his assistants would be. Afterward, public comment about the appointment was heartening for the administration. Senator Morse pronounced it "excellent"; preservationists withheld final judgment but assumed that nobody could be as great a disaster as McKay had been; Republicans were relieved to have a new chance to prove their dependability. As one cartoonist pictured it, a "new tree doctor" would try to heal the controversy-torn trunk of natural resources. Because Seaton shared the president's initial intention of having the federal government share a portion of its responsibility with the states—the first definition of partnership—some observers thought they noticed a modification of the McKay-Tudor later version of partnership as letting local, private facilities do everything except projects that only the government could do. Some of this judgment came from McKay's partisans who were still in the department. They obviously missed their accessible and undemanding old chief. Interior had "shifted about 90 degrees," one grumbled, the day that the new secretary took over. "You know in which direction."[5]

McKay's supporters also expected that the pack of Democrats and conservationist hounds would not be satisfied until the new broom had swept all the way toward the New Deal philosophy. Writing from the refuge of the forced vacation Oregon's voters had given him, McKay refused to believe that his old colleague would shift direction of federal power policy or that the president would tolerate any change. If he were still in office, McKay wrote to frienids, he "would stand and fight on what is right as we have already gone too far down the road toward socialism." Perhaps the most welcome sign that such worn-out phantoms had been replaced by practical thinking was shown in a speech Seaton gave several years earlier, a statement which was read into the record of his nomination hearings by Senator Murray. "It does us no good whatever at the polls," he had reminded fellow Republicans at Topeka, Kansas, "to cry 'Socialism' every time a measure is offered to combat or correct an evil . . . nor is it socialism to conserve our natural resources, to build dams. . . ." Such a nondoctrinaire attitude, the *Washington Post* later observed, was "a good quality in a Secretary of the Interior." Even the formerly critical *Denver Post* was encouraged. Seaton's pragmatic approach represented "a needed fresh viewpoint . . . he is not knowingly allied with the Keystone cops who work overtime guarding the nation against the twin evils of 'creeping socialism' and public power."[6]

Seaton was as cautious and deliberate about choosing his lieutenants as the White House had been about choosing him—and for the same reasons. He had known McKay's men during the preceding years and had assessed their abilities. He has asked most of them to remain at first. Some, like Davis, preferred to leave after the new secretary began his own full tenure in January 1957. Another Nebraskan, George Abbott, became assistant secretary in charge of public land matters. Aandahl stayed on, as did Woozley at the Bureau of Land Management. The men in the Technical Review Section remained to provide continuity in procedure and substance. Wirth continued to direct the National Park Service, perhaps realizing that his position was as important—and certainly more comfortable—as it had been during the Dinosaur controversy. Naturally, Seaton brought in several assistants of his own. One of them, Floyd Dominy, a plain-spoken engineer who respected preservationist values became commissioner of the Bureau of Reclamation.

Seaton's indispensable man was Elmer Bennett of Colorado. A protégé of Senator Eugene Millikan—the connection at first worried preservationists—he had been a legislative counsel in the department's solicitor's office since 1953. His work there involved the creation of an interdepartmental committee to study with the states the problems of jurisdiction over federal reserves and guidance of the vexatious UCB legislation through its final stages. When Seaton was appointed secretary, Bennett became his personal assistant. A year later, he took the "mean job" of department solicitor and, in September 1958, was the widely praised choice to be under secretary of the Interior. At every point in his service, he allayed the worries of those who feared the presence of a Colorado man, those who questioned his sympathies for the "land grabbers" or his objectivity on the Upper Colorado project. Bennett admittedly shared traditional western concern for the rights of resource users; he supported Barrett's bill to make water use laws more equitable. But he was also aware of the sensitivity of conservation organizations to every matter affecting land and resource use. He worked closely with his chief to make it a departmental procedure to inform and consult these organizations in every matter of appointments and relations with the western states. When, for example, a water conference was held in Colorado in 1958, Bennett warned the sponsors that the absence of sessions on wildlife and recreational use of water would confirm conservationists' opinion that the states were indifferent to these subjects. He urged them to deal directly with the issues and thereby promote sounder federal recognition of state water policies. Like Seaton, he quickly compiled a "tremendous record of good will and efficiency" and won the good wishes of men as diverse as Albright, Brower, Persons, and D'Ewart.[7]

It was D'Ewart's presence in the department which gave Seaton his first problem. The same month he assumed the secretaryship, McKay's appointee appeared before the Senate Interior Committee to officially endorse chairman Murray's resolution for a fiftieth anniversary commemoration of the inauguration of federal resource conservation. Again, it was his old enemy who sat at the head of the table when the committee took up the subject of confirmation of the appointment a few weeks later. The questioning necessarily came around to the subject of the 1954 Senate campaign in Montana. D'Ewart denied that the red smear had been made in that contest with his personal knowledge. He insisted that he had refused to use the red-baiting literature himself—and then promised his inquisitors that he would never do it again. Meanwhile, Montanans were engaged in an argument to establish whether their man was needed to influence Interior policy the "proper" way, or whether his presence would be a danger in view of his earlier part in the "giveaway" legislation. Murray was not influenced by either camp or by Seaton's endorsement, preferring instead to extinguish his onetime detractor with a quiet parliamentary maneuver. When Barrett, Watkins, Dworshak, and Goldwater asked him to call the committee into session to vote on reporting the nomination to the Senate, Murray replied that it was already in session but, because he had other business to attend to, it was not convening. Montanans threatened political revenge at the November elections, but Murray would not move. Finally, he asked Senator Anderson of New Mexico to take the chair in his absence, but Anderson declined to call the committee into session on the D'Ewart appointment before Congress adjourned that summer.[8]

It was not an auspicious beginning for the new secretary, but it was quickly forgotten. Seaton soon established a favorable public record in handling the explosive problems he had inherited from McKay. His undramatic but firm approach and the greater confidence he received from the White House advisers enabled him to earn for the department the accolades of "new look" and "goodbye giveaway." He followed Pyle's suggestions concerning solicitude for local pride in the West. For example, stockmen were not the villains that government experts said they were. On the other hand, his former associates at the president's office kept him mindful of minor matters that could turn into political dynamite. He did not respond to a request from the Wyoming Development Commission for the transferral of certain federal holdings to the state. Similarly, he placed a hold order on proposed sale of timber from the Klamath Indian Reservation in Oregon, stating that it would not be done until the lumber market improved. Obviously, he understood that procedural decisions on minor matters might arouse the conservation watchdogs as much as larger subjects.[9]

The development of water and power was the paramount problem of Seaton's tenure, just as it had been for his immediate predecessors. Public power advocates had hoped that Seaton's appointment would put an end to Interior's "warfare" against federal programs. Hells Canyon's proponents immediately launched another effort to get their bill through Congress, but, in the face of "tremendous White House pressure," it was again unsuccessful. When the Democrats retained their control of Congress in the election of 1956 and returned to Washington convinced that the voters had thereby called for a reversal of Republican policies, Interior officials expected a rough time ahead. "I don't know," Bennett wrote to his mentor, Millikan, ". . . but I rather imagine that this will be a year filled with politics of the sort which only a Neuberger or a Morse can generate." That feeling was somewhat mutual; Neuberger considered Bennett "one of the principal spokesmen for this reckless approach to water-resources" and had objected to his confirmation as solicitor.[10] Ever since the campaign of 1956, Democrats had been using the power issue as a rallying cry. Oregon's congresswoman, Edith Green, called it "a symbol of democracy" where fifty years of tradition in federal resource regulation had "come to trial in a test to determine whether natural resources are a national asset or a private windfall." Partnership, said Montana's Senator James Murray, was obviously a giveaway. Clair Engle of California insisted that the outcome of the congressional elections was a mandate for the federal emphasis in power development. As soon as the 1957 session began, the two Oregon senators reintroduced their bill to authorize the high dam at Hells Canyon. The publicity that accompanied it, which Republicans described as "no-holds-barred distortions," made some observers conclude that the sponsors were more interested in keeping Hells Canyon as a political issue than they were in developing water and power. Congressman A. L. Miller of Nebraska, former chairman of the House Interior Committee, called the scheme "a Socialistic brain-storm" and Jack Westland of Washington received assurance from the White House that the president was even more convinced that the partnership emphasis involved in the Idaho Power Company contract was sound.[11]

Seaton's Interior Department defended the stand taken by Tudor and Davis three years earlier, but avoided the way in which their interpretation of limited jurisdiction had contributed to the Democrats' charge of "giveaway" conspiracy. The three-year-old commitment to the IPC could not be canceled without extensive loss of material and investment. The Hells Canyon bill was "little short of expropriation" and a bad precedent that would haunt federal water projects for years to come. Seaton personally preferred a moratorium on any further Snake River dams, but he shrewdly waited to see whether Congress would approve funds for these new units. Rather than leaving the decisions to the Federal Power Commission, as McKay had done, Seaton warned them not to issue a license for another single-purpose project to Hells Canyon. The administration certainly could not afford the distribution of a second Hells Canyon controversy. At the same time, Seaton also recommended the authorization of John Day Dam on the Columbia as a federal undertaking.[12]

Some observers thought these actions were betrayals of the McKay policies, while others believed Seaton was trying to head off a congressional revolt against the administration. "It looks like everybody is playing politics with Hells Canyon," Horan lamented. In fact, many legislators opposed the Morse-Neuberger bill because they felt that western water power development had already received its share of appropriations. O'Mahoney and Watkins wanted the money to go to the UCB project, while other senators were seeking an increase in military spending. Administration officials noted with relief that Democrats were "staying away in droves" whenever the Interior committee voted on the bill. It was not accepted by either house by the end of the session. The following year, Neuberger revived the corpse of CVA. Seaton was just as opposed to that plan as he had been in 1956 when he had promised: "So long as I am Secretary of the Interior Department it will never attempt to impose a basin wide authority on any section of the country."[13]

Like the revival of the Hells Canyon issue, the still-running sore of Dinosaur National Monument put Seaton into another difficult predicament. Before the UCB bill was passed and signed in April 1956, the harmony brought about by the Denver resolution was shattered by persistent rumors that developers still meant to use the sites in the preserve. An engineer from the Bureau of Reclamation reportedly claimed: "We'll have Echo Park absolutely within the next ten years." The Sierra Club found that some Utah officials were "surer now than ever before" that the dams there would be restored to the project. Moreover, the new governor there was George Clyde, former state water engineer in the Lee administration. The preservationists had promised to support the bill so they had to devise some other strategy for heading off the new threat. That same April, Neuberger offered an amendment to the "Mission 66" appropriation measure which would give full national park status to Dinosaur. The item was withdrawn after a flurry of objections from those who had opposed the excluding of the sites from the project. Two months later, Republican John Saylor and Democrat Wayne Aspinall of Colorado jointly sponsored a bill for the creation of Dinosaur National Park.[14]

Seaton was wary at first. Departmental approval of the measure, he knew, would facilitate passage of appropriations for the National Park Service. It would also enable the Eisenhower administration to create the first national park in almost twenty years. He also knew that the president was almost desperately trying to secure funding for the UCB project. Some Republicans, moreover, thought that the park bill was merely Democratic blackmail. There was a hint in the air that its approval would guarantee easy going for the basin appropriations. Seaton was not intimidated by this, nor did he repeat McKay's error of precipitously rejecting the possible subterfuge. The Park Service had unilaterally endorsed the measure, he noticed, and the Bureau of Reclamation had issued an expected protest. Seaton had no intention of getting caught in bureaucratic crossfire as McKay had been. Departmental approval of the bill, he announced, would be contingent upon its clear definition of jurisdiction over the area. Saylor, annoyed by the insistence that procedure was the first concern, wondered if the new secretary was just a shrewder McKay. When Congress adjourned that summer, the Dinosaur park bill was still in committee.[15]

In the spring session of 1957 the legislators returned to their dilemma of UCB funding and Dinosaur. A promising first step was a measure appropriating four million dollars for construction of roads and facilities at the monument. Now Utahans and Coloradans began arguing over whose state should have the preserve's headquarters. Colorado's new Republican senator, Gordon Allott, reintroduced the Saylor-Aspinall bill—and a motion was immediately made for inclusion of water development in the new park. The National Parks Association protested that any bill with such a provision would be unacceptable to preservationist organizations. Several of the latter objected to that claim, however, arguing that it would ruin the chance of getting the park at all. "The word will pass like wildfire," a Sierra Club member wrote,"—and it has already started—that conservationists don't want a Park, they want a fight." It began to look as if these organizations could only work together in the face of a threat to reduce the system but could not retain that unity in order to enlarge it. Similarly, the list of senators for and against the bill ominously resembled the division during the battle to exclude Echo Park. Watkins even objected to the inclusion motion because it implied that there was no such provision in the proclamation of 1938. By now, Seaton was personally interested in securing a Dinosaur National Park, partly as a means of recovering the department's and the administration's prestige. He suggested to the proponents of the bill that the best way to persuade Watkins and others was to point out the immediate economic advantages to their area. Wirth was not convinced that the time was exactly right for taking a final step. Until it was, he advised the preservationists, they must keep their strategy confidential.[16]

The possibility that another long deadlock would bottle up further UCB legislation was an irritating thought for the Eisenhower lieutenants. The issue, they feared, could reopen barely healed wounds of the attacks directed against McKay's policies. After Congress adjourned without acting on the Allott bill, Seaton announced that Interior would not approve any measure that violated the principle of the national parks. Potential water sites must be excluded from the preserve or specifically authorized as part of the UCB project. As he shrewdly expected, the preservationists could not approve of any subtraction from the park, nor could they correctly accuse the secretary of betraying the principle of inviolability. Indeed, they were so confused by the situation that they suddenly withdrew support from the Allott bill and tried to have a substitute introduced. By that time, moreover, the primary purpose of their organizations was to obtain passage of a Wilderness bill, an expansion of federal wilderness preserves in addition to the national parks. The long controversy over Dinosaur had given great impetus to that proposal; now it threatened to impede its fulfillment. As a result, the park bill was tabled while the Wilderness measure was advanced.[17]

Congress approved funding of the UCB that year, but two more years would pass before another Dinosaur National Park bill was introduced. It was immediately opposed by both Utah senators, Republican Wallace Bennett and Democrat Frank Moss. They in turn were charged with bad faith and bad judgment for still wanting dams in Dinosaur. The compromise of 1955, the *Denver Post* claimed, had embodied the agreement that the basin states would wait twenty-five or forty years until the four large dams were completed before the Dinosaur project would be reviewed. Saylor also accused Seaton of "sitting on the Dinosaur report," an unjust criticism that made the secretary "most unhappy." Delays had not originated in Interior, he replied. The department still thought that the monument was "eminently suitable" for full park status and had directed the Park Service to draw up proposed boundaries. But this time he insisted on clear definition of potential use through the insertion of the following clause into the bill: "Any portion of the lands and interest in lands comprising Dinosaur National Park shall be made available upon Federal statutory authorization for public non-park uses when such uses shall be found, in consideration of the public interest, to have a greater public necessity than the uses authorized in this Act."[18]

Both sides of the controversy accused Seaton of acting cynically and deviously, but he was in fact acting realistically. As he explained to Utah state officials, there was no immediate need for a dam in Dinosaur and it would be very unwise to try to restore it to the basin project "particularly in view of the past controversy." If the public ever decided it was necessary, then its construction would be supported. Until then, the department would not disturb "the present situation" concerning exclusion of water development, and monument status would be retained. In Congress, developers were busy inserting reservoir and canal sites into the park bill, and preservationists were busy deleting them. Meanwhile, the Park Service used its "Mission 66" funds to purchase additional acreage for roads, camps, and trails and planned each of these improvements after preliminary consultation with Utah and Colorado officials. Dinosaur retained the wilderness character which preservationists had fought to save, yet it was obviously an accessible attraction and a permanent stimulus to the economy of the border area.[19]

Seaton proved that he was an eminently practical defender of the park system in other cases. Undeterred by the department's discouraging decisions of the Chapman and McKay years, Montanans again sought approval of Glacier View dam. Seaton's response to that pressure was the same as his cautionary explanation to the basin state officials: it was unnecessary and politically unwise. Advised that the waters of the UCB project were backing up and threatening other national monuments in Utah, the department quietly constructed barriers and diversion tunnels and planned to raise the water level of the existing dam units. Developers objected that these projects might jeopardize the feasibility of the entire program and sought legislation which would prohibit use of UCB funds for such purposes. The subsequent debate over priorities in the basin would run on for another decade. Wavering by Republicans also proved embarrassing when the administration recommended a cut in its own "Mission 66" budget in 1958. Referring to the legislative obsession with weapons programs, one Montana newspaper sarcastically commented that if it were renamed "Missile 66" it could get all the money it needed. Because of the determination of Senator Murray's committee majority, however, the Senate increased the authorized budget from 12.4 million dollars to 24 million.[20]

These small differences did not touch the image that Seaton had
with both parties in Congress. Both Democrats and Republicans
preferred the refreshing presence of a competent caretaker in Interior
after the series of controversial secretaries. Seaton did not have the
power that Ickes had, nor did he face the hostility that McKay
encountered. Although he did not launch new programs, his contribution was substantial. He enabled members of an administration
that was naive—even hostile—toward resource policy to find the most
effective way of making sound policy. The Eisenhower men knew
they could rely on his tactful interpretation of procedure and his
estimate of partisan or preservationist publicity. As a result, they
abandoned the wishful political ideology and unilateral decisions that
had brought the "giveaway" brand down on their hides. Early in his
tenure, Seaton said that it was "impossible for any Secretary of the
Interior to win, politically," consequently "any temptation to resort to
political expediency is removed." Yet in a certain sense he did win
politically by enabling his party's administration to regain public
trust. Indeed, he tried to enhance its appeal in the election of 1960
by calling for a "Mission 66" whereby the Bureau of Land Management could develop recreation sites, and a "Mission 76" to provide
federal assistance to the states for their own park and recreation
programs. Seaton's contribution to the best interests of the administration and the party earned him recognition at the Republican National
Convention that July, where he was mentioned as a likely candidate
for the vice presidential nomination.[21]

It would be easy to leap to the assumption that the change from
McKay to Seaton—or from Krug to Chapman—made all the difference
in the acceptance of proposed resource policy. Yet the real forces at
work shown by this narrative had their starting point with the question:
did it make any difference who was "sitting on the lid" as policy maker?
Each of the Interior secretaries expressed in his policies and programs
the needs and issues of his own time. Each of them faced the same
variety of pressures and problems. Harold Ickes was able to stand
especially tall because of the informed support of a powerful president and a host of skilled publicists—development men such as
Michael Straus and preservationists such as Irving Brant. While he
was personally committed to the cause of the latter, he greatly
enhanced the influence of the former because the emphasis on development contributed to his inveterate empire building. When Truman
appointed Julius Krug, and when Krug relied upon "Jebby" Davidson

as well as Straus, that emphasis was so valued by the people and their representatives in Congress that the administration was willing to weaken the Ickes legacy in preservation, at least so far as Dinosaur was concerned. Upon reviewing the momentum of that controversy, an observer may justly wonder whether other "bones" might have had to give way to "farms" had Truman's troubles not overwhelmed him. Krug's technical experience was needed in that administration's early phase. When the fight for CVA was blocked, when bureaucrats compromised and when the Korean conflict precluded all priorities, the Interior Department needed the political juggler, Oscar Chapman.

The Republicans increased the burden carried by McKay and Seaton by promising to restore resource policy to the popular tradition of economic opportunity. Douglas McKay epitomized the righteous determination of his president as much as Ickes had, but as part of the Eisenhower spirit he spurned the publicity and political sophistication that had contributed so effectively to the success of the Democrats. He seemed to epitomize the new broom image early in 1953, but within a year he represented neither the aspirations of men like Barrett in Congress nor the proud managers at the White House. After the former had been ignored and the latter had come forward as guardians of the "Great Crusade," good intentions were no longer sufficient. Once events had shown the paramountcy of shrewd insight, then a Seaton became essential. Like Chapman, his task was not to strike out in a new direction, but to maintain a reasonable compromise between intentions and reality.

In every case, the record of the secretaries was largely determined by the ambitions of their lieutenants. Whether they were preservationists or developers, Democrats or Republicans, they were all more royalist than the king. Davidson was as impervious to suggestions from outsiders for compromise over CVA as Tudor was to suggestions from informed critics of the UCB. Indeed, for all the technological sophistication claimed by each, both were equally blind to any more profound basis for using the natural environment. They readily dismissed the arguments for delay and a more enlightened long-term policy as the schemes of political detractors or the hair-brained visions of the "butterfly" organizations. Several scientists at the time lamented that such controversies as Hells Canyon and Dinosaur indicated a "serious defect" in the federal system and revealed that the proper relationship between science and public policy was still a distant one.[22] Although their appeal occurred during the first phase of the long debate over national security, it came before the advent of Sputnik. As the Dinosaur decision showed, the bureaucrats of both Democratic and Republican administrations drew upon technological advantages only for political purposes. These makers of federal resource policy were preoccupied with traditional concern for economic statistics and political rewards.

That tradition was more decisive than the person of the man "sitting on the lid." When viewed from the White House, there was more continuity between the Truman and Eisenhower administrations than the public comprehended. Both presidents were committed to wide-ranging programs for the development of resources. Both were old-style populists who believed in the greatest possible short-term growth for the largest number of people, whether participants or recipients. Both assumed that they had a mandate to pursue their respective programs. Both were evidently mistaken about the constancy of public expectations and about the possibility of translating generalized yearnings into support for specific legislation. Indeed, although each political party benefited from the mistakes of the other, each assumed that those mistakes would not work the same way against themselves. Thus, the Democrats put on the mantle of Provider and smugly observed how the partisan stinginess of the Republicans on reclamation and power contributed to the political upset of 1948. Yet after CVA was blocked and further projects were suspended because of the Korean conflict, voters concluded that the Republicans could fulfill their promises better than the Democrats. Once in office, however, the promisers of more opportunity with less control preferred to talk about restoring proper balance before they produced any solid results. Although they had reaped the harvest of concern about jobs and contracts, they were now shocked when the voters stocked Congress with more Democratic Providers.

The UCB project demonstrated Republican miscalculation in a nutshell. President Eisenhower's personal interest in it was based on characteristic confidence in the product of the accumulated knowledge of a staff operation. His men at the White House assumed that the public would be as impressed with cost analysis and engineering statistics as they themselves were. Because of the interpretations of the "mandate" of 1952, they underestimated the strength of UCB's critics and assumed that the stigma of the earlier controversy over Dinosaur would not touch an administration ostensibly elected to clean up bureaucratic corruption. They also believed that the public's interest was accurately described by the Reclamation Bureau and by its adherents in Congress. More so than in the case of Hells Canyon or the excessive leaning of Al Sarena, Republican support of UCB was as misplaced as Democratic support of CVA. Both represented maximum planning for minimal impact and, in view of existing governmental machinery, a costliness neither administration desired. In the final analysis, both projects were promoted for their potential political usefulness: to demonstrate each administration's concern for federal development of resources.

Finally, the intersection of the issues of preservation and development of resources during that decade offered striking evidence against the American belief in the effectiveness of party turnover. In that time there occurred one of the most impressive instances of partisan changeover in the nation's history. Yet an examination of federal resource policy in 1956 reveals no substantial alteration in procedure or substance from 1946. The debate over centralism versus localism which raged at the beginning of the period proved to be directed not at the decision makers so much as at the polling booth. When the Republicans were swept into power in 1952, voters evidently were as expectant of change in resource policy as they were of change in other federal policies. But the elections of 1954 and 1956 showed that they were ultimately interested in solid results no matter how labeled. As Republicans recognized before 1956, there was no clear relationship between resource controversies and the outcome of political contests. The McKay-Morse battle was not a struggle between selfishness and altruism. Both men garnered votes by defending policies that promised jobs and contracts. The "giveaway" charge was not an expression of the preservationist emphasis so much as one of the time-honored belief in *equitable* access to resource use. In retrospect the alarms over the national park principle were no more profound in their impact than political expediency permitted.

As a result of these events, that decade brought about but slight alteration in the values held by federal policy makers or in the public's understanding of "necessity" in environmental use. The leaders and publicists of those years addressed themselves only to the immediate issues. When Americans were confronted by a total ecological crisis less than a decade after the quarrels chronicled here, they had nothing more to draw upon to cope with that threat than the economic materialism, the bureaucratic inertia, and the political gamesmanship practiced by the men of the Truman-Eisenhower era.

Notes

FORM OF CITATIONS

Because of the multiplicity of primary sources used herein and because of the details of information involved, the following notes are thus structured: Unless otherwise shown, all sources are letters in the correspondence sections of personal manuscript collections (Papers) or official archives (Records). Individual sources are arranged in each composite note in the order they are used in the text paragraph. Each citation is arranged to read from the specific to the general as follows: item, folder or box title or number, name of file, name of collection or record group, location of collection or record group (at first mention). Further information about these sources is given in the Primary Sources section following the notes.

These abbreviations are used throughout the notes:

BLM–Bureau of Land
    Management

BPA–Bonneville Power
    Administration

BR–Bureau of Reclamation

CVA–Columbia Valley Authority

DDE–Dwight D. Eisenhower

DMK–Douglas McKay

DNM–Dinosaur National
    Monument

EP–Echo Park

FDR–Franklin D. Roosevelt

GAF–General Administrative
    File

HC–Hells Canyon

HLI–Harold L. Ickes

HST–Harry S. Truman

MVA–Missouri Valley Authority

NA–National Archives

NPS–National Park Service

NRC–National Records Center

OF–Official File

ONP–Olympic National Park

PF–Personal File

PPF–Personal, Political File

RG 48–Records of the Office of
    The Secretary of the
    Interior

RG 79–Records of the National
    Park Service

RG 115/4–Records of the Bureau
    of Reclamation, Upper
    Colorado River
    Storage Project
    Subgroup

SCA–Sierra Club Archives

UCB–Upper Colorado River
    Basin Project

PROLOGUE

[1] HLI to Hiram Johnson, January 30, February 10, 14, 15, 1933, Johnson to Charles McClatchy, December 11, 1932, February 28, 1933, Johnson to HLI, February 1, 1933, Hiram Johnson Papers, Bancroft Library, University of California, Berkeley; see also the first volume of *The Secret Diary of Harold L. Ickes* (New York, 1955), esp. pp. viii–ix, hereafter cited as HLI, *Diary.*

[2] The close attention given to resource matters by the president and his secretary of the Interior is documented in HLI, *Diary,* passim, and in Edgar B. Nixon, ed. and comp., *Franklin D. Roosevelt and Conservation* (Hyde Park, N.Y., 1957), hereafter cited as Nixon, *FDR and Conservation.*

[3] HLI to Hiram Johnson, April 6, 1929, February 24, 1930, November 18, 1932, Hiram Johnson Papers; William McAdoo to Daniel Roper, February 13, 1933, McAdoo to FDR, March 10, 1933, William Bechtel to McAdoo, February 21, 1933, John McGrath to McAdoo, December 14, 1932, William G. McAdoo Papers, Bancroft Library, University of California, Berkeley; HLI to Edward Taylor, July 5, 1935, to William Borah, April 25, 1938, Secretary OF, RG 48, NA; Arno Cammerer to HLI, March 19, 1934, State Control, GAF, HLI to Cammerer, February 18, 1935, Conservation, Secretary OF, RG 48, NA.

[4] HLI to Compton White, August 26, 1941, Conservation, Secretary OF, RG 48, NA.

[5] Elmo Richardson, "Western Politics and New Deal Policies: A Study of T. A. Walters of Idaho," *Pacific Northwest Quarterly* 54 (January 1963): 9–18; Oscar Chapman to HLI, December 11, 1934, 67, Oscar Chapman Papers, Harry S. Truman Library, Independence, Missouri; HLI to Farrington Carpenter, October 31, 1935, March 8, 1937, November 8, 1938, HLI to Director Smith, March 15, 1938, Carpenter to HLI, February 9, 1938, Carpenter, "The Taylor Grazing Act," typescript, esp. pp. 4, 14, 16, 17, clippings, and "The Law of the Range," speech typescript, September 28, 1940, Farrington Carpenter Papers, Denver Public Library, Colorado; Carpenter to HLI, July 3, 1936, copy, Secretary OF, RG 48, NA.

[6] C. Watt Brandon to Joseph O'Mahoney, May 2, 1938, Grand Teton National Park, Legislation File, Joseph O'Mahoney Papers, University of Wyoming Library, Laramie.

[7] The Ickes-Albright relationship is delineated in Donald C. Swain, *Wilderness Defender: Horace M. Albright and Conservation* (Chicago, 1970), hereafter cited as Swain, *Albright.*

[8] HLI to Mrs. Wolfe, May 16, 1939, Conservation, Secretary OF, RG 48, NA.

[9] Elmo Richardson, "Olympic National Park: Twenty Years of Controversy," *Forest History* 12 (April 1968): 6–15, describes Ickes's greatest park victory, and Richardson, "Federal Park Policy in Utah: The Escalante National Monument Controversy of 1935–1940," *Utah Historical Quarterly* 33 (Spring 1965): 110–33, unearths one of his greatest failures.

[10] Newton Drury, interview, March 1961, preliminary draft, esp. pp. 349–54, 401–2, 498–99, Regional Oral History Project, Bancroft Library, University of California, Berkeley, hereafter cited as Drury, interview; HLI, *Diary,* 3:72; Robert Marshall to Friends of the Forest Service, copy, November 1, 1940, Irving Clark Papers, University of Washington Library, Seattle; HLI to Earl Warren, April 2, 1951, reel 5, microfilm copy, Franklin D. Roosevelt Library, Hyde Park, New York.

[11] The author is grateful to Donald Swain for clarifying the matter of Ickes's view of the Bureau of Reclamation; Drury, interview, pp. 403, 412–15, 511–16; Frank Flint to James Murray, April 13, 1936, Legislation-Interior, James Murray Papers, University of Montana Library, Missoula.

[12] Rosalie Edge to Irving Brant, October 7, 1940, Brant to Edge, October 17, 1940, Edge to J. Burke, October 18, 1940, Brant Papers.

13 Frank Horton, statement, *Rock Springs* (Wyoming) *Miner,* December 29, 1939; Irving Brant to William Van Name, November 21, 1940, Van Name to HLI, November 7, 1940, copy, Brant Papers; Leslie Miller to FDR, November 11, 1940, PPF, Franklin D. Roosevelt Papers, Roosevelt Library, Hyde Park, New York.

14 William Van Name to Newton Drury, June 25, 1941, Irving Brant to Rosalie Edge, November 24, 1941, Brant Papers; H. Parkes to Joseph O'Mahoney, December 9, 1941, Legislation-Interior, O'Mahoney Papers; Abe Murdoch to FDR, November 25, 1940, OF 928, FDR Papers; Drury, interview, pp. 403–7, 412–15.

15 The discussion of the Sitka spruce episode in these paragraphs is based upon the following sources: Irving Clark to Irving Brant, April 26, 1941, Brant to William Van Name, April 12, 1942, Brant Papers; *Seattle Post-Intelligencer,* March 18, 1942; HLI to FDR, December 21, 1942, March 29, 1943, Frank Brundage to J. Taylor, December 31, 1942, Newton Drury to HLI, June 2, 1943, printed in Nixon, *FDR and Conservation,* 2:567, 572–73 and note; Oscar Chapman to HLI, July 5, 1943, HLI to Chapman, July 6, 1943, to Donald Nelson, July 1, 1943, not signed, July 12, 1943, Nelson to HLI, September 23, 1943, copies of these letters in the possession of Newton Drury; this correspondence is also found in Sitka Spruce, ONP, 17, Drury File, RG 79, NA; Brant to FDR, March 2, 1943, to Rosalie Edge, July 5, 1943, HLI to Nelson, September 14, 1943, copy, Brant to Edge, September 21, November 8, 1943, Brant to Clark, September 21, 1943, to HLI, July 7, 1943, to Edge, April 2, 1944, Brant Papers; the lumberman's complaint is in E. Bishop to Drury, February 24, 1943, copy, NPS, 225, Carl Russell Papers, Washington State University Library, Pullman; Drury to Brant, June 29, 1944, Brant Papers.

16 Newton Drury, interview, pp. 521–22; Herbert Evison and Drury, "Comments on Conservation: The National Park Service and the Civilian Conservation Corps," typescript of interview, 1963, preliminary draft, pp. 106, 112, Regional Oral History Project, Bancroft Library, University of California, Berkeley, hereafter cited as Drury-Evison, interview.

17 Newton Drury to HLI, January 25, 1945, and comment by Ickes, February 9, 1945, copy 14. Bernard De Voto Papers, Stanford University Library, California; Michael Straus to HLI, February 6, 1945, 19, Drury File, RG 79, NA; Straus to Newton Drury, October 4, 1945, Drury to HLI, September 25, 1945, HLI to K. Riede, January 17, 1946, 9, 12, GAF, RG 48, NA; HLI to Ansel Adams, December 20, 1945, 41–51, 1, Drury File, RG 79, NA.

18 FDR, "Message . . . on the Missouri River Development Plan," September 21, 1944, and press conference statement, November 14, 1944, *Public Papers and Addresses of President Franklin D. Roosevelt* (New York, 1938–1946), 8:274–76, 419–22.

19 James Murray to Sam Ford, February 12, 1944, copy, Murray to F. Hagie, November 24, 1944, Missouri River Basin, pamphlets, clippings, resolutions, MVA, Anti-MVA Lobby, S. Small to Elbert Thomas, September 29, 1944, copy, L. Maury, "Missouri Valley Authority and Governor Ford" [1944], Ford, Reclamation, Murray Papers; Wesley D'Ewart, biographical information, 1, Wesley D'Ewart Papers, University of Montana Library, Missoula; D'Ewart, interview, Columbia Oral History Project, July 5, 1967, copy in Dwight D. Eisenhower Library, Abilene, Kansas, hereafter cited as D'Ewart, interview; Ford, statement, Ford to E. Duncan, April 26, 1945, Northwest States Development Association, Columbia River, Sam C. Ford Papers, University of Montana Library, Missoula; Walt Horan to J. Berry, May 4, 1945, CVA, 134, Walt Horan Papers, Washington State University Library, Pullman.

20 Clarence Dill to FDR, December 29, 1933, printed in Nixon, *FDR and Conservation,* 1:234–36; M. Smith to FDR, April 23, 1935, OF 402, Lewis Schwellenbach to FDR, August 3, 1936, PPF 2754, FDR Papers; the author is grateful to

Wesley Dick for permission to read his manuscript "Power to the People" and to Philip Funigello for permission to consult his manuscript "The Bonneville Power Administration and the New Deal"; see also Dill, *Where White Water Falls* (Spokane, Wash., 1971), passim.

[21] Walt Horan to H. Carstenson, June 3, 1944, James O'Sullivan to E. Davis, September 25, 1944, Horan to N. Mackenzie, December 27, 1944, A. Zickler to Horan, June 27, 1945, Power 1943–1945, 420, 421, Horan Papers.

[22] N. Mackenzie to Walt Horan, March 12, 1945, "Regional Meeting . . . Spokane, March 9, 1945," copy, G. Jewett to Horan, March 23, April 19, 1945, Horan to Kirby Billingsly, April 11, 1945, Clarence Dill to Horan, April 30, 1945, Horan to James O'Sullivan, May 7, 1945, CVA, 133, 134, Horan Papers.

[23] Frank Corcoran to FDR, October 27, 1934, Oswald West to James Farley, July 24, 1934, OF 300, Clarence Dill to FDR, August 6, 1940, Clarence Martin to FDR, November 17, 1934, PPF, Morris Cooke to FDR, February 20, 1937, OF 2575, FDR Papers; David Lilienthal, *The Journals of David Lilienthal* (New York, 1964–1968), 1:62, 638, 659, hereafter cited as Lilienthal, *Journals;* George Norris to FDR, June 7, 1941, printed in Nixon, *FDR and Conservation*, 2:313–16; Roy Bessey to E. Cooper, February 15, 1943, CVA, 45, Julius Krug Papers, Library of Congress, Washington, D.C.

[24] FDR to George Norris, May 29, 1941, printed in Nixon, *FDR and Conservation*, 2:511–13.

CHAPTER ONE

[1] HST, *Memoirs* (New York, 1955), 1:254; HST, "Address . . . Kentucky Dam," October 10, 1945, *Public Papers of the Presidents of the United States* (Washington, D.C., 1952–   ), volume per calendar year, pp. 301–2, 392, hereafter cited as *Public Papers;* HST to O. Bundy, CVA, 2, Charles Murphy File, HST Records, Harry S. Truman Library, Independence, Missouri; Lilienthal, *Journals,* 2:2–5, 18–20; P. Sifton to J. Loeb, Jr., November 6, 1945, CVA, Reclamation, Murray Papers.

[2] Richard Neuberger to Walt Horan, June 19, 1945, Clifford Stone, "The 'Authority' Issue," copy, 133, CVA, Horan Papers; R. Reynolds to Sam Ford, May 24, 1945, Northwest Development Association, BR, Ford Papers.

[3] HLI to HST, November 23, 1945, 1050, OF 360, HST Records; F. Huntington to James Murray, May 1, 1945, D. Anderson to Murray, June 18, 1945, MVA, Reclamation, Murray Papers; R. Seelig to Walt Horan, May 1, 1945, 133, CVA, Horan Papers.

[4] Samuel Rosenman to HST, August 14, 1945, HLI, 8, Samuel Rosenman Papers, HST Library; HST, "Message . . . ," January 27, 1946, *Public Papers*, pp. 60–61; Lilienthal, *Journals,* 1:661–67, 94–95.

[5] HST, *Memoirs*, 1:607-9; HST, press conference statements, June 2, July 5, August 23, 1945, *Public Papers*, pp. 133, 164, 230; Irving Brant to Rosalie Edge, June 15, 1945, Brant Papers; Harold D. Smith, "Diary," entries for February 7, 9, 1946, copy, Submerged Lands, 5, Warner Gardner File, HST Library.

[6] Incoming correspondence concerning the Pauley affair and Ickes's resignation, 56, OF 6, HST Records; Horace Albright to Newton Drury, March 1, 1946, 1, Drury File, RG 79, NA.

[7] Endorsements for Secretary of the Interior, February 1946, 57, 58, OF 6, HST Records; Lilienthal, *Journals,* 2:18–20; HST, *Memoirs*, 2:221–22; Irving Brant to William Van Name, April 23, 1945, to Rosalie Edge, April 23, 1945, Brant Papers; HST, press conference statements, February 21, March 8, 1946, *Public Papers*, pp. 128–29, 132–33, 146.

8 Lilienthal, *Journals,* 2:6, 38, 24–25; Horace Albright to Newton Drury, March 1, 1946, Drury File, RG 79, NA; Albright to Oscar Chapman, March 15, 1946, Chapman Papers.

9 HLI to HST, November 11, 1945, BR, 59, OF 6c, HST Records; HST, press conference statement, December 12, 1945, *Public Papers,* pp. 537–38; Joel Wolfsohn to Abe Fortas, May 9, 1946, 12, Joel Wolfsohn Papers, HST Library; Ernest Gruening to Charles Ross, April 21, 1948, PPF 3804, HST Records; Harold Smith, "Diary," entries for April 10, May 2, 1946, Submerged Lands, 5, Gardner File, HST Records.

10 Newton Drury, interview, pp. 521–22; Drury-Evison, interview, pp. 106, 112; Julius Krug to C. Girard Davidson, January 27, 1948, 13, to Davidson, August 29, 1947, Davidson to Krug, September 13, 1947, NPS, 79, Julius Krug Papers; Warner Gardner to D. Myer, July 22, 1946, 1, 3, Coordinating Committee, 4, Gardner File, HST Records.

11 HLI, "Memorandum on Power Policy . . . ," January 3, 1946, copy, 47, 3, President's Water Resources Policy Commission File, B. Lyons to Charles Ross, April 5, 1946, BR, 59, OF 6c, HST Records; HST to Robert Sawyer, drafts, October 1, 1946, October 8, 1947, NRA, PPF 2167, HST Records.

12 Joel Wolfsohn to G. Sundborg, August 6, 1946, Wolfsohn Papers; Warner Gardner, address to National Reclamation Association, October 10, 1946, Reclamation, 45, Gardner File, HST Records; C. Girard Davidson to E. MacNaughton, July 22, 1946, copy, Sawyer Papers.

13 Robert Sawyer to E. MacNaughton, February 16, 1946, Sawyer Papers; *Salem* (Oregon) *Statesman,* March 28, 1946; D. Baker to Walt Horan, August 5, 1946, 133, CVA, Horan Papers; *New York Times,* March 12, 1946, Lilienthal, *Journals,* 2:94–95; E. MacNaughton to Sawyer, ca. February 1946, Sawyer Papers; Sawyer to Harry Polk, February 16, 1946, Polk to Sawyer, ca. February 1946, Sawyer Papers.

14 The seven-year debate over CVA and the several alternatives to it is viewed through the perspective of Governor Langlie's role in it by George W. Scott's "Arthur Langlie: Republican Governor in a Democratic Age" (Ph.D. diss., University of Washington, 1972), a massive, detailed work based on a variety of primary sources, hereafter cited as Scott, "Langlie." HST, press conference statement, January 8, 1946, *Public Papers,* p. 11; Walt Horan to W. DeLong, November 29, 1946, J. Ford to Horan, November 26, 1946, 584, Politics in Congress, Horan Papers.

15 Walt Horan to Richard Neuberger, September 28, 1945, Horan to D. Baker, August 5, 9, 1946, Horan to A. Thiele, April 30, 1946, 133, CVA, Horan Papers.

16 Walt Horan to James O'Sullivan, December 27, 1946, Fred Johnson, April 10, 1946, 133, CVA, Horan Papers.

17 Walt Horan to Wilson Compton, November 21, 1946, 133, CVA, Horan to Rufus Woods, January 22, 1947, 584, Politics in Congress, Compton to Kenneth Wherry, May 15, 1947, copy, 422, Power, B. Cist to John Taber, June 21, 1947, Horan to Wesley D'Ewart, November 13, 1947, 584, Politics in Congress, Horan Papers.

18 F. Hagie to Guy Cordon et al., May 21, 1947, Harry Polk to Hagie, December 26, 1947, Sawyer Papers; Warner Gardner to HST, October 7, 1947, BR, 59, OF 6, HST Records; A. Garton to Clarence Dill, January 17, 1947, Columbia Basin Commission, Director's General Correspondence, Conservation and Development Commission Records, Washington State Archives; Hugh Mitchell to C. Girard Davidson, May 17, 1948, Hugh Mitchell Papers, University of Washington Library.

19 Clark Clifford, "Memorandum for the President . . . ," ca. Spring 1948, copy, pp. 3, 24, 33, 38, Clark Clifford File; John McCormack, press release, July 4, 1948, copy, Republican National Committee, GF 267C, HST Records; Michael

Straus to HST, August 17, 1948, HST to Straus, August 20, 1948, BR, 59, OF 6, HST Records.

20 HST, remarks, Seattle, June 10, 1948, Colorado Springs, Colorado, and Denver, September 20, 1949, Grand Junction, Colorado, Salt Lake City, Utah, September 21, 1948, Public Papers, pp. 24, 513–14, 522–23, 530–31.

21 Walt Horan to Rufus Woods, April 21, 1948, 422, Power, Woods to Mrs. Horan, February 2, 1948, 550, Politics, Horan Papers.

22 Thomas E. Dewey, statements, St. Louis Post-Dispatch, September 22, 1948, New York Times, May 7, August 22, September 22, 1948.

23 For Oscar Chapman's political efforts see items in 84, 85, Michael Straus to Chapman, September 5, 1948, 85, Chapman Papers; Straus, recollections, Washington (D.C.) Star, February 4, 1952.

24 Mark Anderson, "Republican Defeat and Western Conservation," November 9, 1948, copy, 7, Bernard De Voto Papers, Stanford University Library, California; E. Rising to Robert Sawyer, November 8, 1948, Sawyer Papers.

25 Paul Raver to HST, December 21, 1948, BPA, 60, OF 6, HST Records; I. Block to H. Roback, February 3, 1949, 10, 106, Mitchell Papers; C. Girard Davidson to Charles Murphy, January 28, 1949, CVA, 2, David Bell to Murphy, June 24, 1949, CVA, 1, David Bell File, HST Records; HST to Harry Polk, draft, November 6, 1949, PPF 2167, HST Records; Oscar Chapman, memorandum on White House conference, February 4, 8, 1949, 73, Chapman Papers.

26 David Bell to Charles Murphy, June 29, 1949, CVA, 1, Bell File, Murphy to C. Moore, April 25, 1949, CVA, Murphy File; Bell to R. Greenleaf, April 27, 1949, CVA, 1, Bell File; Bell to Murphy, June 29, 1949, CVA, 21, Murphy File, HST Records.

27 HST, "Special Message . . . ," April 13, 1949, Public Papers, pp. 208-13; David Bell to R. Greenleaf, April 27, 1949, CVA, 1, Bell File, HST Records.

28 Misc. endorsements of CVA, OF 360A Misc., HST Records; Pendleton East Oregonian, September 5, 7, 1949; L. Dugh to Walt Horan, March 2, 1949, 131, Columbia Interstate Commission, Horan Papers; C. Girard Davidson to Charles Murphy, January 28, 1949, CVA, 21, Murphy File, HST Records; Arthur Langlie and DMK to HST, January 24, 1949, C. Robins to HST, January 27, 1949, HST to L. Wallace, January 31, 1949, OF 360A Misc., HST Records.

29 Walt Horan to John Rogers, January 27, 1949, Conservation and Development Commission Records, Washington State Archives; Rufus Woods to Horan, February 1, 1949, 551, Politics, Horan Papers; Clarence Dill to HST, February 17, 1949, 1050, OF 360, HST Records; J. McCauley to Stephen Mitchell, January 27, 1949, 108, 1, Stephen Mitchell Papers, HST Library.

30 Walt Horan to Arthur Langlie, January 24, 1949, 133, CVA, Horan Papers; Horan to John Rogers, January 27, 1949, CVA-Horan, Conservation and Development Records, Washington State Archives; Horan to Kirby Billingsly, January 31, 1949, 423, Power, Horan to Wesley D'Ewart et al., January 26, 1949, Horan to E. Weston, May 16, 1949, M. Swick to Horan, March 26, 1949, E. Tollefson to Julius Krug, March 19, 1949, copy, 131, Columbia Interstate Commission, Horan Papers.

31 Hugh Mitchell to Walt Horan, February 16, 1949, copy, Stephen Spingarn File, HST Records.

32 Arthur Langlie to Hugh Mitchell, February 10, 1949, 109, 15, Hugh Mitchell Papers; Spokane (Washington) Spokesman-Review, May 17, 1949; Elbert Thomas to Walt Horan, April 11, 1949, R. Sullivan to Horan, October 17, 1949, Horan to Dennis Chavez, June 1, 1949, Horan to James O'Sullivan, December 21, 1949, 131, Columbia Interstate Commission, Horan Papers.

33 DMK, statements, ca. March 1950, statements by spokesmen for Montana Chamber of Commerce, ca. June 1950, Arizona Pulp and Paper Association, March

1, 1950, by L. Karrick, October 17, 1950, by J. W. Penfold, March 22, 1950, by H. Linke, July 5, 1950, by F. Schrack, June 16, 17, 1950, by J. W. Penfold, March 22, 1950, by Leslie Miller, ca. June 27, 1950, transcript of testimony, 5, President's Water Resources Policy Commission File, HST Records.

34 *Sprague* (Washington) *Advocate,* July 28, 1949; *Olympia* (Washington) *Olympian,* July 20, 1949; Socialist Party, statement, May 4, 1949, copy, 5–16, VI, Arthur Langlie Papers, University of Washington Library, Seattle; *Oregon City Enterprise,* September 23, 1949; *Spokesman-Review,* September 23, 1949.

35 Reva Bosone to Oscar Chapman, October 23, 1950, 41, Chapman Papers; Arthur Watkins to J. Bracken Lee, July 6, 1950, J. Bracken Lee Records, Utah State Archives, Salt Lake City; HST to W. Norbald, August 28, 1950, 1050, OF 360, HST Records; David Bell to Charles Murphy, November 13, 1950, CVA, 21, Murphy File, HST Records; Robert Sawyer to Guy Cordon, January 16, February 6, 1951, Sawyer Papers; Gus Norwood to Cordon, December 28, 1951, 1, CF, Gus Norwood Papers, University of Washington Library, Seattle; Oscar Chapman to Arthur Langlie, July 30, 1951, 9–12, VI, Langlie Papers. The author is grateful to Robert Tininenko whose "Middle Snake River Development: The Origins of the Hells Canyon Controversy" (Master's thesis, Washington State University, 1967) enhanced understanding of the issue of Hells Canyon.

36 *New York Times,* May 13, 1950; C. Girard Davidson to Oscar Chapman, January 3, 1950, 58, Chapman Papers; Compton White to HST, January 17, 1950, HST to White, January 19, 1950, BR, 59, OF 6, HST Records; Andrew Schoeppel, press release, September 5, 1950, copy, especially pp. 16–22, misc. letters to Chapman, HST to Chapman, September 8, 1950, and Michael Straus to Chapman, September 7, 1950, 65, 66, Chapman Papers; HST, press conference statement, September 7, 1950, *Public Papers,* p. 621.

37 HST, remarks, May 10, 1950, *Public Papers,* p. 357; Glen Taylor to D. Dawson, March 4, 1950, 1050, OF 360, HST Records; C. Welteroth to Taylor, April 12, 1950, C. A. Robins Records, Idaho State Archives, Boise; Robert Sawyer to Guy Cordon, March 18, 1950, Sawyer to R. Parkman, February 14, 1950, Sawyer Papers; Oscar Chapman to Taylor, July 27, 1950, Taylor to Chapman, June 20, 1950, Congressional correspondence, 5, C. Girard Davidson File, RG 48, NA. The author is grateful to F. Ross Peterson whose "The Public Career of Senator Glen H. Taylor" (Ph.D. diss., Washington State University, 1968) provides a perceptive analysis of Taylor's political campaigns.

38 Oregon Political Survey, 1950, Presidential Correspondence, 1, William Boyle File, HST Records; DMK, remark, *Milton* (Oregon) *Eagle,* September 22, 1949; *Great Falls* (Montana) *Tribune,* December 21, 1951.

39 Davidson rumor is in Anon. to Oscar Chapman, February 12, 1952, 58, Chapman Papers; on Weaver-Newell, C. Girard Davidson to C. Skinner, July 4, 1949, 45, Krug Papers.

40 HST to Morris Cooke, July 28, August 1, 1951, Cooke to HST, August 1, 1951, to Leland Olds, November 28, 1951, Morris L. Cooke Papers, FDR Library; see also HST, "Special Message . . . ," January 19, 1953, *Public Papers,* pp. 1208-15.

CHAPTER TWO

1 HST, "Special Message . . . ," May 16, 1946, *Public Papers,* pp. 262–63; Horace Albright to Oscar Chapman, July 29, 1946, Albright, 13, Chapman Papers; miscellaneous material, BLM, 64, OF 6–2, HST Records; misc. material, grazing controversy, 11, Secretary OF, RG 48, NA; misc. material, Great Land Grab, Arthur Carhart Papers, Conservation Library, Denver, Colorado; C. Moynihan to Chapman, April 10, 1947, 26, Farrington Carpenter to Chapman, October 25, 1947,

16, Izaak Walton League, press release, October 23, copy, 21, Carhart to Chapman, October 16, 1947, 16, Chapman Papers; *Denver Post*, September 11, 1947.

[2] H. Chapman to Oscar Chapman, October 22, 1947, 21, Chapman Papers; J. Patton to HST, October 17, 1947, copy, Arthur Carhart to W. Booth, October 15, 1947, Julius Krug to W. Wright, September 17, 1947, copy, Carhart Papers; U.S., Congress, Senate, Committee on Interior Affairs, *Natural Resources Policy: Hearings . . .* , 82d Cong., 1st sess., January 7, 1949, p. 320.

[3] Arthur Demaray to C. Girard Davidson, August 30, 1948, Priority Legislation, 15, Davidson File, RG 48, NA; HST, "Address on Conservation at the Dedication of Everglades National Park," December 6, 1947, *Public Papers*, pp. 505–8.

[4] Arthur Carhart to Oscar Chapman, December 26, 1949, 42, William Voigt to Newton Drury, December 14, 1949, copy, 55, Chapman Papers. The long fight for the addition of Jackson Hole National Monument to Grand Teton National Park and Albright's vital role in that struggle is chronicled in Swain, *Albright*, pp. 253ff, 280–83. In addition, see Grand Teton National Park files in the O'Mahoney Papers and the C. Watt Brandon Papers, University of Wyoming Library, and Drury, interview, esp. pp. 664-85.

[5] Newton Drury to Julius Krug, November 29, 1946, Drury to William Greeley, March 13, 31, 1947, May 12, 1948, Oscar Chapman to Henry Jackson, March 14, 1947, copy, Drury to Irving Clark, March 18, 1947, ONP, 17, Drury File, RG 79, NA; Chapman to William Van Name, May 2, 1947, Brant Papers; Jackson to Clark, March 3, 1947, Clark Papers; David Brower, "Trouble on Olympus," Irving Clark, "Olympic National Park—Is It Too Large?" copies, Pacific Northwest Lumbermen's Association Papers, University of Washington Library, Seattle; D. Goldy to C. Girard Davidson, July 15, 1947, NPS, Davidson File, RG 48, NA; Krug to F. Waldrop, July 22, 1947, ONP, 17, Drury File, RG 79, NA.

[6] HLI to Irving Brant, April 1, 1947, Rosalie Edge to O. Case, March 25, 1946, copy, Brant to Monrad Wallgren, May 10, 1947, Brant Papers; Julius Krug to HLI, July 24, 1946, 20, Krug Papers; HLI, column, *Seattle Times*, April 10, 1947; Brant to Newton Drury, June 17, 1949, Brant Papers.

[7] HLI to Eleanor Roosevelt, July 23, 1947, copy, Roosevelt to Krug, July 31, 1947, copy, ONP, 17, Drury File, RG 79, NA.

[8] Julius Krug to Eleanor Roosevelt, July 23, 1947, copy, Roosevelt to Krug, July 31, 1947, copy, Newton Drury to J. Cudahay, October 7, 1947, ONP, 17, Drury File, RG 79, NA; Irving Brant to Rosalie Edge, February 9, 1948, Edge to Brant, October 6, 1947, Brant to Charles Ross, October 22, 1947, C. Girard Davidson to Edge, November 2, 1947, Brant to Drury, June 17, 1947, Drury to Brant, September 5, 1947, Edge to Brant, November 17, 1947, February 4, 1948, Brant to Edge, December 15, 1947, Brant to Ross, December 28, 1947, Brant Papers; Drury to Davidson, March 25, 1947, Drury to Edge, May 22, 1947, Davidson File, RG 48, NA; Ross to Brant, October 22, 1947, Brant to HST, December 28, 1947, HST to Brant, January 5, 1948, OF 6P, HST Records; Ted Goodyear to Arthur Langlie, May 27, 1947, ONP, Arthur Langlie Records, Washington State Archives, Olympia.

[9] Julius Krug to Hugh Butler, July 30, 1949, copy, Parks, Monrad Wallgren Records, Washington State Archives, Olympia; Newton Drury to Oscar Chapman, December 16, 1950, ONP, Horace Albright to Drury, April 11, 1947, 17, Drury File, RG 48, NA.

[10] Bernard De Voto to Richard Neuberger, May 31, 1948, Personal General File, Richard Neuberger Papers, University of Oregon Library, Eugene; *Seattle Times*, February 25, 1947; Monrad Wallgren to R. Welch, February 25, 1947, Conservation and Development Commission Records, Washington State Archives; F. Hagie to E. Eiffany, June 5, 1947, Harry Polk to Robert Sawyer, January 24, May 17, 1948, Harry Bashore to Polk, May 23, 1948, copy, Sawyer to Polk, July 5, 1948,

Guy Cordon to Sawyer, July 19, 1948, J. Shively to Sawyer, September 28, 1948, Sawyer to Cordon, June 10, December 10, 1948, Sawyer Papers.

11 Irving Brant, "Open Letter to . . . Dewey," *New York Star*, July 28, 1948; HLI, column, *New York Post*, September 27, 1948; HLI to Thomas Dewey, October 5, 1948, copy, to Bernard De Voto, October 19, 1948, 19, De Voto Papers.

12 HST, "Remarks, Alpine, Texas," September 25, 1948, *Public Papers*, p. 572; Irving Brant to R. Provines, September 10, 1948, to Rosalie Edge, November 7, 1948, Brant Papers.

13 Pacific Northwest Travel Association, resolution, Spokane, November 14–15, 1949, copy, H. Hoss, "Comments on the Testimony of . . . Davidson . . . ," National Parks and Monuments, 80th Congress legislation, Murray Papers.

14 HST, press conference statement, January 1, 1949, *Public Papers*, p. 84; Horace Albright to Oscar Chapman, May 25, 1948, 11, 12, GAF, RG 79, NA; Drury, interview, pp. 480–81, 688–89; Drury to Emmanuel Fritz, February 8, 1946, 8, to Julius Krug, January 13, 1947, BR, 19, Albright to Drury, October 6, 1949, Drury File, RG 79, NA; Arthur Demaray to Krug, April 7, 1947, Davidson File, RG 48, NA; Krug to Waldo Leland, July 22, 1946, Warner Gardner to Krug, May 13, 1946, 9, 12, C. Girard Davidson to Concessions Advisory Committee, April 23, 1947, to Krug, September 19, 1947, Drury to Krug, October 29, 1947, 10, 12, GAF, RC 79, NA.

15 James Murray to Julius Krug, February 25, 1948, Reclamation, Murray Papers; Krug to A. Houghton, March 1, 1948, 11, 12, GAF, RG 79, NA; Bernard De Voto to Mike Mansfield, August 1, 1950, 5b, De Voto Papers; Drury, interview, p. 512; Drury to De Voto, August 11, 1948, to L. Tonner, November 1, 1948, Glacier Dam, 8, Drury File, RG 79, NA; Montaineers, statement, 7, Kenneth Hechler File, HST Records; HST, press conference statement, February 17, 1949, *Public Papers*, p. 138.

16 HST, statement, Phoenix, Arizona, September 24, 1948, *Public Papers*, pp. 566–67; HST to J. Vivian, July 1, 1947, Julius Krug to HST, July 16, 1946, Joseph O'Mahoney to HST, May 7, 1949, UCB Compact, OF 165, HST Records.

17 H. Baker to T. Vint, August 19, 1935, Arno Cammerer to HLI, July 30, 1935, 2163, National Monument File, RG 79, NA; HLI to Cammerer, June 8, 1936, copy, 118, 10, RG 115/4, NRC.

18 William King to HLI, July 31, 1936, 2163, to Arno Cammerer, November 22, 1937, Arthur Demaray to Abe Murdoch, November 29, 1937, 2159, Conrad Wirth to T. Moskey, ca. October 1937, 2164, National Monument File, RG 79, NA.

19 David Madsen to Arthur Demaray, June 11, 18, 1936, 2163, National Monument File, RG 79, NA.

20 W. Little to B. Thompson, February 2, 1938, 2164, National Monument File, RG 79, NA.

21 R. Walter to J. McLaughlin, March 20, 1939, and attached draft of agreement, 2163, Arthur Demaray, note attached to T. Allen to Demaray, March 27, 1940, 2163, Conrad Wirth to Newton Drury, December 11, 1941, National Monument File, RG 79, NA.

22 "Notes on a Memorandum of Understanding Re: Proposed Survey of Recreational Resources of the Colorado River Basin, Dated November 4, 1941, and attached correspondence," copy, Brant Papers.

23 *Vernal* (Utah) *Express*, August 23, 1945, article by former park ranger, July 11, 1948, and misc. clippings and memoranda, 1943, 1947, 1949, 2162, National Monument File, RG 79, NA.

24 A. Knox to T. Moskey, November 3, 1943, Dan Beard to Charles Merriam, October 3, November 26, 1943 (bearing Drury's comment), J. Doen to Merriam, October 14, 1943, Newton Drury to Herbert Maw, November 26, 1943, 2164, NMF, RG 79, NA.

[25] *Rocky Mountain News* (Denver), October 31, 1943; Dan Beard to Newton Drury, October 3, 1943, Drury to G. Blackman, draft and letter sent, November 26, 1943, Drury to Charles Merriam, December 14, 1943, to Michael Straus, December 1, 1943, Conrad Wirth to Arthur Demaray, October 28, 1948, EP, 6, Drury File, Wirth to Drury, August 21, 1944, "roost" statement is in B. Thompson to Wirth, September 18, 1943, 2164, National Monument File, RG 79, NA.

[26] Michael Straus to Julius Krug, October 12, 1948, 71, Krug Papers; Krug to A. Houghton, March 1, 1948, 11, 12, GAF, RG 79, NA; W. Miller, "The Concern of the Federal Security Agency for Recreation," March 20, 1947, copy, NPS, Davidson File, RG 48, NA; C. Girard Davidson to National Parks Advisory Board, April 23, 1947, to Krug, September 19, 1947, Newton Drury to Krug, October 25, 1948, 10, 12, GAF, RG 79, NA; Drury, interview, pp. 397, 427; Krug to Straus, April 6, 1949, 11, 12, GAF, RG 79, NA.

CHAPTER THREE

[1] *New York Times,* November 5, 11, 12, 1949; HST, press conference statements, December 2, 1948, November 10, 11, 1949, *Public Papers,* pp. 558–59 and 563–64 respectively.

[2] Julius Krug to Oscar Chapman, December 19, 1949, 20, Krug Papers; M. Costy to Chapman, 42, Chapman Papers; Richard Neuberger, "Daring Young Man from the West," *Nation* 166 (January 1949); 129–30; T. Sancton, "The Gentle Crusader," *Nation* 168 (March 1949): 267–68.

[3] Lilienthal, *Journals,* 2:20; Drury-Evison, interview, pp. 28, 103–6, 117; Drury, interview, p. 523.

[4] Arthur Carhart to Oscar Chapman, December 26, 1949, 42, Chapman Papers; U.S., Congress, Senate, Interior Committee, *Hearings on the Nomination of Oscar Chapman . . . ,* 81st Cong., 2d sess., 1949, esp. pp. 23–26.

[5] Arthur Watkins to J. Bracken Lee, February 3, 1950, Lee to Oscar Chapman, January 30, 1950, "Bulletin of . . . Committee of Twenty One Counties," February 5, 1950, and attached items, H. Linke, "Brief on Dinosaur National Monument for the Attention of . . . Chapman," January 31, 1950, Linke to Granger, February 6, 1950, Reva Bosone to Linke, February 6, 1950, Linke to Bosone, February 10, 1950, Colorado River Commission, State Engineer File, J. Bracken Lee Records; L. Knous to Chapman, February 9, 1950, copy, EP, 8a, Edwin Johnson Records, Colorado State Archives, Denver.

[6] Newton Drury to Michael Straus, January 5, 1950, 19, Drury File, RG 79, NA; Vernal Chamber of Commerce, resolution, December 6, 1949, copy, H. Linke to Oscar Chapman, January 30, 1950, State Engineer File, Lee Records; excerpts from preservationist organizations' testimony are in Water Gate-Dinosaur folder, J. W. Penfold to Bernard De Voto, August 9, 1950, "Ding" Darling to Arthur Carhart, October 6, 1950, Carhart Papers; Newton Drury to Regional Directors, II and III, February 3, 1950, to Ira Gabrielson, March 21, 1950, to Chapman, March 3, June 16, 1950, DNM, 6, "A Survey of the Recreational Resources of the Upper Colorado Basin," 1950, Drury File, RG 79, NA.

[7] Irving Brant to Oscar Chapman, April 3, 1950, Brant Papers.

[8] Oscar Chapman to Elbert Thomas, June 27, 1950, Interior Department, press release, June 27, 1950, copy, 6, Drury File, RG 79, NA; Thomas to Chapman, June 26, 1950, 117, 1, RG 115/4, NRC.

[9] Horace Albright to Bernard De Voto, July 21, 1950, 7, De Voto to H. Frank, July 29, 1950, 5b, HLI to De Voto, December 12, 1950, 19, De Voto Papers.

[10] Arthur Carhart, statement to the author, June 19, 1968; Bernard De Voto to Carhart, March 8, 1954, William Voigt to Carhart, December 11, 1950, Jess

Penfold to Carhart, December 11, 1950, EP, Carhart Papers; James Murray to W. Nye, December 9, 1950, Glacier View, Reclamation, Murray Papers.

[11] Arthur Carhart, testimony, J. W. Penfold, statement quoted by F. Clark, March 28, 1950, transcript of testimony, 5, President's Water Resources Policy Commission File, HST Records.

[12] William Warne to Paul Raver, November 3, 1950, Glacier, 8 Michael Straus to Oscar Chapman, January 17, 1952, 12–47, part 2, Glacier Administration, Newton Drury to Regional Director, II, May 3, 1950, 4, Drury File, RG 79, NA.

[13] Horace Albright to Bernard De Voto, July 21, 1950, 7, De Voto to J. Knight, August 28, 1950, De Voto to Robert Sawyer, January 15, 1950, De Volto to Elmer Bennett, August 15, 1950, 5b, De Voto Papers; Ulysses Grant III, "The Dinosaur Dams Are Not Needed," *Living Wilderness* 15 (Autumn 1950): 17–24.

[14] B. Ward to Reva Bosone, December 15, 1950, copy, Colorado River, H. Linke to B. Hibbs, July 20, 1950, Linke to B. Stringham, May 26, 1950, H. Simpson to Linke, July 20, 1950, State Engineer File, Lee Records; Ward to Commissioners, ca. June 2, 1950, transcript of testimony, 5, President's Water Resources Policy Commission File, HST Records; Bernard De Voto to Palmer Hoyt, August 1, 1950, 5b, De Voto Papers.

[15] Arthur Carhart to Oscar Chapman, September 10, 12, 1950, Chapman to Carhart, August 30, 1950, contains quoted statement, October 3, 1950, EP, Carhart Papers; Horace Albright to Bernard De Voto, August 8, 1950, 7, De Voto Papers.

[16] William Voigt to J. W. Penfold and to Carhart, December 11, 1950, EP, Carhart Papers.

[17] Newton Drury to Irving Brant, April 7, 1950, Brant Papers; Drury to Bernard De Voto, July 19, 1950, De Voto to Oscar Chapman, August 15, 1950, 24, De Voto Papers; Chapman to William Warne, May 10, 1950, copy, Warne to Chapman, August 18, 1950, DNM, 6, Drury File, RG 79, NA; William Voigt and J. W. Penfold to Arthur Carhart, December 11, 1950, EP, Carhart Papers; Drury-Evison, interview, pp. 107–9; Drury, statement to the author, August 23, 1968; an earlier version of the "evaporation" phrase is in Drury to Chapman, June 16, 1950, DNM, 6, Drury File, RG 79, NA.

[18] Newton Drury to Oscar Chapman, May 23, 1950, 44, Reva Bosone to Chapman, October 23, 1950, 41, Chapman Papers; "Recommendations of the Advisory Committee . . . November 20, 21, 1950," especially item 5, copy, EP, Carhart Papers.

[19] Oscar Chapman to Newton Drury, December 13, 1950, Drury to Chapman, December 15, 1950, January 10, 19, 1951, copies, 24, Bernard De Voto to E. Lee, May 17, 1951, 5b, De Voto Papers; J. Patton to Chapman, August 15, 1950, 51, Chapman to Drury, February 6, 1951, Drury to Chapman, March 30, 1951, 44, Chapman Papers; Swain, *Albright*, pp. 290-91.

[20] Newton Drury to Charles Sauers, January 28, 1951, 13, De Voto Papers; Drury-Evison, interview, p. 107.

[21] HLI, appointment for January 3, 1951, Matthew Connolly File, HST Records; HLI, column, *San Francisco Examiner*, August 25, 1948, May 30, 1951; *Los Angeles Daily News*, April 7, 1951; *New York Times*, March 11, 1951; HLI to Earl Warren, April 2, 1951, copy, to Irving Brant, April 6, 1951, Brant Papers; *Washington Post*, February 17, 18, 1951.

[22] Bernard De Voto to E. Lee, May 17, 1951, 5b, Charles Sauers to De Voto, January 28, 31, 1951, 13, February 5, 1951, 27, to Oscar Chapman, February 3, 1951, copy, 27, De Voto Papers.

[23] Howard Zahniser to HST, January 13, 1951, copy, William Voigt to HST, January 16, 1951, copy, 44, Chapman Papers; Oscar Chapman to William Hassett, April 6, 1951, 60, OF 6, HST Records; Newton Drury to George Kelly, March 23,

1951, George Kelly Papers, Denver Conservation Library; Clinton Anderson to Bernard De Voto, February 14, 17, 1951, 7, Arthur Carhart to De Voto, February 17, 1951, 11, De Voto Papers; Irving Brant to HST, February 16, 1951, HST to Brant, February 20, 1951, Brant Papers.

[24] Irving Brant, notation March 16, 1957, at end of HST to Brant, February 20, 1951, Brant Papers; Waldo Leland to Charles Sauers, February 22, 1951, 21, De Voto to E. Lee, May 17, 1951, 5b, De Voto Papers.

[25] Newton Drury to Olaus Murie, January 23, 1951, Wilderness Society, 25, Drury File, RG 79, NA; Michael Straus to Oscar Chapman, June 7, 1951, 12.0, 16, GAF, RG 79, NA; *Deseret News* (Salt Lake City), February 17, 1951; J. W. Penfold to the editor, *Deseret News*, May 30, 1951, copy, 13, De Voto Papers.

[26] Newton Drury, report to the Sierra Club, May 15, 1951, notes made by Carl Russell, 74, Russell Papers, Washington State University Library, Pullman; National Parks Advisory Board, minutes of meetings May 7, 8, 1951, 1, Wirth File, RG 79, NA; Chapman to Olas Murie, March 15, 1951, Alfred Knopf to Chapman, December 1, 1951, Michael Straus to Chapman, March 28, 1951, 12–46, part 2, 3847, Secretary OF, RG 48, NA; Straus to H. Collins, March 6, 1951, Brant Papers.

[27] *Salt Lake Tribune*, March 1, 1952; George Kelly to R. Howell, May 4, 1951, Kelly Papers; Dan Thorton to Edwin Johnson and Eugene Millikan, July 16, 1951, 6, GF, Dan Thorton Records, Colorado State Archives, Denver; J. Bracken Lee to H. Linke, August 28, 1950, State Engineer File, Lee Records; J. W. Penfold to Michael Straus, July 24, 1951, copy, EP, Carhart Papers; Howard Zahniser to Oscar Chapman, November 23, 1951, Kelly to Chapman, December 11, 1951, Kelly Papers; *Denver Post*, November 15, 1951.

[28] Swain, *Albright*, p. 292; Conrad Wirth to Oscar Chapman, June 10, 12, 1952, Alfred Knopf to Chapman, December 12, 1951, 12–46, part 2, 3847, Secretary OF, RG 48, NA; Wirth to William Voigt, November 21, 1951, Izaak Walton League, 2, Wirth File, RG 79, NA.

[29] Oscar Chapman to Arthur Watkins, November 21, 1951, copy, UCB, Arthur Carhart to Elbert Thomas, February 20, 1954, EP, Carhart Papers; Chapman to George Kelly, February 28, 1952, Kelly Papers; Michael Straus to Chapman, June 7, 1951, 12.0, 16, April 1, 1952, 12–46, part 2, 3847, Secretary OF, and April 29, 1952, 12.0, 17, GAF, RG 48, NA; S. Vinke to James Murray, November 8, 1952, Parks and Monuments, EP Legislation, Murray Papers.

[30] Arthur Watkins to Oscar Chapman, December 2, 1952, Chapman to Watkins, November 21, 1952, copies, 117, 1, RG 115/4, NRC; Chapman to B. Ward, August 29, 1952, 125, Reading File, Chapman Papers; H. Bradley to James Murray, May 14, 1951, EP Legislation, Parks and Monuments, Murray Papers.

[31] Oscar Chapman to DMK, December 16, 1952, January 2, 1953, to HST, January 7, 1953, 6, Reading File, Chapman Papers; *Denver Post*, December 10, 1952.

CHAPTER FOUR

[1] C. Bennett to Dan Thorton, August 25, 1952, J. Hall to Thorton, July 2, 1952, J. Frost to Thorton, October 18, 1952, DDE, Dan Thorton Records, Colorado State Archives, Denver; R. Ruhl to Robert Sawyer, August 4, 1949, Sawyer Papers; *Wrangell* (Alaska) *Sentinel*, September 5, 1952; Mrs. J. Fischer to DMK, January 5, 1954, PF, Douglas McKay Papers, University of Oregon Library, Eugene; *Seattle Post-Intelligencer*, September 17, 1952.

[2] Harry Cain, statement is in speech, "The Grab Is On," March 11, 1952, copy, Tidelands, Arthur Langlie Records.

3 Western Forest Industries Association, study, February 1953, and accompanying items, NPS, J. Byrd to P. Remly, December 3, 1952, Bureau of Mines, Secretary OF, RG 48, NA; L. Longwood to Arthur Langlie, August 4, 1953, Conservation and Development Commission Records, Washington State Archives; *Denver Post,* February 10, 1952; Dan Thorton, inaugural message, press releases, and speeches, Dan Thorton Records; G. Stanfield to DMK, December 6, 1952, PF, DMK Papers; Robert Smylie to DMK, December 29, 1952, PF, Robert Smylie Records, Idaho State Archives, Boise.

4 Arthur Watkins to J. Bracken Lee, July 6, 1950, Lee Papers; H. Houston to I. Lewis, October 11, 1951, 9–12, VI, Langlie Papers; Charles Sprague to Robert Sawyer, January 8, 1952, Sawyer Papers; Sidney T. Harding, "A Life in Western Water Development," interview, 1967, Oral History Project, University of California Library, Berkeley, p. 373, hereafter cited as Harding, interview; *Los Angeles Times,* November 29, 1951; [Memorandum for Governor Stevenson] ca. September 1952, Kenneth Hechler File, HST Records; C. Erdahl to Marshall Dana, December 23, 1952, copy, PF, DMK Papers.

5 Natural resources plank, Republican platform, 1952, copy, Republican National Committee Clippings and Publication File, Dwight D. Eisenhower Library, Abilene, Kansas.

6 *Salt Lake Tribune,* cited in *Denver Post,* July 18, 1952.

7 DDE, campaign statements, Denver, August 18, 1952, copy, Land Matters, OF 125, Boise, Idaho, August 20, 1952, Seattle, October 6, 1952, Fresno, California, October 9, 1952, Sacramento, California, October 8, 1952, Portland, Oregon, October 7, 1952, Casper, Wyoming, October 13, 1952, Fargo, North Dakota, October 4, 1952, "Campaign Statements of . . . Eisenhower," copies, DDE Records, DDE Library; H. Powell to Arthur Langlie, December 3, 1956, 6–26, VI, Langlie Papers.

8 Richard Neuberger, "Adlai Stevenson in the Far West," copy, '52 Campaign, Oregon, Washington, 88, Neuberger to Oscar Chapman, September 8, 1952, 87, Chapman Papers; Adlai Stevenson, campaign statements, Seattle, September 8, 1952, *Major Campaign Speeches of Adlai Stevenson* (New York, 1953), pp. 83–90; *Oregon Journal* (Portland), August 17, 1952.

9 H. Linke to Arthur Watkins, April 13, May 21, 1951, Watkins, Lee Records.

10 W. Pilgeram to J. Watson, June 18, 1952, copy, Lands and BLM, Murray Papers; HST, address, May 7, 1952, *Public Papers,* esp. p. 345; Julius Krug to Oscar Chapman, July 13, 1949, 10, Krug Papers; M. White to Chapman, June 6, 1950, Tidelands, 34, HLI to Joseph O'Mahoney, September 24, 1951, copy, Chapman to Maury Maverick, August 30, 1952, 125, Reading File, Chapman to Adlai Stevenson, August 12, 1952, 54, Chapman Papers; Lyndon Johnson to HST, January 13, 1953, 25, Murphy File, HST Records.

11 HST, campaign remarks, Shelby, Montana, September 30, 1952, Whitefish, Montana, October 1, 1952, Bonners Ferry and Sandpoint, Idaho, October 1, 1952, Hungry Horse Dam, Kalispell, Montana, October 1, 1952, Spokane, Washington, October 1, 1952, Redding, California, October 3, 1952, Rifle and Grand Junction, Colorado, October 6, 1952, *Public Papers,* pp. 345, 638, 645–46, 655, 657, 659–65, 695–96, 716–19.

12 T. Davis to E. Ellis, September 9, 1952, Michael Straus to Oscar Chapman, ca. September 1952, Politics General, Platform Proposals, Democratic National Committee, 87, Chapman Papers; Joel Wolfsohn to William Warne, November 12, 1952, 26, Wolfsohn Papers, HST Library; G. Ruele to F. Gross, August 29, 1952, Colorado, 5, Hechler File, HST Records; Carl Hayden, memorandum, August 29, 1952, "The Losing of the West," Politics General, 87, Chapman Papers; J. Little to B. Gross, Graham to Gross, August 29, 1952, Colorado Background, Hechler File, HST Records.

[13] Robert Smylie, memorandum for DDE, August 16, October 1, 1952, memorandum for Sherman Adams, October 1, 1952, "Memorandum Concerning the Political Situation in the Mountain West . . . ," October 3, 1952, memorandum for General Cutler, October 11, 1952, PPF, Robert Smylie Records, Idaho State Archives, Boise.

[14] R. Weber to C. Hendrickson, October 21, 1952, 56–23, VI, Langlie Papers; J. Brock to Hugh Butler, September 16, 1952, Wyoming, Hugh Butler Papers, Nebraska State Historical Society, Lincoln; Scott, "Langlie," esp. pp. 356ff.; E. Kerr to Robert Smylie, November 17, 1952, PPF, Smylie Records.

[15] HST to Dennis Chavez, January 10, 1952, Federal Power Commission, OF 235, HST Records; William Warne to Oscar Chapman, February 18, 1952, 56, Chapman Papers; *Salt Lake Tribune,* August 7, 1952; HST, "Annual Message . . . ," January 16, 1952, *Public Papers,* esp. pp. 87–89.

[16] Irving Clark to J. Osseward et al., March 6, 1952, Clark Papers; K. Whitaker to Oscar Chapman, December 22, 1952, 56, Chapman Papers; W. Mumaw to F. Kimball, copy, December 24, 1951, Conservation and Development Commission Records, Washington State Archives; *Aberdeen* (Washington) *World,* February 25, 1952, March 2, 1953.

[17] Arthur Langlie to HST, December 2, 1952, ONP Review Committee, Langlie Records; HST, press conference statement, January 6, 1953, *Public Papers,* p. 1069; *Seattle Times,* December 5, 1952; Monrad Wallgren to Langlie, December 5, 1952, ONP Review Committee, Langlie Records; *Aberdeen World,* December 11, 1952.

[18] HST to Arthur Langlie, December 6, 1952, ONP Review Committee, Langlie Records; Irving Brant to HST, December 24, 1952, HST to Brant, December 31, 1952, Brant Papers; HST, statement, January 6, 1953, *Public Papers,* pp. 1113–14.

[19] G. Lee to Arthur Langlie, November 19, 1952, Conservation and Development Commission Records, Washington State Archives; G. Collingwood and L. Lee, statements, *American Forests* 59 (February 1953): 14, 28, 30, 32; *Washington Star,* January 7, 1953; *Washington Post,* January 10, 1953; R. Heminger to Walt Horan, February 26, 1953, 553, Politics, Horan Papers; Robert Smylie to W. Smylie, November 13, 1952, PPF, Smylie Records.

[20] *Washington Post,* November 18, 1952; Raymond Moley, column, *Newsweek* (November 17, 1952), p. 20.

[21] *Idaho Statesman,* November 11, 1952; Arthur Carhart to Bernard De Voto, November 18, 1952, 6, De Voto Papers.

[22] K. Miller to DMK, November 11, 1952, Sawyer to Miller, December 10, 1952, to Raymond Moley, January 5, 1952, to Harry Polk, January 5, February 24, 1952, Moley to Sawyer, December 8, 1952, Sawyer Papers.

[23] DMK's political career is documented in the collection of his papers as governor of Oregon and secretary of the Interior deposited in the University of Oregon Library. See also Franklyn D. Mahar, "Douglas McKay and the Issues of Power Development in Oregon, 1953–1956" (Ph.D. diss., University of Oregon, 1968) hereafter cited as Mahar, "McKay"; the Nixon episode is in Richard Nixon, *Six Crises* (New York, 1962), p. 92.

[24] DMK, speech, Montesano, Washington, June 23, 1951, copy, PF, Langlie Records.

[25] DDE, *Mandate for Change* (New York, 1961), pp. 121–22; Mabel McKay, statement, Mahar, "McKay," pp. 308–9; DMK to M. Hamilton, December 5, 1952.

[26] M. Hamilton to DMK, November 22, 1952, DMK to F. Molling, November 28, 1952, Ray Wilbur, Jr., to DMK, December 24, 1952, PF, DMK Papers; DMK to Robert Smylie, November 25, 1952, PPF, Smylie Records; Joel Wolfsohn to M. Bisgyar, November 20, 1952, 26, Wolfsohn Papers; Robert Sawyer to L. Wehle, December 1, 1952, Sawyer Papers; H. Whitney to DMK, December 2, 1952,

Federal Power Commission, 388, GF 43 A, DDE Records; *Idaho Statesman*, November 22, 1952; Thomas Dewey to DMK, December 20, 1952, PF, DMK Papers.

27 Bernard De Voto to Arthur Carhart, November 23, 1952, Carhart Papers; De Voto to Butler, December 1, 1952, 6, De Voto Papers; Irving Brant to HST, December 24, 1952, Brant Papers; Wayne Morse, quoted in *Idaho Statesman*, November 21, 1952; Al Ullman to Gus Norwood, November 24, 1952, HC, Northwest Public Power Association Papers; Norwood to R. Lewis, November 21, 1952, Norwood Papers.

28 U.S., Congress, Senate, Interior Committee, *Hearings on the Nomination of Douglas McKay . . .* , Senate Report 2270, 83d Cong., 1st sess., 1953, esp. pp. 12, 15, 20, 29–30, 32, 38, 43, 54–56.

29 Bernard De Voto to Henry Jackson, ca. February 1953, 6, Elmer Davis to De Voto, May 6, 1953, De Voto Papers.

CHAPTER FIVE

1 Merlo J. Pusey, *Eisenhower the President* (New York, 1956), pp. 64–65; John Franklin Carter, *Republicans on the Potomac* (New York, 1953), pp. 204–8; DMK's expression quoted by Horace Albright in Swain, *Albright*, p. 302.

2 DMK to C. Brownell, December 20, 1952, PF, DMK Papers.

3 Oscar Chapman to HST, January 13, 1953, DDE Administration Briefings, 21, Murphy File, HST Records; Emmet Hughes, *Ordeal of Power: A Political Memoir of the Eisenhower Years* (New York, 1963), pp. 67, 136; DMK to F. Anderers, April 22, 1953, PF, DMK Papers; DMK to Robert Sawyer, March 14, 1953, 7, McCrillis File, Secretary OF, RG 48, NRC.

4 DMK to Joseph Dodge, February 15, 1954, Dodge to Sherman Adams, February 18, 1954, 115, OF 3WW, DDE Records.

5 Charles Willis to Sherman Adams, February 3, 1953, 115, OF 3WW, DDE Records; Ralph Tudor, "I'm Glad I Went to Washington," *Saturday Evening Post* (November 27, 1954), pp. 28, 37–40; Tudor to Robert Sawyer, January 7, 1952, Sawyer Papers; Tudor, *Notes Recorded While Under Secretary of the Interior* (privately printed, undated, not consecutively paged), entries for July 19, November 15, 1953, hereafter cited as Tudor, *Notes*. There are copies of this journal in the DMK Papers and at the DDE Library.

6 D. Swim to Herbert Brownell, December 25, 1952, Raymond Moley to Arthur Langlie, February 26, 1953, 14–15, VI, Langlie Papers; J. Jennings to Leonard Hall, December 4, 1952, Appointments, Secretary OF, RG 48, NA.

7 DDE to Herbert Brownell, November 24, 1952, Dan Thorton to Brownell, December 5, 1952, Len Jordan to Brownell, December 24, 1952, DMK to Brownell, December 20, 1954, copy, BPA, Appointments, Secretary OF, RG 48, NA; Robert Sawyer to Raymond Moley, December 12, 1952, Sawyer Papers; Hugh Butler to DMK, December 29, 1952, PF, DMK Papers.

8 Clarence Davis to DMK, November 3, 1953, PF, DMK Papers; Ralph Tudor, *Notes*, entry for March 20, 1954; Davis to DMK, August 28, 1955, OF 125, DDE Records; Robert Sawyer to Harry Polk, January 5, 1953, Polk to Sawyer, February 20, 1953, Sawyer Papers.

9 M. Young to Arthur Summerfield, December 20, 1952, copy, T. Coleman to H. Talbot, December 6, 1952, Howard Pyle to Summerfield, November 25, 1952, Barry Goldwater to Summerfield, December 5, 1952, Styles Bridges to Summerfield, December 5, 1952, Appointments, Secretary OF, RG 48, NA; J. Bermingham to Robert Smylie, February 5, 1953, PF, Smylie Records; DMK to DDE, January 30, 1953, ca. February 1953, 115, OF 3WW, DDE Records; T. Coleman to H. Talbot, December 6, 1952, Goldwater to Summerfield, December 19, 1952, Ap-

pointments, Orme Lewis to DMK, July 27, 1955, Secretary OF, RG 48, NA; C. Cole to Frank Barrett, March 19, 1954, BLM, Interior, Frank Barrett Papers, University of Wyoming Library, Laramie; Ralph Tudor, "I'm Glad I Went to Washington," p. 37; Glenn Emmons, McKay's Commissioner of Indian Affairs, to the author, November 19, 1971; Tudor to Lewis, August 17, 1954, Secretary OF, RG 48, NA; U.S., Congress, Senate, Interior Committee, *Hearings on the Nominations of . . . Tudor . . . Aandahl . . . Lewis . . . Davis . . .* , 83d Cong., 1st sess., February 5, 1953, esp. pp. 5–7, 15, 44.

10 Ira Gabrielson to DDE, January 27, 1953, Natural Resources, OF 134, DDE Records; R. Emmons to DMK, March 13, 1953, N. Harlan to DMK, May 4, 1953, Walter Hallanan to DMK, September 4, 1953, DMK to O. Brownson, July 9, 1954, to R. Ostrander, January 26, 1954, to Sherman Adams, May 26, 1953, PF, DMK Papers; Ralph Tudor, "I'm Glad I Went to Washington," pp. 37–38; Tudor, *Notes,* entries for November 7, 1953, and March 20, 1954.

11 DDE to DMK, September 29, 1953, and Tudor note attached, PF, DMK Papers; Tudor to DMK, August 18, September 13, 1953, January 15, 1954, Secretary OF, RG 48, NA; *Oregonian,* October 13, 1953; *Spokane* (Washington) *Chronicle,* November 3, 1953; "Action Taken by Interior to Avoid or Reduce Expenditures . . . ," 1956, copy, Budget, Secretary OF, RG 48, NA.

12 *Salem* (Oregon) *Capital Journal,* December 16, 1952; Tudor, *Notes,* entry for April 19, 1953; Michael Straus to DDE, January 20, 1953, DDE to Straus, February 9, 1953, copies, BR, Case File, Paul Douglas Papers, Chicago Historical Society; Straus to DMK, February 9, 1953, statement attached, BR, Secretary OF, RG 48, NA; Harding, interview, p. 375.

13 DMK to Robert Sawyer, February 1953, 7, McCrillis File, RG 48, NRC; K. Miller to Sawyer, February 6, 1953, Sawyer to Miller, February 11, 1953, W. Welsh to Sawyer, March 16, 1953, Sawyer Papers; Barry Goldwater to Ralph Tudor, February 9, 1953, copy, Tudor to Goldwater, February 9, 1953, copy, PF, DMK Papers; DDE, press conference statement, July 1, 1953, *Public Papers,* p. 420; Tudor, *Notes,* entry for April 11, 1953; F. Champ to Arthur Watkins, December 24, 1952, copy, Lee Records; D. Stringfellow to DMK, July 11, 1953, PF, DMK Papers.

14 Harding, interview, pp. 373–75; John Rogers to DMK, December 13, 1952, DMK Papers; Harry Polk to Robert Sawyer, July 6, 1953, Sawyer Papers; DMK to DDE, July 18, 1953, 118, OF 4 E, DDE Records.

15 Wall to Robert Sawyer, June 12, 1953, Sawyer Papers; P. Lyon to DMK, April 18, 1953, Marion Clawson to DMK, April 21, 1953, PF, DMK Papers.

16 Tudor, *Notes,* entry for April 19, 1953; DDE, press conference statement, April 23, 1953, *Public Papers,* p. 204; Robert Smylie to Ralph Cake, December 18, 1953, to J. Bermingham, March 6, 1953, PF, Smylie Records; Bernard De Voto to Sawyer, April 29, 1953, De Voto Papers; Edward Woozley to James Murray, July 3, 1951, Lands and BLM, Murray Papers; Woozley to Smylie, March 22, 1954, PF, Smylie Records.

17 Horace Albright to Robert Sawyer, February 10, 1953, Sawyer Papers; C. Woodbury to Irving Clark, April 28, 1953, Clark Papers; Alfred Knopf to Conrad Wirth, March 20, 1953, Wirth to Knopf, March 25, 1953, 6, Wirth File, RG 79, NA.

18 DDE to Horace Albright, October 2, 1952, copy, PF, DMK Papers; Stuart Moir to Robert Sawyer, February 5, 1953, Sawyer Papers; W. Hogenstein to Corydon Wagner, March 9, 1953, West Coast Lumbermen's Association File, Corydon Wagner Papers, University of Washington Library, Seattle; A. Shankland to Sawyer, April 30, 1953, Sawyer Papers; C. Woodbury to Irving Clark, April 28, 1953, Clark Papers; Ted Stephens to DDE, February 12, 1953.

19 DMK to Ted Stephens, February 12, 1953, Natural Resources, OF 134, DDE Records; Ralph Tudor to DMK, ca. April 1953, PF, DMK Papers.

[20] Horace Albright to Bryce Harlow, November 27, 1953, Gabriel Hauge to Harlow, November 30, 1953, 4, Bryce Harlow File, DDE Records; R. Lord to Morris Cooke, April 6, 1953, Cooke to V. Boughton, October 9, 1953, HST to Cooke, November 3, 1953, J. Patton et al. to Albright, November 10, 1953, copy, National Rural Electric Cooperative Association, press release, November 30, 1953, copy, "Corporate and Association Representation . . . ," copy, R. Gustavson, form letter, November 16, 1953, copy, Morris Cooke Papers, Roosevelt Library; DDE to Albright, March 6, 1953, *Public Papers,* pp. 91–92; for a full discussion of the conference, see Swain, *Albright,* pp. 294–301.

[21] C. Woodbury to Irving Clark, April 28, 1953, Clark to Woodbury, May 4, 1953, Clark Papers; Horace Albright, memorandum, quoted in Swain, *Albright,* pp. 301–2; Joseph Dodge, "Conservation and Development of Natural Water Resources: A Proposed General and Interim Policy," draft and memorandum, November 23, 1953, pp. 6–7, OF 155, DDE Records; Resources for the Future, "The Nation Looks at Its Resources," proceedings, December 2–4, 1953, copy, Cooke Papers.

[22] William Dawson to DMK, December 1, 1952, DDE to Herbert Brownell, December 4, 1952, Appointments, Secretary OF, RG 48, NA; Bernard De Voto to Hugh Butler, December 1, 1952, to Robert Sawyer, January 31, 1953, 22, to Eugene McCarthy, March 19, 1953, 6, De Voto Papers.

[23] Arthur Langlie, statements, *New York Times,* May 4, 26, 1953; Horace Albright to Nelson Rockefeller, March 10, 1953, copy, PF, DMK Papers; F. Gabocan to Corydon Wagner, American Forestry Association, Wagner Papers; John Rogers to Robert Sawyer, February 26, 1953, Sawyer to Rogers, March 3, 1953, to Guy Cordon, March 2, 21, 1953, Cordon to Sawyer, February 20, 1953, 24, Forestry, Sawyer Papers.

[24] DDE, statement, April 24, 1953, *Public Papers,* pp. 217–19; undated, unidentified memorandum, evidently copies of Sherman Adams to Ezra Benson, Tidelands, Langlie Records; Walt Horan to Jack Westland, December 12, 1952, 584, Politics in Congress, Horan Papers; *Oregonian,* October 8, 1955.

[25] Wesley D'Ewart, interview, pp. 79–80, DDE Library; Frank Barrett to George Aiken, June 24, 1953, Agriculture-Grazing, Barrett Papers; Aiken, statement quoted by Stephen Mitchell, Western Tour, 1953, 42, Mitchell Papers, Truman Library; L. Lokke to McKitrick, May 18, 1953, R. J. to Director, May 22, 1953, Joseph Dodge to Sherman Adams, June 30, 1953, Adams to Elmer Bennett, June 26, 1953, C. Moore to Adams, September 15, 1953, Land Matters and Grazing Lands, OF 125, DDE Records.

[26] Frank Barrett to S. Hyatt, July 22, 1953, Frank Mollin to Barrett, July 31, August 4, 1953, Barrett to Mollin, August 1, 31, 1953, F. Cooper to Barrett, July 2, 1953, Agriculture-Grazing, Barrett Papers.

[27] U.S., Congress, Senate, *Hearings on S. 2548,* 83rd Cong., 1st sess., 1953; DDE to Albert Miller, March 20, 1953, Land Matters, OF 125, DDE Records; W. Ralston et al. to James Murray, May 30, 1953, Murray, form reply, BLM, Murray, press release, April 7, 1953, C. Merritt to Lee Metcalf, copy, May 28, 1954, Murray Papers; Bernard De Voto to H. Chollis, April 10, 1953, to Thomas Dodd, April 29, 1953, 6, De Voto Papers; Kirby Billingsly to Walt Horan, May 4, 1953, 559, Politics, Horan Papers; E. Wentworth to Frank Barrett, July 29, 1953, Barrett to Wentworth, July 31, 1953, Lester Hunt to Dear Friend, copy, July 14, 1953, Agriculture-Grazing, Barrett Papers; *Rocky Mountain News,* May 30, 1953.

[28] R. Leuss to DMK, June 16, 1953, G. Knowles to Sherman Adams, copy, June 16, 1953, Wesley D'Ewart to DMK, June 4, 1953, DMK to D'Ewart, June 29, 1953, DMK to Arthur Langlie, June 20, 1953, PF, DMK Papers.

[29] Robert Sawyer to Harry Polk, July 10, 1953, Polk to Sawyer, June 16, 1953, Sawyer Papers; Farrington Carpenter to Frank Barrett, July 5, August 1, Barrett

to B. Friggens, October 26, 1953, J. Wilse to R. Hall, copy, August 8, 1953, Agriculture-Grazing, Barrett Papers; Sawyer to Richard Neuberger, August 31, 1953, Sawyer Papers; Olaus Murie to J. Welland, January 10, 1954, copy, Wilderness Society, Clark Papers; Barrett to Frank Mollin, February 25, June 14, to J. Jones, March 21, 1955, J. Wilson to Barrett, June 20, 1955, Mollin to R. Hope, August 16, 1954, copy, Agriculture-Grazing, Barrett Papers; Sawyer to Ralph Tudor, January 12, 1954, Sawyer Papers.

[30] DDE, "Annual Message . . . ," January 7, 1954, "Letter to . . . McKay," "Message . . . ," August 25, 1954, *Public Papers*, pp. 17–18; 713–14, 775–76; President's Commission on Intergovernmental Relations, committee minutes and reports, pp. 34–35, OF A 67–5, DDE Records; Frank Mollin to R. Hope, August 16, 1954, copy, Agriculture-Grazing, Barrett Papers.

[31] Horace Albright to Robert Sawyer, February 10, 1953, Sawyer Papers; C. Woodbury to Irving Clark, April 28, 1953, Clark Papers; Alfred Knopf to Conrad Wirth, March 20, 1953, Wirth to Knopf, March 25, 1953, 6, Wirth File, RG 79; NA; Joseph Dodge to DMK, September 15, 1953, NP, 121, OF 4Q6, DDE Records; DMK, statements, *US News and World Report* (October 9, 1953), p. 107; *Oregonian*, May 27, 1953; *Port Angeles* (Washington) *News*, July 18, 1953.

[32] Conrad Wirth to DMK, January 21, 1953, H. Oehlmann to Orme Lewis, copy, August 6, 1954, Lewis to DMK, September 21, 1954, Horace Albright to DMK, February 25, 1955, PF, DMK Papers; Bernard De Voto to editor, *Cut Bank* (Montana) *Pioneer Press*, September 21, 1954, 6, De Voto Papers.

[33] DMK to Horace Albright, March 3, 1955, PF, DMK Papers; Joseph O'Mahoney to J. Harlan, March 31, 1955, Yellowstone, O'Mahoney Papers; Conrad Wirth to Warren Magnuson, July 28, 1954, copy, DMK, Norwood Papers.

[34] DMK to Paul Patterson, March 26, 1953, Oregon, 6, McCrillis File, RG 48, NRC; Russell Mack to A. Prial, attached to Corydon Wagner to Arthur Langlie, February 4, 1953, C. Paul to Langlie, February 6, 1953, Langlie to Mack, February 18, 1953, Mack to Langlie, March 3, 1953, ONP Review Committee, Langlie Records; M. Deggler to Mack, March 5, 1953, ONP, General Correspondence, Wagner Papers; Miller Freeman to Langlie, May 27, 1955, Jack Westland to Langlie, July 28, 1953, and attachments, "Proceedings of the Olympic . . . Review Committee . . . September 27, 1953," Vol. 1, October 2, 1953, Vol. 2, October 16, 1953, Gordon Marckworth to Langlie, September 10, 1953, February 18, 1954, ONP Review Committee, Langlie Records; "Is the Olympic National Park Too Big?" pamphlet, W. DeLoong to Irving Clark, June 29, 1954, "Memorandum of Facts Re the Olympic National Park," August 1955, copies, Pacific Northwest Lumbermen's Association Papers, University of Washington Library, Seattle; J. Osseward to Irving Clark, May 1955, Clark Papers; Horace Albright to DMK, April 1, 1954, PF, DMK Papers.

[35] DMK to Stuart Moir, May 12, 1953, PF, DMK Papers.

[36] Horace Albright to DMK, July 16, 29, 1953, DMK to Albright, July 28, PF, DMK Papers; Albright to David Brower, October 5, 1953, SCA; F. Northrup to DMK, February 5, 1953, 12–47, part 2, Glacier, RG 79, NA; L. Markham to Walt Horan, June 3, 1953, C. Chorpenning to Horan, June 23, 1953, 426, Power, Horan Papers; A. Zahn to DMK, July 20, 1953, 12.0 part 18, GAF, RG 79, NA; Mike Mansfield to DMK, March 18, 1954, John Marr to Orme Lewis, February 26, 1954, DMK to Mansfield, March 18, 1954, Glacier, Parks and Sites, 139, 6PS, RG 79, NRC; Albright to DMK, April 1, 1954, PF, DMK Papers.

[37] I. Axelson to Orme Lewis, January 26, 1954, D.K. to C. Johnson, ca. February 19, 1954, C. Nicol to Conrad Wirth, March 31, 1954, Everett Dirksen to DMK, February 10, 1954, Lewis to R. Baker, August 6, 1954, DMK to Nicol, April 2, 1954, Lewis to Nicol, May 19, 1954, Lewis to Dirksen, March 9, 1954, Everglades, 139, Parks and Sites, 6PS, RG 79, NRC.

38 Arthur Langlie to DMK, May 5, September 21, 1954, PF, DMK Papers; Sherman Adams to H. Bradley, March 10, 1955, R. Davis to R. Butcher, May 29, 1955, 117, 9, RG 115/4, NRC; F. McNeil to Richard Neuberger, May 4, 1955, General Correspondence, Neuberger Papers; see also Arthur Martinson, "Mountain in the Sky: A History of Mount Rainier National Park" (Ph.D. diss., Washington State University, 1966), pp. 153–55.

39 William Voigt to DMK, March 30, 1954, DMK to Voigt, April 16, 1954, Everglades, 139, Parks and Sites, 6PS, RG 79, NRC.

40 DMK to DDE, Ralph Tudor to DDE, both undated but ca. July 1954, 115, OF 3WW, DDE Records; Tudor to Robert Sawyer, January 13, 1954, Sawyer Papers; Tudor to DMK, August 11, 1954, Secretary OF, RG 48, NA; "Summary . . . Reorganization of the Bureaus of . . . Interior," August 11, 1954, 115, OF 3WW, DDE Records.

41 Wesley D'Ewart, interview, pp. 79–80; John D. Rockefeller, Jr., to DDE, December 10, 1953, OF 4Q3, DDE Records; DDE to DMK, January 9, 1954, PF, DMK Papers.

42 Bradley Patterson, Jr., interview, March 30, 1959, copy, DDE Library; Maxwell Rabb to DMK, January 20, 1956, 15, Gerald Morgan File, DDE Records; DMK to DDE, February 1, 1956, DDE to Sam Rayburn, February 2, 1956, and attachments, "Mission 66 for The National Park Service," Ezra Benson to Sherman Adams, February 20, 1956, Rowland Hughes to Adams, February 29, 1956, Adams to Benson, March 5, 1956, OF 4Q3, DDE Records; DDE, "Letter to the President of the Senate and the Speaker of the House . . . ," February 2, 1956, Public Papers, pp. 223–24.

43 H.Z.N. to Earl –, August 27, 1959, NPS, Dworshak Papers; "Scenic Resources Review," DNM, 21, Solicitor File, RG 48, NRC; C. Woodbury to Irving Clark, May 18, 27, 1954, Clark Papers; Bernard De Voto to C. Brandt, February 1, 16, 1955, 6, Fred Packard to Alfred Knopf, February 14, 1955, 24, De Voto Papers; Carl Russell to A. Josephy, October 23, 1963, Russell Papers.

CHAPTER SIX

1 DDE, "Annual Message . . . ," February 2, 1953, statement, August 18, 1953, "Special Message . . . ," July 31, 1953, "Remarks . . . ," August 4, 1953, Public Papers, pp. 26–27, 573–74, 528–33, 538–39 respectively.

2 DDE, "Special Message . . . ," July 31, 1953, Public Papers, pp. 528–33; Robert Sawyer to Ralph Cake, March 30, 1953, W. Welch to Sawyer, March 16, 1953, Sawyer Papers; Robert Donovan, Eisenhower: The Inside Story (New York, 1956), pp. 79-81; C. Johnson to Herbert Brownell, January 5, 1953, Appointments, Secretary OF, RG 48, NA.

3 "Budget Bureau Policy . . . ," 87, Interior Appropriations Committee, notation by Walt Horan on L. Smith, list of reclamation projects, 373, Irrigation and Reclamation, Horan Papers; Ralph Tudor speech, Idaho State Reclamation Association, Boise, November 4, 1953, copy, 10, Personal, Elmer Bennett Papers, DDE Library; Fresno (California) Bee, March 27, April 20, 1955; DDE, "Annual Budget Message . . . ," January 17, 1955, Public Papers, pp. 156–58, statement, August 6, 1956, pp. 648–50.

4 DMK, statements, New York Times, December 18, 31, 1952; Robert Sawyer to DMK, January 13, 1953, Charles Sprague to Sawyer, December 1, April 24, 1953, Sawyer Papers.

5 DMK to C. Brownell, December 20, 1952, Appointments, BPA, Secretary OF, RG 48, NA; DMK to Gus Norwood, February 19, 1953, Norwood Papers; B. Jensen, statements, March 27, 1953, Congress, Secretary OF, RG 48, NA; J. Price

to DMK, February 16, 1953, copy, 6–15, VI, Langlie Papers; O. Hurd to F. Northrup, April 6, 1953, PF, Northwest Public Power Association Papers; DMK to W. Greve, April 21, 1953, PF, DMK Papers; DMK, speech, Boston, May 14, 1953, copy, PNE Power, General Conservation and Development Commission Records, Washington State Archives.

6 DMK, speech, March 3, 1953, copy, 64, PF, DMK Papers; DMK, quoted in *Oregonian*, June 2, 1953; Republican National Committee correction, *Denver Post*, October 30, 1955.

7 Clarence Davis to DMK, January 22, 1953, PF, DMK Papers; J. Houston to Arthur Langlie, April 20, 1953, 9–20, VI, Langlie Papers; Ralph Tudor to DMK, May 7, 1954, PF, DMK Papers.

8 Ralph Tudor, *Notes*, entries for July 6, September 27, October 11, 1953; DMK to E. Newby, May 4, 1954, T. Hedges to Walt Horan, May 5, 1953, 87, Interior Appropriations Committee, Horan Papers.

9 *Idaho Statesman*, March 1, 1953; DMK, testimony, February 17, 1956, in U.S., Congress, Senate and House, Interior Committee, *Hearings Before the Joint Committee* . . . , 84th Cong., 2d sess., 1956; Ralph Tudor, *Notes*, entries for April 11, May 10, August 5, 29, 1953; HC, undated items, 61, PF, DMK Papers; Tudor to DMK, ca. April 1953, Secretary OF, RG 48, NA; DMK to James Murray, November 2, 1953, PF, DMK Papers; Eugene Millikan to Scott Lucas, May 26, 1953, copy, Personal Book 1 (2), 8, Elmer Bennett to J. Martin, October 29, 1953, copy, Power, 6, Bennett Papers; E. Cooper to Julius Krug, May 13, 1953, 45, Krug Papers.

10 Sherman Adams to Palmer Hoyt, June 6, 1953, Hoyt to Adams, May 25, 1953, 838, OF 155 E 1, DDE Records; DDE, press conference statement, May 14, 1953, *Public Papers*, pp. 286–87; *Denver Post*, May 13, 20, 1953; DMK to T. Delzell, May 11, 1953, Delzell to DMK, May 8, 1953, 2, McCrillis File, Secretary OF, RG 48, NRC; Ralph Tudor to DMK, August 5, October 16, 1953, Secretary OF, RG 48, NA.

11 DDE, quoted by Hughes, *Ordeal of Power*, p. 152; DDE, press conference statement, June 17, 1953, *Public Papers*, pp. 433–34.

12 Bureau of the Budget, unsigned memorandum, May 11, 1953, TVA, OF 51, Gabriel Hauge to DDE, June 22, 1953, 1, Gabriel Hauge File, DDE Records; Homer Gruenther to Sam Ervin, August 21, 1953, 234, TVA, OF 51, DDE Records; DDE, press conference statement, October 8, 1953, *Public Papers*, p. 544, statement, press conference, November 10, 1954, *Public Papers*, p. 1054.

13 Lilienthal, *Journals*, 3:408; David Lilienthal to Palmer Hoyt, September 10, 1953, copy, Gordon Clapp to Lilienthal, June 18, 1953, Clapp to Hoyt, September 10, 1953, 2, Gordon Clapp Papers, HST Library; Gabriel Hauge to DDE, October 12, 1953, 1, Hauge File, DDE Records.

14 Bureau of the Budget, memorandum, ca. November 23, 1953, and Joseph Dodge, "Proposed Statement Regarding the Tennessee Valley Authority," draft, November 27, 1953, OF 155, DDE Records.

15 Walt Horan to DDE, October 12, 1953, Ralph Tudor, draft, October 29, 1953, DMK to Horan, November 4, 1953, 828, OF 155A-1, DDE Records; *Spokesman-Review*, December 21, 1952; Paul Raver to Horan, September 30, 1953, 426, Power, Horan to Kirby Billingsly, May 13, 1953, Billingsly to Horan, December 5, 1953, 553, Politics, Horan Papers; Henry Dworshak to N. Sharp, April 27, 1953, and unidentified item, January 12, 1953, Interior-Reclamation, Dworshak Papers; J. Houston to Arthur Langlie, ca. March 1953, 9–20, VI, Langlie Papers; Harris Ellsworth to DMK, November 13, 1953, DMK to Paul Patterson, April 17, 1953, copy, McCrillis File, Secretary OF, RG 48, NRC; Ralph Tudor, *Notes*, entries for April 11, July 6, September 6, October 24, 1953; Tudor to Fred Aandahl, Appointments, Secretary OF, RG 48, NA; B. Hallock

to DMK, October 24, 1953, DMK to Hallock, November 13, 1953, PF, DMK Papers; Tudor to M. Frey, December 22, 1953, Secretary OF, RG 48, NA.

16 Ralph Tudor to Robert Sawyer, January 27, 1954, Sawyer Papers; G. Scott to Elmer Bennett, November 12, 1956, Personal, II–2, 8, Bennett Papers.

17 Sherman Adams to S. Tunney, January 26, 1954, Adams-DDE correspondence and dossiers, A. Morgan to DDE, March 1, 1951, TVA, 254, OF 51, DDE Records.

18 DDE, press conference statement, August 4, 1954, *Public Papers*, p. 182; Lilienthal, *Journals*, vol. 3, entries for August 11, September 29, 1954; Adams to Joseph Dodge, May 13, 1953, H. Vogel to R. Hughes, November 14, 1955, TVA, 235, OF 51, DDE Records.

19 Ralph Tudor, *Notes*, August 29, 1953; Tudor to DMK, August 5, October 16, 1953, Secretary OF, RG 48, NA; Fred Aandahl, statements, *New York Times*, August 24, November 6, 14, 1953; memorandum to L. Smith, October 15, 1953, 115, OF 3WW, Joe Martin to Warren Magnuson, October 29, 1953, OF 141, Bryce Harlow to Wilton Persons, December 14, 1953, TVA, 234, OF 51, DDE Records.

20 Arthur Langlie to S. Aders, February 16, 1954, Paul Patterson to Langlie, March 1, 1954, 6–20, VI, Langlie Papers; Walt Horan to J. Jones, March 30, 1953, 426, Power, Horan Papers; Henry Dworshak to L. Crandall, February 1, 1954, Dworshak to A. Curtis, January 26, 1954, Interior-Reclamation, Dworshak Papers; W. Hagenstein to C. Cucanter, November 6, 1953, American Forestry Congress, 1, Wagner Papers; W. O'Neil to DMK, October 27, 1953, PF, DMK Papers; see also Scott, "Langlie," p. 401.

21 Bureau of the Budget, memorandum, November 23, 1953, and "Conservation and Development of National Water Resources . . . ," draft, 825, OF 155, DDE Records.

22 U.S., Congress, Senate, Interior Committee, *Hearings . . . December 29, 1954, January 4, 1955*, 84th Cong., 1st sess., 1955, esp. pp. 181–91; Water Power Committee, statement, August 6, 1954, Correspondence and Meetings, 35, President's Commission on Intergovernmental Relations File, DDE Records; Edwin Johnson to Gus Norwood, January 22, 1954, President's Correspondence, Northwest Public Power Association Papers; Walt Horan to C. Peterson, June 18, 1953, Horan to DMK, November 16, 1953, 426, Power, Horan Papers; C. Ellis to A. Radin, American Public Power Association, Northwest Public Power Association Papers; W. Holden to Henry Dworshak, November 24, 1954, Interior-Reclamation, Dworshak Papers.

23 D. Bandemann to DDE, April 22, 1953, W. Weyer to DDE, April 23, 1953, 388, GF 43–A, DDE Records; *Oregonian*, April 26, 1953, March 21, 1954; S. Anderson to DMK, November 9, 1953, copy, Leland Olds to Morris Cooke, August 4, 1953, Clyde Ellis to Cooke, March 5, 1954, Morris Cooke Papers; Frank Clement to Henry Dworshak, May 1, 1953, Interior-Reclamation, Dworshak Papers; Lilienthal, *Journals*, 4:87; David Lilienthal to Gordon Clapp, May 19, 1953, 2, Clapp Papers; Michael Straus to Joseph O'Mahoney, September 24, 1954, 1954 Campaign, O'Mahoney Papers.

24 Herblock cartoons reproduced in Herbert Block *Here and Now* (New York, 1955), esp. pp. 213–27, 242; C. Keiser to Walt Horan, February 6, 1954, G. Markham to Horan, September 13, 1954, Horan to Markham, September 17, 1954, 427, Power, Horan Papers; D. Bandemann to DDE, April 22, 1953, W. Weyer to DDE, April 23, 1953, 388, GF 43–A, DDE Records; Al Ullman to James Murray, May 8, 1953, HC, 7, Reclamation, Murray to G. Horsford, May 14, 1953, Political Misc., Murray Papers; Wayne Morse to DDE, December 28, 1953, copy, Ralph Tudor to Estes Kefauver, December 24, 1953, copy, Personal, 10, Bennett Papers; Warren Magnuson et al. to DDE, December 30, 1954, Congres-

sional Correspondence Index, DDE Records; T. Roach to Bernard De Voto, August 18, October 4, 1954, 19, C. Girard Davidson to De Voto, September 13, 1954, De Voto Papers.

25 U.S., Congress, Senate, Interior Committee, *Monopoly in the Power Industry . . . Report . . .*, 84th Cong., 2d sess., 1955, misc. items in HC, Power Hearings, Interior Committee, O'Mahoney Papers; James Weschler to Richard Neuberger, April 3, 1956, Lyndon Johnson to Neuberger, August 31, 1955, Senators, Neuberger Papers; Sherman Adams to Arthur Langlie, April 7, 1955, Langlie to Adams, April 11, 1955, 9–18, VI, Langlie Papers; DMK to E. Alldredge, May 19, 1955, PF, DMK Papers.

26 Wendell Wyatt to Sherman Adams, July 19, 1955, copy, Misc. Political Correspondence, E. Newby to DMK, April 27, 1954, DMK to Newby, May 4, 1954, PF, DMK Papers; Gus Norwood to C. Ellis and A. Radin, August 26, 1954, American Public Power Association, Northwest Public Power Association Papers; Scott, "Langlie," pp. 401, 413; *Seattle Post-Intelligencer*, February 26, 1954; *Lewiston* (Idaho) *Tribune*, January 22, 1954; Walt Horan to Adams, March 1, 1955, 554, Politics, Horan Papers; Adams to DMK, June 1, 1955, White House, PF, DMK Papers; Ralph Tudor to P. Young, September 30, 1954, copy, Secretary OF, RG 48, NA; Tudor to Robert Sawyer, December 23, 1954, Sawyer Papers; Tudor, address, Chicago, May 5, 1954, copy, Personal Book I, 10, Bennett Papers.

27 Ralph Tudor, briefs and copy of opinion survey, "The Voter Looks at Public Power," ca. February 1954, Secretary OF, RG 48, NA; "The Situation in Idaho," April 4, 1955, 38, Pyle File, DDE Records; DMK to DDE, October 15, 1954, 44, John Bragdon File, G. Morgan to DDE, ca. October 15, 1954, Homer Gruenther to DDE, October 18, 1954, 825, OF 155, DDE Records; Len Jordan to DMK, August 8, 1955, PF, DMK Papers; DMK to James Murray, March 2, 1955, DDE to DMK, March 26, 1954, 825, OF 155, DDE Records; DDE, "Statement . . . February 10, 1954," and press conference statement, March 10, 1954, *Public Papers*, pp. 256, 307–8; DMK to Marshall Dana, July 25, 1955, PF, DMK Papers; Gabriel Hauge to DMK, April 6, 1955, 115, 3WW, survey of congressional mail, October 1955, 825, OF 155, DDE Records; DDE, "Annual Message . . . ," January 6, 1956, *Public Papers*, pp. 18–19.

CHAPTER SEVEN

1 Arthur Watkins, statement, *Deseret News*, December 6, 1952; "A Conversation with Arthur V. Watkins," *Dialogue* (Winter 1968), pp. 113–20.

2 J. Bracken Lee to DMK, June 18, 1953, Wilbur Dexheimer to Lee, October 5, 1953, UCB, Lee Records; Conrad Wirth to DMK, April 22, 1953, attached to Wirth to Orme Lewis, March 18, 1953, Alfred Landon to Wirth, March 10, 1953, Fred Aandahl to Wirth, April 6, 1953, 12–46, part 2, 3847, Secretary OF, RG 48, NA; Ralph Tudor to J. Will, July 16, 1953, State Engineer File, Lee Records.

3 Ralph Tudor, *Notes*, entry for April 19, 1953; Tudor to Orme Lewis, 1953, 12–46, part 2, 3847, Secretary OF, RG 48, NA; Fred Aandahl to J. Bracken Lee, June 18, 1953, UCB, J. Will to J. Tracy, June 18, 1953, State Engineer File, Lee Records; G. Maltes to Tudor, May 15, 1953, 12–46, part 2, Secretary OF, RG 48, NA; Tudor to Will, July 16, 1953, UCB, Thorton Records.

4 David Brower to R. Dally, May 12, 1953, Richard Leonard to P. Orcutt, October 13, 1953, SCA; Fred Packard to G. Kahn, November 29, 1954, copy, 24, Bernard De Voto to John Fischer, March 23, 1953, 6, De Voto Papers; Ralph Tudor to Robert Sawyer, January 8, 1954, 117, 1, RG 115/4, NRC; Tudor, *Notes*, entries for September 27, November 22, 1953; Horace Albright to David Brower,

October 16, 1953, "Special Bulletin #6," with Brower notation, February 18, 1954, SCA; *Salt Lake Tribune*, October 19, 1953; Tudor, *Notes*, entry for November 22, 1953.

5 David Brower to R. Dally, May 12, 1953, SCA; Arthur Carhart to Horace Albright, December 24, 1953, EP, Carhart Papers; DMK, statement quoted is in DMK to DDE, December 10, 1953, copy, 1, Aandahl File, RG 48, NA; all federal correspondence to and from the Interior Department on the subject of UCB is printed in U.S., Congress, House, *Colorado River Storage Project*, House Document No. 364, 85th Cong., 2d sess., 1955.

6 Edwin Mecham to DDE, March 26, 1954, UCB, part 1, 828, OF 115 A 2, DDE Records; *New York Times*, December 29, 1953; Arthur Carhart, drafts of letters and pamphlets, December 1953, EP, Carhart Papers.

7 Conrad Wirth to Ralph Tudor, December 16, 1953, John Marr to Wirth, January 18, 1954, 117, 1, RG 115/4, NRC; Arthur Carhart to DDE, January 4, 1954, EP, Carhart Papers; Ulysses Grant III to DDE, December 19, 1953, Grant to DMK, January 20, 1954, copies, EP, 24, RG 79, NA; Charles Sauers to DDE, January 15, 1954, copy, 6, De Voto Papers; Alfred Knopf to DDE, January 4, February 5, 1954, Gabriel Hauge to Sherman Adams, January 25, 1954, DDE to DMK, January 26, 1954, EP, 838, OF 155 E 1, DDE Records; Donovan, *Eisenhower: The Inside Story*, pp. 140–41; T. Jukes to DDE, December 28, 1953, Ansel Adams to DDE, December 28, 1953, copies, Richard Leonard to W. Olney, January 16, 1954, SCA.

8 The Sierra Club Archives and Library, San Francisco, holds much of the literature issued by the preservationist organizations on the Dinosaur issue. These tracts may also be found in the Arthur Carhart Papers and the Bureau of Reclamation record sub-group at the National Records Center. Herblock's cartoons are in the *St. Louis Post-Dispatch*, March 15, April 19, 1954; Somdal's cartoon is in the *Sacramento Bee*, January 12, 1954; Wallace Stegner, ed., *This Is Dinosaur* (New York, 1954). Two contemporary studies engendered by the controversy are Robin W. Winks, "The Preservation Movement" (Ph.D. diss., Johns Hopkins University, 1956), and Owen Stratton and Phillip Sorotkin, *The Echo Park Controversy*, "Cases in Public Administration and Policy Formation," vol. 46 (University of Alabama, 1959).

9 Arthur Carhart to Meyer Litton, December 19, 1953, Litton to Richard Leonard, September 19, 1953, SCA; Howard Zahniser to Carhart, December 21, 1953, Carhart to Buz Hatch et al., December 16, 1953, to John Saylor, February 24, 1954, to Ira Gabrielson, March 23, 1954, Bernard De Voto to Carhart, March 8, 1954, EP, Carhart Papers; Alfred Knopf to DDE, April 26, 1954, EP, 838, OF 155 E 1, DDE Records.

10 J. Stoker to Henry Dworshak, February 3, 1954, NPS, Dworshak Papers; DDE, "Statement . . . upon Approving Recommendations for the Development of the Upper Colorado River Basin," March 20, 1954, DDE to DMK, May 26, 1954, *Public Papers*, pp. 338–39, 415, 509–10; Sherman Adams to H. Crowe, May 15, 1954, Bryce Harlow to Adams, May 15, 1954, EP, 838, OF 155 E 1, DDE Records.

11 "Conservation . . . A Misinformed President," March 22, 1954, copy, SCA; "A Conversation with . . . Watkins," *Dialogue* (Winter 1968), pp. 114–15.

12 DDE, *Mandate for Change*, p. 550; DMK to C. Whitehead, February 19, 1954, 117, 2, RG 115/4, NRC; DMK to Arthur Carhart, March 20, 1954, EP, Carhart Papers; Frank Barrett to E. Crippen, March 15, 1954, Barrett to O. Bertagnolli, March 15, 1954, UCB, Interior-Reclamation, Barrett Papers.

13 Robert Sawyer to Ralph Tudor, January 17, 1954, Tudor to Sawyer, January 8, 1954, Sawyer Papers; William Dawson, comment quoted in *Sierra Club Bulletin* #6, February 10, 1954, SCA; J. Bennett to Tudor, September 1, 1953, 12.0, part

18, GAF, RG 79, NA; H. Donohoe to Barry Goldwater, January 13, 1954, DMK to Sherman Adams, March 5, 1954, 117, 2, RG 115/4, NRC.

14 Editorials, *Denver Post,* March 5, 9, August 5, September 15, 1954. The arguments issued by the proponents of the UCB dams, issued as pamphlets, resolutions, and correspondence, are contained in the files of the Upper Colorado River Basin Commission and the records of the governors of Utah and Colorado located in the archives of those states.

15 Wesley D'Ewart to Kern, February 1, 1954, Absaroksa Conservation Committee, D'Ewart Papers; J. Stone, statement, in Stone to DDE, March 19, 1954, 117, 3, RG 115/4, NRC.

16 DDE, press conference statement, February 9, 1956, *Public Papers,* p. 265.

17 *Deseret News,* July 31, October 11, 1954; *Salt Lake Tribune,* June 18, 1954.

18 Visitor statistics at DNM are in H. Baker to Conrad Wirth, December 11, 1954, DNM, 1, Wirth File, RG 79, NA.

19 Bernard De Voto to Palmer Hoyt, March 1, 1954, 6, De Voto Papers; Arthur Carhart to B. Strong, January 25, 1954, De Voto to Carhart, March 8, 1954, EP, Carhart Papers; De Voto to John Kennedy, September 15, 1954, 6, De Voto Papers.

20 Howard Pyle to DMK, March 18, 1954, 117, 3, John Saylor to DMK, March 6, 1954, 117, 2, RG 115/4, NRC.

21 Bestor Robinson to DMK, February 17, 1954, DMK to Robinson, March 9, 1954, 117, 2, John Marr to Ralph Tudor, January 15, 1954, 117, 1, H. McPhail to Marr, February 15, 1954, Fred Aandahl to Joseph Dodge, March 2, 1954, 117, 2, RG 115/4, NRC.

22 David Brower to Howard Zahniser, February 7, 1955, SCA; DMK to Arthur Watkins, February 24, 1955, 139, DNM, 6 NPS, RG 48, NRC; Brower to editor, *Salt Lake Tribune,* January 9, 1955, SCA.

23 Conrad Wirth to John Bricker, January 29, 1954, 1, Wirth to Orme Lewis, February 3, 1954, 117, 2, T. Tolson to Acting Director, NPS, September 15, 1955, 118, RG 115/4, NRC; to B. Thompson, February 17, 1954, DNM, 1, to Alfred Knopf, March 31, 1954, 6, Wirth File, RG 79, NA.

24 Arthur Carhart, press release, ca. February 8, 1954, Carhart to Ira Gabrielson et al., February 8, 1954, Carhart to —, March 8, 1954, EP, Carhart Papers; J. W. Penfold to DMK, February 10, 1954, 117, 2, RG 115/4, NRC.

25 Ralph Tudor to William Harrison, May 13, 1954, copy, EP, 838, OF 155 E 1, DDE Records; "Official Statement of the Committee for a Glen Canyon National Park," 1954, copy, UCB, 1954, Lee Records; H. Bradley to David Brower, April 7, 1954, SCA; Tudor to Robert Sawyer, April 14, 1954, Sawyer Papers; *Denver Post,* May 21, 1954; Sherman Adams to DMK, April 15, 1954, Adams, 1, McCrillis File, RG 48, NRC.

26 David Brower to Robert Sawyer, May 7, 1954, Sawyer to Richard Leonard, ca. June 1, 1954, Leonard to C. Mauk, copy, July 9, 1954, Sierra Club, Sawyer Papers; Wilbur Dexheimer to Fred Aandahl, June 8, 1954, 117, 8, RG 115/4, NRC.

27 Elmer Bennett to Wilbur Dexheimer, May 26, 1954, Ralph Tudor to R. Davis, July 15, 1954, 117, 8, RG 115/4, NRC; Sam Coon to Robert Sawyer, May 21, 1954, Sawyer Papers; David Brower to Sherman Adams, May 26, 1954, copy, SCA; Brower to Tudor, June 1, 1954, DMK to Dexheimer, August 10, 1954, 117, 8, Tudor to F. Whitman, August 30, 1954, 117, 9, RG 115/4, NRC.

28 Bernard Shanley to D. Lowe, August 23, 1954, J. W. Penfold to E. Halliday, July 22, 1954, EP, Carhart Papers; Dan Thorton to Herbert Brownell, October 4, 1954, Thorton Records; John Saylor to DDE, April 5, 1954, Congressional Correspondence Index, DDE Records; Walt Horan to Saylor, March 10, 1954, 373, Irrigation and Reclamation, Horan Papers; Gracie Pfost, statement, April 8, 1954, SCA; Arthur Carhart to William Voigt, October 13, 1954, EP, Carhart Papers; Bernard De Voto to F. Huntington, 6, De Voto Papers.

29 DDE, "Remarks at Natrona Airport . . . ," September 4, 1954, *Public Papers*, pp. 835–36; statement quoted is in D. Bradley to Sherman Adams, October 16, 1954, 117, 9, RG 115/4, NRC.

30 A. Harrington to Joe Martin, February 23, 1955, UCB, 1, OF 155 A 2, DDE Records; DMK to R. Penguilly, March 19, 1955, Sherman Adams to H. Bradley, March 10, 1955, 117, 9, RG 115/4, NRC.

31 *Sierra Club Bulletin* (January 1955), Alfred Knopf to Orme Lewis, April 26, 1955, copy, H. Severance to David Brower, February 4, 1955, SCA; Roderick Nash, *Wilderness and the American Mind* (New Haven, Conn., 1967), p. 218, n59.

32 L. Snarr to H. Simpson, February 24, 1955, John Fischer to J. Bracken Lee, January 27, April 7, 1955, UCB, Lee Records.

33 U.S., Congress, House, *Colorado River Storage Project*, House Doc. 364, 83d Cong., 2d sess., 1955; George Clyde to J. Bracken Lee, April 21, 1955, UCB, Lee Records; *Deseret News*, April 23, 1955; Robert Lucas to Richard Neuberger, April 13, 1955, Conservation-EP, Neuberger Papers; Arthur Watkins to DDE, February 16, 1955, UCB, 1, OF 155 A 2, DDE Records; S. Southard to Everett Dirksen, copy, October 19, 1955, 117, 14, RG 115/4, NRC; DDE, press conference statement not released for quotation, March 16, 1955, *Public Papers*, pp. 330–31; David Brower to D. Brinegar, January 20, 1955, SCA; J. Price to Neuberger, January 28, 1955, Lewis, Wirth File, RG 79, NA; C. Baker to Neuberger, April 13, 1955, Conservation-EP, Neuberger Papers; statement quoted is in Arthur Watkins to Richard Leonard, April 5, 1955, SCA.

34 Milward Simpson to Frank Barrett, January 4, 13, 1955, Interior-Reclamation, UCB, Barrett Papers; Richard Neuberger to David Brower, April 20, 1955, SCA; Bernard De Voto to Paul Douglas, April 26, 1955, 6, De Voto Papers; Neuberger to Robert Lucas, April 21, 1955, to John Kennedy, April 22, 1955, to Clinton Anderson, April 23, 1955, to Joseph O'Mahoney, April 23, 1955, to Alfred Knopf, April 21, 1955, Knopf to Neuberger, April 21, 25, 27, 1955, Conservation-EP, Neuberger Papers.

35 Edwin Johnson to George Kelly, February 1, 1954, Kelly Papers; Johnson to Arthur Carhart, July 6, 1954, UCB, Carhart Papers; Bernard De Voto to Ira Gabrielson, December 3, 1954, 30, De Voto Papers; Carhart to David Brower, December 11, 21, 1954, SCA; Carhart to E. Graves, December 19, 1954, UCB, Carhart Papers.

36 Izaak Walton League, "Report of the Governor's Meeting . . . January 4, 1955," copy, Carhart Papers; Milward Simpson to Joseph O'Mahoney, January 6, 1955, O'Mahoney, "Echo Park Dam Is Essential," copy of article in *Collier's*, O'Mahoney to T. Roncalis, August 23, 1954, H. Hagen, February 18, 1955, G. Sertesy to O'Mahoney, February 26, 1955, O'Mahoney to Leslie Miller, January 3, 1955, O'Mahoney to Arthur Watkins, April 23, 1955, Watkins to O'Mahoney, April 29, 1955, UCB, O'Mahoney Papers; see also Clinton Anderson, *Outsider in the Senate* (New York, 1970), pp. 238–42.

37 Edwin Johnson to J. W. Penfold, December 31, 1953, Kelly Papers; Johnson to H. Ferrill, May 25, 1955, Johnson to Mrs. S. Wheeler, May 27, 1955, UCB, 8a, Johnson Records; T. Eliot to Wayne Aspinall, April 5, 1955, copy, SCA; James Murray to F. Bronson, February 21, 1955, to H. Bradley, April 25, 1955, EP-Reclamation, Murray Papers; "Handed Out at a Republican Caucus, July 25, 1955," copy, Joseph O'Mahoney to D. Scoll, August 12, 1955, UCB, O'Mahoney Papers; George Clyde to J. Bracken Lee, May 4, 1955, Governor, Arthur Watkins to Lee, August 6, 1955, Lee Records.

38 Cartoon by Conrad, *Denver Post*, August 26, 1955; F. Smith to David Brower, June 8, 1955, SCA; J. W. Penfold, statement, July 22, 1955, UCB, 8a, Johnson Records; *Denver Post*, October 31, 1955; John Saylor, press release, June 8, 1955, copy, Charles Hosmer, press release, copy, June 8, 1955, DNM, 1, Wirth File, RG

79, NA; "Tomorrow's Playground for Millions of Americans," Pamphlet, Utah State Historical Society, Salt Lake City; Arthur Watkins, statement quoted in O. Dick to Conrad Wirth, September 19, 1955, DNM, 1, Wirth File, RG 79, NA.

[39] Edwin Johnson to Robert Lucas, July 25, 1955, to Milward Simpson, November 2, 1955, UCB, 8a, Johnson Records; "Conference on the Upper Colorado River Storage Project . . . November 1, 1955," copy, Clinton Anderson to Wilbur Dexheimer, November 9, 1955, copy, both items kindly supplied to the author by Senator Anderson; "Actions of Conference on Upper Colorado River Legislation," copy, UCB, O'Mahoney Papers.

[40] J. Bracken Lee to Edwin Johnson, December 22, 1955, UCB, Lee Records; T. Bolack to Joseph O'Mahoney, November 10, 1955, J. Moynihan to Johnson, March 3, 1956, copy, UCB, O'Mahoney Papers; Conrad Wirth to J. W. Penfold, December 1, 1955, Izaak Walton League, 2, Wirth File, RG 79, NA; Alfred Knopf to Bernard De Voto, November 7, 1955, 22, De Voto Papers; Paul Douglas to James Murray, January 15, 1960, Reclamation, 6, Murray Papers.

[41] Wesley D'Ewart to DMK, November 23, 1955, DMK to D'Ewart, November 23, 1955, 118, 14, RG 115/4, NRC; J. W. Penfold to Joseph O'Mahoney, January 9, 1956, UCB, O'Mahoney Papers; Interior Department, press release, "Statement on Echo Park," November 29, 1955, copy, DNM, 21, Solicitor File, RG 48, NRC; DMK to David Brower, January 30, 1956, SCA.

[42] Edwin Johnson to State and Congressional Delegations, February 14, 1956, Wayne Aspinall to Johnson, February 16, 1956, J. Simms to I. Golson, copy, February 20, 1956, F. Peterson to Johnson, May 17, 1956, Johnson to Wilbur Dexheimer, May 21, 1956, to J. Bracken Lee, November 25, 1955, UCB, 8a, Johnson Records.

[43] A. Hildebrand to David Brower, December 19, 1955, SCA; J. W. Penfold to Milward Simpson, copy, November 23, 1955, UCB, 8a, Johnson Records; Ira Gabrielson et al. to Joseph O'Mahoney, December 15, 1955, Horace Albright et al. to O'Mahoney, January 23, 1956, UCB, O'Mahoney Papers; Fred Packard to David Brower, December 20, 1955, and attached note, "Conservation Policy Guide—Abstract of Directors' Actions, 1946–1964," entry for December 1955, pp. 3–4, SCA; C. Graves to Arthur Watkins, December 24, 1955, copy, UCB, 8a, Johnson Records; *Oregonian,* March 9, 1956.

CHAPTER EIGHT

[1] Ralph Tudor, *Notes,* entry for May 10, 1953.

[2] Stephen Mitchell, speeches, Western Tour, 1953, D.C. Conference of Western Congressmen, 1954, 42, Mitchell Papers.

[3] Paul Douglas to R. Weigel, May 28, 1953, N. Long to Douglas, March 8, 1953, A. Pine to Herbert Lehman, July 25, 1953, copy, Interior, Paul Douglas Papers; Ernest Gruening to Richard Neuberger, August 4, 1954, Oregon Politics—1954 Campaign, PF, Neuberger Papers. The caricatures of "boob" Eisenhower and "giveaway" McKay were perpetuated most tellingly by Herbert Block's syndicated newspaper cartoons, reprinted in his *Here and Now* and *Special for Today* (New York, 1955 and 1958).

[4] E. Hartwick to D. Kendall, July 20, 1953, copy, DMK to Harris Ellsworth, March 18, 1954, PF, DMK Papers; Wendell Wyatt to DMK, August 17, 1954, 9, McCrillis File, RG 48, NRC; F. Cooper to Frank Barrett, July 21, 1953, Agriculture-Grazing, Barrett Papers.

[5] I. Jones to Walt Horan, May 6, 1953, Horan to Jones, May 8, 1953, 426, C. Keiser to Horan, February 6, 1954, 427, Power, Horan Papers; Robert Sawyer to J. Murphy, May 8, 1954, copy, Tudor, Sawyer Papers.

⁶ Wesley D'Ewart, speech, October 8, 1954, copy, 1, D'Ewart Papers; copies of campaign literature against James Murray are in D'Ewart folder, Murray Papers.

⁷ Misc. newspaper clippings, Montana, Wyoming, Republican National Committee Clippings and Publications File, DDE Library.

⁸ FDR to Richard Neuberger, February 21, 1941, copy, General, PF, Neuberger Papers.

⁹ Richard Neuberger to M. Bauer, October 16, 1953, PF, Neuberger Papers.

¹⁰ Clarence Dill to Richard Neuberger, May 18, 1953, General, PF, Neuberger Papers; Bernard De Voto to Garrett Mattingly, May 19, 1954, 6, De Voto Papers.

¹¹ Richard Neuberger to Charles Sprague, June 19, 1954, to J. Ruhl, October 23, 1954, to Sam Rosenman, April 12, 1954, to M. Frey, October 9, 1954, to the editor, *Roseburg* (Oregon) *News*, March 29, 1954, to Palmer Hoyt, April 27, 1954, to Irving –, July 15, 1954, to Wendell Wyatt, December 8, 1954, Oregon Political–1954 Campaign, PF, Neuberger Papers.

¹² D. Simpson to Robert Sawyer, March 26, 1954, Cordon, Sawyer Papers; DMK to Robert Smylie, March 9, 1954, PPF, Smylie Records; DMK to C. Edwards, May 22, 1954, PF, DMK Papers; DMK to Sherman Adams, May 29, 1953, to Wendell Wyatt, September 2, 1954, McCrillis File, RG 48, NRC; Ralph Tudor, *Notes*, entry for July 4, 1954; Paul Patterson to DMK, September 9, 1954, copy, 14–47, VI, Langlie Papers.

¹³ DDE, "Remarks at Natrona Airport, Casper, Wyoming," and "Address at the Dedication of McNary Dam, Walla Walla, Washington," September 23, 1954, *Public Papers*, pp. 835–36, 855; DMK to Walt Horan, ca. December 6, 1954, 373, Irrigation and Reclamation, Horan Papers.

¹⁴ Richard Neuberger to Wendell Wyatt, December 8, 1954, Oregon Politics–1954 Campaign, PF, Neuberger Papers; Neuberger to C. Girard Davidson, November 15, 1954, C. Girard Davidson Papers, University of Oregon Library, Eugene; Wayne Morse to Gus Norwood, November 8, 1954, HC, Northwest Public Power Association Papers; C. Fisher to James Murray, December 2, 1954, D. Reed to Murray, November 17, 1954, HC, Reclamation, Murray Papers; DDE, press conference statement, December 8, 1954, *Public Papers*, p. 645; Neuberger to editor, *US News and World Report*, November 11, 1954; Oregon Politics–1954 Campaign, PF, Neuberger Papers.

¹⁵ "Hells Canyon and Other Public Power Issues in the Pacific Northwest," distributed by Northwest Associated Businessmen, Inc., Spokane, ca. January 1955, copy, HC, Douglas Papers.

¹⁶ Paul Douglas to T. Ludlow, April 27, 1954, to DMK, January 21, August 3, 1954, to Wayne Morse, September 3, 1954, General Outgoing Correspondence, Douglas Papers.

¹⁷ James Murray to D. Reed, December 1, 1954, 7, Michael Straus, draft, post-campaign program, 6, Reclamation, Murray Papers; Stuart Moir to Richard Neuberger, February 17, 1955, Forest Service, PF, Horace Albright to Neuberger, August 16, 1955, Conservation General, PF, Neuberger Papers; Neuberger to C. Girard Davidson, November 13, 1954, Davidson Papers; U.S., Congress, Senate, Interior Committee, *Colorado River Storage Project: Hearings . . . ,* 84th Cong., 1st sess., 1955; U.S., Congress, Senate, Interior Committee, *Report . . . ,* Senate Doc. 128, 84th Cong., 1st sess., 1955; David Brower to Paul Douglas, May 20, 1955, P. Taylor to Douglas, November 28, 1955, Case File, Interior, Douglas Papers; Raymond Moley, column, *Philadelphia Bulletin,* April 20, 1955; American Enterprise Association, Inc., "What Price Federal Reclamation," booklet No. 455 (New York, 1955), copy, Douglas Papers; Straus to Neuberger, September 27, 1955, Conservation General, Neuberger Papers.

¹⁸ R. Saul to David Brower, ca. February 8, 1955, SCA; Arthur Carhart to Neuberger, September 15, 1955, Conservation General, Neuberger Papers.

[19] Howard Pyle to Clarence Davis, August 23, 1955, Pyle to P. Baker, August 23, 1955, I. Kennedy to Davis, August 25, 1955, 6, Pyle File, DDE Records; *Eugene* (Oregon) *Register-Guard*, September 27, 1955.

[20] Bert Swanson and Deborah Rosenfield, "The Coon-Neuberger Debates of 1955," *Pacific Northwest Quarterly* 55 (April 1964): 55–66; Richard Neuberger to Michael Straus, October 8, 1955, Conservation General, Neuberger Papers.

[21] Wayne Morse, press release, September 9, 1955, copy, 4, HC, National Hells Canyon Association Papers, University of Oregon Library, Eugene; International Woodworkers of America, Inland Empire District Council, Spokane, resolution, July 31, 1955, copy, OF 17 A, DDE Records; Richard Neuberger to James Murray, October 16, 1955, Senate Interior Committee, Hubert Humphrey to F. Griffith, August 25, 1955, PF, T. Balke to Neuberger, September 25, 1955, Conservation General, Neuberger Papers.

[22] *Denver Post*, August 2, 1955.

[23] DMK to Robert Sawyer, December 6, 1956, Sawyer Papers; DMK to Walt Horan, ca. December 6, 1954, 373, Irrigation and Reclamation, Horan Papers.

[24] DMK to E. Linn, cited in *Glasgow* (Montana) *Mountain Courier*, December 8, 1955; DMK, statement, St. Louis, cited in *Washington Post*, October 12, 1955; DMK to Wesley D'Ewart, October 18, 1955, Gordon Allott to DMK, July 28, 1955, PF, DMK Papers; D'Ewart folder, Secretary OF, RG 48, NA; Sherman Adams to DDE, September 6, 1955, 115, OF 3WW, DDE Records.

[25] *Washington Star*, October 25, 1955; V. Reinheimer to J. Megler, November 3, 1955, D'Ewart, Murray Papers; *Oregonian*, October 8, 1955; *Denver Post*, October 14, 1955.

[26] Wesley D'Ewart, interview, pp. 79, 103; DMK to D'Ewart, November 10, 1955, PF, DMK Papers; James Murray to Richard Neuberger, October 21, 1955, Murray, press release, October 6, 1955, Neuberger, press release, October 11, 1955, copies, Interior Committee, O'Mahoney Papers; W. Fraser to Murray, November 16, 1955, Murray to J. Umber, November 5, 1955, D'Ewart, Murray Papers.

[27] The chronology and documents of the Al Sarena affair are printed in U.S., Congress, Senate, House, *The Al Sarena Case: Report Submitted . . . by the Senate Subcommittee . . . and the House Subcommittee . . .*, Item 1040 and 1016, 84th Cong., 2d sess., 1956, hereafter cited as *Al Sarena;* Frank Boykin to M. White, copy, June 13, 1951, F. Libby to Harris Ellsworth, June 9, 1953, copy, Davis, Secretary OF, RG 48, NA.

[28] Wendell Wyatt, December 13, 1955, Wyatt to DMK, December 5, 1955, 1956 File, DMK to L. Wallace, February 23, 1956, Al Sarena, PF, DMK Papers.

[29] DMK to Robert Kerr, February 7, 1956, printed in *Al Sarena*, pp. 35–36; Clarence Davis, testimony, *Al Sarena*, esp. pp. 661ff.; *Lincoln* (Nebraska) *Evening Journal*, April 14, 1956; cartoon by Bimrose, *Oregonian*, January 30, 1956.

[30] Barry Goldwater, statement, *Al Sarena*, pp. 34, 38; *Chicago Tribune*, January 27, 1956; Robert Kerr, statement, *Al Sarena*, pp. 57–58.

CHAPTER NINE

[1] DMK to D. Hood, December 26, 1953, P. Patterson to DMK, February 6, 1954, PF, DMK Papers; *New York Herald Tribune*, August 26, 1955; DMK to C. Steifel, October 20, 1954, to J. Bracken Lee, February 10, 1956, PF, DMK Papers.

[2] *Washington Star*, December 22, 1955, January 31, February 14, 1956; C. Willis to Leonard Hall, March 12, 1955, Oregon, OF 109 A 2, DDE Records; G. Scott to DMK, April 11, 1956, Robert Sawyer to DMK, March 14, 1956, J. Patterson to DMK, February 17, 1956, Orme Lewis to DMK, February 19, 1956, Henry

Dworshak to DMK, February 27, 1956, DMK to F. McCaslin, February 7, 1956, PF, DMK Papers.

[3] For the Ballinger precedent see Elmo Richardson, *The Politics of Conservation: Crusades and Controversies, 1897–1913* (Berkeley and Los Angeles, 1962), pp. 127–28.

[4] DMK to Robert Sawyer, March 20, 1956, 1956 File, DMK Papers; Mabel McKay, statement, Mahar, "McKay," pp. 305–8; Ezra Benson, *Cross Fire: The Eight Years with Eisenhower* (New York, 1962), pp. 86–87, 550; Sawyer to Ralph Cake, June 13, 1956, Sawyer Papers; Charles Sprague, column, *Oregon* (Portland) *Statesman*, November 11, 1956; Cake to the author, September 5, 1968; *Oregonian*, March 6, 1956; Glenn Emmons to the author, November 1971; Appointments, Sherman Adams File, DDE Records; Adams, *First Hand Report*, pp. 235–37.

[5] Mabel McKay, statement, Mahar, "McKay," pp. 308–9; DMK to Robert Sawyer, March 20, 1956, Sawyer Papers; *Oregonian*, March 7–10; *Oregon Statesman*, March 10, April 16, 1956; H. Kane to M. Snyder, March 10, 1956, Oregon, OF 109 A 2, DDE Records; Wendell Wyatt to DMK, March 30, 1956, DMK to Wyatt, April 5, 1956, Wyatt to W. Phillips, ca. April 1956, 1956 File, DMK Papers.

[6] Howard Pyle to Sherman Adams, March 28, 1956, 115, OF 3WW, N. Heath to DDE, April 28, 1956, OF 138 A 5, DDE Records; DDE, press conference statement, June 6, 1956, *Public Papers*, pp. 565–66; DDE to DMK, March 8, 9, 27, 28, 29, 1956, PF, DMK Papers (the letters of March 9 and 29 are printed in *Public Papers*, pp. 299–300, 348–49).

[7] *Denver Post*, March 12, 1956; O. Fitz-Simmons to DMK, March 4, 1956, Derogatory, Miscellaneous, 1956 File, DMK Papers.

[8] DMK to Robert Smylie, May 25, 1956, PF, Smylie Records; misc. congratulatory letters, March-April 1956, 69, 1956 File, DMK Papers; DMK, address, Chandler, Arizona, April 3, 1956, "Public Addresses," bound volumes, vol. 2, pt. 2, esp. pp. 520–26; *Washington Post*, April 2, 1956.

[9] DMK, radio addresses, March 2, May 10, 1956, copies, 16, DMK, Pyle File, DDE Records; DMK to editor, *Oswego* (Oregon) *Review*, April 3, 1956, DMK to F. Barber, April 3, 1956, Wendell Wyatt to DMK, March 12, 1956, PF, DMK Papers; *Idaho Statesman*, March 27, 1956; DMK to Sherman Adams, May 19, 1956, DMK, 16, Pyle File; "Abstract of Votes, Primary Election . . . May 23, 1956," copy, 69, 1956 File, DMK Papers.

[10] Lyndon Johnson to Richard Neuberger, August 31, 1955, Senators, Neuberger Papers; *New York Times*, March 29, 1956; U.S., Congress, Senate, Hubert Humphrey, extended remarks, 84th Cong., 2d sess., June 20, 1956, *Congressional Record*, Appendix, 4898–99; Wayne Morse, address, August 14, 1956, and HST, address, August 17, 1956, *Official Proceedings of the Democratic National Convention . . . 1956* (Richmond, Va., 1956), esp. pp. 141–43, 495.

[11] Charles Sprague, column, *Oregon Statesman*, November 11, 1956; DMK to Sherman Adams, June 25, 1956, Oregon, OF 109 A 2, DDE Records; Corydon Wagner to H. Bahr, October 4, 1956, General, Northwest Lumbermen's Association File, Wagner Papers; O. Yokum to DMK, September 7, 1956, PF, DMK Papers; *New York Times*, September 5, 1955; Clarence Davis to DMK, June 27, 1956, Interior Staff, *International Woodworkers* (October 10, 1956), T, 1956 File, DMK Papers.

[12] J. Tooze to DMK, May 25, 1956, W. Adams to DMK, September 28, 1956, Robert Sawyer to A. Phillips, August 15, 1956, "The Documented Record of Senator Wayne Morse," copy, 70, 1956 File, DMK Papers.

[13] Howard Pyle to DMK, March 23, 1956, DMK, 16, Pyle File; D. Weider to V. Schenck, September 10, 1956, Emmons, T. Purcell, reports on index cards, ca. May 1956, C. Walls to DMK, September 8, 20, 1956, Ralph Cake to O. Bronson, October 3, 1956, Unfavorable Publicity, 1956 File, DMK Papers; Sherman Adams,

campaign memorandum, Adams, 1, 28, Pyle File, DDE Records; "Fact Sheet," 5, Norwood Papers; M. Bauer to Richard Neuberger, July 16, 1956, PF, Neuberger Papers.

[14] Mabel McKay to Sherman Adams, October 13, 1956, Oregon, OF 109 A 2, DDE Records; Robert Gray, *Eighteen Acres under Glass* (London, 1962), p. 70; DMK to R. Rodman, October 12, 1956, Leonard Hall to DMK, July 1, 1956, Interior Staff, 1956 File, DMK Papers; Howard Pyle to DMK, March 23, 1956, DMK, 16, Pyle File, DDE Records; Pyle to Adams, July 6, 1956, Oregon, OF 134 B 2, DDE Records; DDE, remarks, Portland, October 18, 1956, address, October 18, 1956, *Public Papers*, pp. 956–57, 961.

[15] Wayne Morse, statement, *Washington Post*, February 22, 1956; William R. Burch, "Ordeal by Sophistry: The McKay-Morse Campaign of 1956" (Ph.D. diss., University of Oregon, 1957), esp. pp. 172–80; Democratic State and National Committees, 1956, Campaign File, Davidson Papers; Richard Neuberger to R. Frazier, June 25, 1956, Wildlife Refuges, Lyle Watts to Neuberger, July 6, 1956, Forest Service, Neuberger Papers.

[16] Howard Pyle to Sherman Adams, May 22, 1956, Adams, 1, 28, Pyle File, DDE Records; Pyle to Adams, July 6, 1956, Oregon, OF 109 A 2, DDE Records; DMK, statement, *Oregon Statesman*, November 5, 1956.

[17] DMK to Sherman Adams, November 12, 1956, D.C., 1956 File, DMK Papers; "Abstract of Votes, Regular General Election, November 6, 1956," Oregon, OF 109 A 2, DDE Records; DMK to Wilton Persons, November 20, 1956, PPF 20X56, DDE Records.

[18] DDE to DMK, November 8, 1956, Wilton Persons to DMK, November 7, 1956, and attached T. Cross, "Memorandum for the Vice President," B. McKelvey to N. Schuttle, November 11, 1956, copy, Wendell Wyatt to Sherman Adams, November 11, 1956, M. Brown to Adams, July 20, 1957, Oregon, OF 109 A 2, DDE Records.

[19] Charles Sprague, column, *Oregon Statesman*, November 11, 1956.

[20] DMK to Sherman Adams, November 12, 1956, to Edgar Eisenhower, December 29, 1956, 1956 File, DMK Papers; DMK to Robert Sawyer, December 6, 27, 1956, Sawyer Papers; H. Short to C. Masterson, November 14, 1956, copy, 43, Wendell Wyatt to Adams, November 18, 1956, Oregon, OF 109 A 2, DDE Records; *Oregon Journal*, November 19, 1956.

[21] Republican platform, 1956, copy, 98, Republican National Committee Clippings and Publications File, DDE Library; Leonard Hall, memorandum, March 23, 1956, 16, Pyle File; DDE to H. Magie, October 15, 1956, OF 134 B 2, DDE Records; DDE, "Letter to Horace Albright Concerning the Administration's Conservation Program," November 2, 1956, *Public Papers*, pp. 1074–75.

[22] Misc. clippings, Colorado, Montana, Idaho, Republican National Committee Clippings and Publications File, DDE Library; Robert Smylie to J. Bermingham, September 18, 1956, Correspondence, Smylie Records; Callison Marks to Walt Horan, June 27, 1956, Power, 429, Horan Papers; *Idaho Statesman*, November 7, 1956.

[23] *Wenatchee* (Washington) *World*, September 19, 1956; Corydon Wagner to Arthur Langlie, April 17, 1956, Federal Departments, Langlie Records.

[24] H. Powell to Arthur Langlie, December 3, 1956, 6–22, Langlie to Powell, December 17, 1956, 6–27, VI, Langlie Papers; Walt Horan to Sherman Adams, March 1, 1956, to Harry Cain, March 1, 1956, 554, Politics, Horan Papers; "The Situation in Washington," March 30, 1956, 38, Pyle File, DDE Records; *Washington Post*, April 12, 1956; DDE to Langlie, September 20, November 10, 1956, OF 138 A 5, DDE Records; DDE, "Address at a Rally . . . Seattle . . . ," October 17, 1956, *Public Papers*, p. 942; statement quoted is in F. LaBelle to Horan, July 15, 1956, 429, Power, Horan Papers.

25 "A Survey of Public Opinion on Power . . . ," June 29, 1956, 429, "The Electric Power Issue in the 1956 Oregon and Washington Elections," and "Power as an Issue . . . ," copies, 430, Power, Horan Papers.

26 *Idaho Statesman,* November 10, 12, 1956; Wendell Wyatt to Sherman Adams, November 16, 1956, Howard Pyle to Wyatt, November 23, 1956, M. Brown to Adams, July 20, 1957, Oregon, OF 109 A 2, DDE Records.

27 "Post Election Survey, 4th Congressional District of Oregon," and "Oregon Survey, November-December, 1956," 42, Pyle File, DDE Records.

28 P. Keller to DDE, November 16, 1956, Oregon, OF 109 A 2, P. Ewing to Fred Seaton, November 21, 1956, Oregon Political Situation, 43, Staff File, DDE Records; DDE, press conference statement, May 23, 1956, *Public Papers,* p. 515.

29 Charles Sprague, column, *Oregon Statesman,* November 11, 1956.

EPILOGUE

1 DDE, press conference statement, June 6, 1956, *Public Papers,* pp. 565–66; recommendations for Secretary of the Interior, GF 17A, DDE Records; Milward Simpson to DMK, March 12, 1956, PF, DMK Papers; John Osseward to Irving Clark, March 15, 1956, Olympic Park Association, Clark Papers; O. Malmquist to Robert Smylie, June 13, 1956, CF, Smylie Records.

2 Recommendations for Clarence Davis, 116, OF 4 and GF 17A, DDE Records; *Nashville Tennessean,* March 10, 1956; *Washington Post,* April 12, 1956; Ralph Tudor to DMK, May 21, 1956, DMK to Tudor, June 8, 1956, California, 1956 File, DMK Papers.

3 Howard Pyle to Sherman Adams, May 22, 1956, Adams 1, 28, Pyle Records; *Chicago Sun-Times,* May 30, 1956; DDE, press conference statement, June 6, 1956, *Public Papers,* pp. 565–66.

4 Fred Seaton to Paul Douglas, August 3, 1952, Douglas Papers; Seaton folder, OF 2A2, DDE Records; Gray, *Eighteen Acres,* p. 31; Robert Smylie to Seaton, January 12, 1956, PF, Smylie Records; Robert Monohan to Sherman Adams, ca. June 1956, copy, SCA; Robert Sawyer to Ralph Cake, June 13, 1956, copy, 1956 File, DMK Papers.

5 U.S., Congress, Senate, Interior Committee, *Hearings on the Nomination of . . . Seaton . . . ,* 84th Cong., 2d sess., 1956, esp. pp. 19, 23, 26–27, 29–30; *Chicago Sun-Times,* May 30, 1956; *Idaho Statesman,* May 29, June 2, 1956; Robert Sawyer to William Whele, July 3, 1956, Sawyer Papers; William Strand to DMK, June 9, 1956, Interior Staff, 1956 File, DMK Papers.

6 DMK to Robert Sawyer, December 6, 1956, Sawyer Papers; *Medford* (Oregon) *Mail-Tribune,* June 5, 1956; Fred Seaton, statement, Topeka, Kansas, January 29, 1952, reprinted in *Hearings . . . ,* p. 15; *Washington Post,* October 15, 1956; *Denver Post,* May 30, October 15, 1956.

7 Biographical information on Elmer Bennett, Personal Books, III/1, N. Ely to Thomas Kuchel, A. Forkner to Bennett, May 17, 1957, 111/2, Bennett to R. Sargent, June 22, 1956, to William Kelly, March 31, 1956, I/1, R. Holbrook to Bennett, May 7, 1957, II/1, Bennett to J. Barnard, May 28, 1958, Horace Albright to Bennett, May 17, 1957, III/2, Wesley D'Ewart to Bennett, May 9, 1957, II/I, Elmer Bennett Papers, DDE Library.

8 Wesley D'Ewart, testimony, U.S., Congress, Senate, Interior Committee, *Hearings on S. J. R. 139,* 84th Cong., 2d sess., June 7, 1956, pp. 25–37; U.S., Congress, Senate, Interior Committee, *Nomination of . . . D'Ewart,* 84th Cong., 2d sess., 1956, passim; A. Schlact to Joseph O'Mahoney, July 30, 1956, O'Mahoney to Schlact, July 21, 1956, O'Mahoney Papers; Richard Neuberger, Wayne Morse, statements, U.S., Congress, Senate, 84th Cong., 2d sess., June 30, 1956, *Congres-*

sional Record, p. 14577; *Miles City* (Montana) *Star,* June 24, 1956; D'Ewart to James Murray, May 10, 1956, M. Emmett to Murray, July 25, 1956, J. Clark to Murray, July 13, 1956, R. Jeudeman to Murray, July 25, 1956, Frank Barrett et al. to Murray, July 24, 1956, Murray to Joseph Aronson, July 21, 1956, Clinton Anderson to Murray, July 20, 1956, D'Ewart folder, Murray Papers; *Billings* (Montana) *Yellowstone News,* August 2, 1956; *Billings Gazette,* August 1, 1956.

9 Robert Smith, series of articles, November-December 1956, *Oregonian; Denver Post,* January 12, 1957; Robert Sawyer to Ralph Cake, June 13, 1956, 24, Sawyer to DMK, December 2, 10, 1956, Sawyer Papers; Clarence Davis to DDE, December 7, 1956, OF 4, DDE Records; Howard Pyle to Fred Seaton, January 4, 19, 1957, Seaton, 22, Pyle Records.

10 C. Cochran to James Murray et al., June 4, 1956, copy, HC, O'Mahoney Papers; Warren Magnuson to Gus Norwood, July 1, 25, 1956, Edith Green to Norwood, July 25, 1956, HC, Northwest Public Power Association Papers.

11 Albert Miller to Sherman Adams, July 12, 1957, drafts of DDE to Jack Westland, HC-2, 838, OF 155 E 1, DDE Records; Elmer Bennett to Eugene Millikan, February 1, 1957, II/1, Bennett Papers.

12 Fred Seaton to Charles Jensen, December 21, 1956, copy, John Taber to Sherman Adams, August 30, 1957, copy, Jensen to Seaton, December 30, 1957, Seaton to Jensen, January 2, 1958, copy, Paradise Dam, 22, Solicitor File, RG 48, NRC; Sherman Adams to Taber, September 19, 1957, Snake River, OF 155 A 10, Jack Anderson to Wilton Persons, ca. April 1957, Jack Anderson Records, DDE Library; Elmer Bennett to Charles Francis, February 14, 1957, II/1, Bennett to Frank Hoag, June 28, 1956, II/3, Bennett to Seaton, February 15, 1957, II/2, Bennett Papers; Russell Mack to Leonard Peoples, April 29, 1957, Richard Neuberger to Gus Norwood, May 14, 1957, HC, Byron Brinton to Wayne Morse, April 15, 1957, copy, HC Development Association, Northwest Public Power Association Papers; T. Heath to Henry Dworshak, November 21, PF, Smylie Records.

13 Walt Horan to J. Nesbitt, July 21, 1957, Horan to W. Nordeen, July 18, 1957, 430, Power, Horan Papers; Sherman Adams to John Taber, September 19, 1957, Snake River, OF 155 A 10, DDE Records; Fred Seaton to E. Itchner, June 20, 1956, Glacier, Parks and Sites, RG 79, NRC; Arthur Langlie to Hickman Powell, December 17, 1956, VI, 6–22, Langlie Papers; Seaton, statements, *Denver Post,* November 17, 1956; *Christian Science Monitor,* January 11, 1958.

14 Craig Hosmer to David Brower, January 6, 1956, W. Chaillie to H. Bradley, May 11, 1956, Ned — to Jess Lombard, March 25, 1956, Lombard to Brower, March 15, 1956, H. Crowe to Conrad Wirth, Wirth to Crowe, April 26, 1956, SCA; Edwin Johnson to Wirth, July 30, 1956, Federal Government, 31, Johnson Records; Richard Neuberger to Brower, May 4, 1956, Robert Monohan to Sherman Adams, ca. June 1956, copy, SCA.

15 Fred Seaton to F. Smith, April 18, 1956, copy, John Saylor to Seaton, June 4, 1956, DNM, 21, Solicitor File, RG 48, NRC.

16 Misc. correspondence, DNM, 139, 6P, RG 48, NRC; U.S., Congress, Senate, 85th Cong., 1st sess., *Congressional Record,* pp. 10828–31; Gordon Allott to DMK; March 2, 1956, Edwin Johnson to Wesley D'Ewart, March 28, 1956, William Dawson to Conrad Wirth, March 17, 1956, DNM, 139, 6P, RG 48, NRC; Fred Seaton to F. Smith, July 26, 1957, copy, III/1, Bennett Papers; Smith to Trustees of the National Park Association, August 3, 1957, Meyer Litton to David Brower, August 15, 1957, Brower to Alfred Knopf, August 30, 1957, draft, H. Kallman to A. Chamberlain, undated copy, SCA.

17 *Salt Lake Tribune,* August 19, 1957; *Vernal Express,* August 17, 1957; *Ogden* (Utah) *Standard Examiner,* August 16, 1957; *Grand Junction Sentinel,* August 19, 1957; George Clyde to Arthur Watkins, August 7, 22, 1957, Watkins to Clyde,

August 16, 1957, Wilderness Act, George Clyde Records, Utah State Archives; *Sierra Club Bulletin*, August 22, 1957, David Brower to Fred Seaton, ca. September 1957, draft, Bestor Robinson to Brower, September 5, 1957, SCA.

[18] Ted Stevens to R. Andrews, April 11, 1958, OF 133 A 1, DDE Records; *Denver Post*, January 5, 1959; *Salt Lake Tribune*, January 2, 7, 10, 1959; F. Smith to National Park Advisory Board, August 19, 1959, copy, Fred Seaton to Wayne Aspinall, August 23, 1959, copy, DNM, 21, Solicitor File, RG 48, NRC.

[19] Fred Seaton to George Clyde, September 24, 1959, Seaton, provision for insertion into the bill, Seaton to Frank Moss, September 29, 1959, DNM, 21, Solicitor File, RG 48, NRC.

[20] L. O'Neil to James Murray, December 21, 1959, Murray to O'Neil, January 4, 1960, Glacier Valley, Reclamation, Murray Papers; Elmer Bennett, "Current Issues," Briefing Book, Bennett Records; Murray, press releases, April 11, 16, 1958, Conrad Wirth to Murray, April 17, 1958, Murray, testimony to Senate Interior Appropriations Subcommittee, March 28, 1958, copy, Murray to Associated Press of Helena, Montana, April 1958, Mission 66, Murray Papers.

[21] Fred Seaton, address, Inland Daily Press Association, Chicago, October 14, 1957, copy, 1956 File, DMK Papers; Ted Stevens to Seaton, July 11, 1960, Campaign, Bennett Papers; *New York Times*, July 21, 1960.

[22] Paul Sears, statement quoted in Melvin Price, press release, June 13, 1955, copy, DNM, Wirth Records; John Bennett to Peter Sorotkin, September 15, 1955, 118, 13, RG 115/4, NRC.

Primary Sources

This study is based upon primary sources—official and personal correspondence and documents. Since such sources have not been used extensively by students of federal resources policy, the essential building blocks of scholarly monographs are not available. Gordon B. Dodds has compiled a list of background secondary sources in his "Conservation and Reclamation in the Trans-Mississippi West: A Critical Bibliography," *Arizona and the West* 13 (Summer 1971): 143–71. Yet there are no overall studies of resource policy of either the Democratic or Republican presidential administrations, no published biographies of the men who shaped resource legislation at the White House, in Congress, or on the state level. No comprehensive histories of the proposals for the development of the Missouri or Columbia rivers have been written, nor any full account of the Upper Colorado Basin project. The persistent, certainly wasteful, conflicts over development and preservation among the Bureau of Reclamation, the Army Corps of Engineers, and the Park Service have been dealt with only in piecemeal fashion. The pressures of private organizations and quasi-public agencies, as decisive now as they were in the period discussed herein, have not been described or evaluated. The great body of contemporary commentary on these subjects is primarily polemical. The handful of doctoral dissertations about some of them were necessarily based on secondary, printed sources.

Consequently, the following information is offered as a guide to the scholars whose efforts are needed to produce the detailed monographs upon which an accurate and comprehensive assessment can be based. Because of the past and undoubtedly future controversies connected with resource policy, researchers cannot be satisfied with official statements and single sources. Only after examining literally tons of evidence can they fill in the total picture of the nation's use and abuse of its natural heritage. Although this is not an exhaustive list of available primary sources, the collections noted here are voluminous and important enough to provide information for a host of scholars working for many years to come.

The National Archives in Washington holds the records of the Interior Department, its secretaries, bureau chiefs, and administrative assistants. Details concerning specific policies, programs, and problems can be found in the records of the Bureau of Reclamation and the National Park Service. The material therein consists of communications among department officials—both staff and field—and the correspondence of these men with private persons and organizations, state officials, state and federal administrators and legislators. Segments of these record groups, especially for the years after 1953, are deposited at the National Records Center in Suitland, Maryland. They include the Park Service's National Monuments File, the application of "Mission 66," and the files of the Bureau of Reclamation relating to the Upper Colorado Storage Project. Although some of the papers of Secretary McKay's assistants are located there, his own papers are at the University of Oregon Library in Eugene. That depository also contains the papers of Secretary Krug's assistant, C. Girard Davidson. Krug's papers are at the Library of Congress.

The presidential libraries contain not only the official correspondence of the chief executives but also that of their policy advisers and special appointees as well. The Franklin Roosevelt Library in Hyde Park, New York, for example, has the papers of Morris L. Cooke, presidential adviser on water and power for both Roosevelt and Truman. The Harry S. Truman Library in Independence, Missouri, holds, among others, the files of resource policy advisers David Bell and Charles Murphy and those of Interior officials Joel Wolfsohn and Warner Gardner. It also has the extensive official and personal papers of Secretary Oscar Chapman. The Dwight D. Eisenhower Library collections at Abilene, Kansas, include the files of White House assistant Howard Pyle and the official correspondence of Elmer Bennett of the Interior Department. Because Secretary Fred Seaton's papers are not yet available, the latter group is especially useful.

The administration of resources by state officials can be traced in the records of Governors Edwin Johnson and Dan Thorton at the Colorado State Archives, Denver, the records of Governors George Clyde and J. Bracken Lee (containing significant correspondence of Senator Arthur Watkins) at the Utah State Archives, Salt Lake City, the less extensive files of Governors Len Jordan and Robert Smylie at the Idaho State Archives, Boise, the records of several governors held by the Universities of Montana and Wyoming, and the records of Governors Arthur Langlie and Monrad Wallgren at the Washington State Archives, Olympia. In every one of these archives, gubernatorial correspondence on the subject of resource policy may be supplemented by the files of the state engineers, state water commissions, and various river development agencies.

Two of the greatest treasure troves for research in recent American history are the papers of state and federal legislators. They have been comparatively unexploited because they are usually voluminous and only generally arranged according to content. The Frank Barrett Papers at the University of Wyoming, Laramie, are concerned primarily with grazing policy. Those of Hugh Butler at the Nebraska State Historical Society are more useful for the years before he was chairman of the Senate Interior Committee than after 1953. The papers of Paul Douglas at the Chicago Historical Society are enormous in extent and presently unarranged. Henry Dworshak's Papers at the Idaho State Archives are very useful on all aspects of resource development in the Northwest. The segment on Hells Canyon, not available for examination when this study was prepared, is now included in the collection. The 600 document boxes containing the Walt Horan Papers at Washington State University, Pullman, are well arranged and cataloged and constitute one of the richest primary sources on the subjects of water and land development for the period 1942–1964. The Hugh Mitchell Papers at the University of Washington Library, Seattle, are devoted almost entirely to the controversy over CVA. The James Murray Papers at the University of Montana Library, Missoula, are extensive and generally arranged and cover the long period of his tenure in Congress. The Richard Neuberger Papers at the University of Oregon Library include material on his publicist activities before he ran for the United States Senate as well as correspondence concerning his crusading efforts in that body. The largest and most comprehensive collection of a legislative expert on resource problems is the Joseph O'Mahoney Papers at the University of Wyoming Library, Laramie. These have recently been arranged and cataloged.

The attitudes and procedures of resource developers can be examined in several collections at the University of Washington Library. The Corydon Wagner Papers include business records as well as the files of Pacific Northwest lumbering organizations. Both the Gus Norwood Papers and the files of the Northwest Public Power Association are concerned with cooperative action among private, local, district, state, and federal water and power agencies in that region. At the University of Oregon Library, Robert Sawyer's correspondence is alphabetized by the names of the correspondents—businessmen, conservationists, and legislators who were among his many acquaintances.

The papers of Irving Brant, prominent among the preservationists, are at the Library of Congress but a microfilm copy of the material dealing with his role as publicist and adviser on resource matters may be obtained from the Roosevelt Library. Arthur Carhart's papers at the Denver Conservation Library, not yet arranged, are very valuable. The concerns and efforts of a Pacific Northwest preservationist are disclosed in the papers of Irving Clark at the University of Washington Library. Although small in volume, the papers of Bernard De Voto at the Stanford University Library in California contain many excellent items concerning federal resource policy from the New Deal to the middle 1950s. The archives of the Sierra Club in San Francisco may be used with the permission of that organization which has been so outspoken and effective in preservationist battles for more than seventy years.

Finally, I would like to remind my fellow researchers in resource history that it is necessary to exploit human resources. Although apparently breaking new ground, I have not been without help in the wilderness. This study can stand as an expression of gratitude to the continuing assistance of these friends: Richard Berner, archivist of the University of Washington Library; Eugene Gressley, curator of Manuscripts at the University of Wyoming Library; Sid McAlpin, director of the Washington State Archives; Robert Maxwell of the National Archives; Martin Schmidt of the Manuscripts Division of the University of Oregon Library; and Merle Wells, state archivist of Idaho. Briefer but no less helpful association was extended by the directors and staffs of the following depositories: the Bancroft Library and Oral History Project at the University of California, Berkeley; the Denver Conservation Library; the Stanford, Montana, and Washington State University libraries; the National Records Center; the historical societies of Nebraska and Utah; the archives of Colorado and Utah; and the special cordiality and patience of those at the Roosevelt, Eisenhower, and Truman libraries. The Truman Library generously provided funds for the final phase of travel and research.

Several people extended particular courtesies: Oscar Chapman, Irving Brant, and Conrad Wirth gave me permission to use their papers and records; Newton Drury and Arthur Carhart also answered some prying questions; Ralph Cake, Paul Douglas, Palmer Hoyt, Clinton Anderson, and Glenn Emmons responded to specific inquiries. Professor Eugene Trani kindly let me read his manuscript survey of the secretaries and undersecretaries of the Interior Department. Professors Donald Swain and Roderick Nash were notably courageous in endorsing the publication of this study.

The following persons and publishers kindly granted permission to quote from copyrighted materials: Newton Drury and the Bancroft Library for the preliminary versions of the Drury and Drury-Evison interviews; Wesley D'Ewart and the Columbia Oral History Collection for the D'Ewart interview, copy used at the Eisenhower Library; The University of Chicago Press for Donald Swain's *Horace Albright;* Simon and Schuster, Inc., for *The Secret Diaries of Harold Ickes;* Harper and Row for *The Journals of David Lilienthal;* Random House for *The Major Campaign Speeches of Adlai Stevenson;* Atheneum for Emmet Hughes's *Ordeal of Power.*

Although I found it necessary to step around the detractions leveled by some academic Talleyrands, I had the encouragement of two players of the academic game: Professor Robert Burke of the University of Washington has boosted me up so many times that words could never adequately acknowledge his faith and solicitude; Professor Donald McCoy of the University of Kansas—unsinkable "Ollie"—put up with my mercurial personality for about fifteen years and three weeks of mutual productivity and laughter.

Index